## Access Your Online Resources

All the activity sheets included in *The Power of Emotional Intelligence* are downloadable for easy printing to ensure this resource best supports your professional needs.

Go to https://resourcecentre.routledge.com/speechmark and click on the cover of this book.

Answer the question prompt using your copy of the book to gain access to the online content.

# THE POWER OF EMOTIONAL INTELLIGENCE

We've all been told emotional intelligence is a good thing, but are we really clear about what it is and how we can all get more of it? We know it helps children self-regulate, be more motivated, maintain relationships and be more resilient, but how do we go about accessing these benefits?

*The Power of Emotional Intelligence* will help primary school teachers and leaders to increase their awareness and use of emotional intelligence to improve the wellbeing of the whole school community. It includes everything you need to embed emotional intelligence at the core of your school's ethos. This practical book:

- explores key issues relating to emotional intelligence to help develop adults' understanding;

- contains a wealth of activities that can be used with children to help develop their emotional intelligence, with extra focus given to anger and anxiety, as well as the impact emotions can have on learning and relationships;

- covers the beneficial impact of emotional intelligence when supporting challenging behaviour;

- outlines a straightforward emotional intelligence curriculum that ties into the personal, social, health and economic education (PSHE) schemes of work; and

- provides ideas for developing a whole-school approach to putting emotional intelligence firmly on the agenda.

This comprehensive resource has been written with teachers and school leaders in mind – particularly PSHE leads, special educational needs coordinators and those who work in pupil referral units and alternative provisions; but it is a useful tool for all adults working with children who are looking to improve children's self-awareness and wellbeing.

**Molly Potter** has worked as a mainstream teacher, a teacher in a pupil referral unit, a PSHE adviser, a trainer and writer; has provided one-to-one support for children; and is the author of more than 35 books on topics, many relating to emotional intelligence and wellbeing.

# THE POWER OF EMOTIONAL INTELLIGENCE

## A PRIMARY SCHOOL TOOLKIT

Molly Potter

Routledge
Taylor & Francis Group

LONDON AND NEW YORK

Designed cover image: © Sarah Hoyle

First published 2025
by Routledge
4 Park Square, Milton Park, Abingdon, Oxon OX14 4RN

and by Routledge
605 Third Avenue, New York, NY 10158

*Routledge is an imprint of the Taylor & Francis Group, an informa business*

*British Library Cataloguing-in-Publication Data*
A catalogue record for this book is available from the British Library

*Library of Congress Cataloging-in-Publication Data*
Names: Potter, Molly, author.
Title: The power of emotional intelligence : a primary school toolkit / Molly Potter.
Description: Abingdon, Oxon ; New York, NY : Routledge, 2024. | Includes
bibliographical references. | Summary: -- Provided by publisher.
Identifiers: LCCN 2024005461 (print) | LCCN 2024005462 (ebook) | ISBN
9781032690766 (hardback) | ISBN 9781032690759 (paperback) | ISBN
9781032690773 (ebook)
Subjects: LCSH: Education, Primary--Psychological aspects. | Emotional
intelligence. | Emotions in children. | Behavior modification. |
Children with mental disabilities--Education (Primary)
Classification: LCC LB1513 .P67 2024 (print) | LCC LB1513 (ebook) | DDC
370.15/2--dc23/eng/20240403
LC record available at https://lccn.loc.gov/2024005461
LC ebook record available at https://lccn.loc.gov/2024005462

ISBN: 978-1-032-69076-6 (hbk)
ISBN: 978-1-032-69075-9 (pbk)
ISBN: 978-1-032-69077-3 (ebk)

DOI: 10.4324/9781032690773

Typeset in DINPro
by Deanta Global Publishing Services, Chennai, India

Access the Support Material: https://resourcecentre.routledge.com/speechmark

For Mikey Potter – my brother, mentor and ridiculous playmate!

# CONTENTS

Contents

Contents

# INTRODUCTION

I think emotional intelligence (or 'EQ') is a superpower! This might seem like a very bold statement (and it possibly is if you're thinking in terms of time travel, flying or turning into a human-sized spider); but considering that it impacts on how well we perceive, evaluate and express our emotions, and that emotions are a vital part of being human, it does appear to be key to unlocking how well we manage life.

Unfortunately, though, emotions tend to be considered a bit of an inconvenience. Perhaps this is why we're inclined to ignore, suppress, dismiss and even apologise for them. It's usually logic that we would like to pretend always provides the interface between us and all we do – certainly in our professional interactions. However, most of us will have experienced how hard it is to concentrate when we're consumed with worry or have engaged in less than helpful behaviours while in the grips of a powerful emotion. Emotions that we don't learn to manage end up controlling us – sometimes with disastrous effects.

Because emotions play a significant role in our day-to-day experiences, rather than ignoring them, it's considerably better to work towards understanding and mastering them. When we become increasingly curious about our emotions and reactions, not only do we become more skilled at making better choices about how we respond in situations that trigger emotions, we also improve our motivation, our interpersonal skills, how effective we are at looking after our wellbeing and our resilience (to name just a few things)!

It's also great to acknowledge that emotional intelligence is a superpower that all of us can develop. Some people have more than others to start with; but the good news is we can all work to improve how well we manage our emotions – especially as children – and this is where this book comes in.

DOI: 10.4324/9781032690773-1

1

## What is this book?

This is a book for primary schools that wish to put emotional intelligence well and truly on the agenda. It provides a comprehensive toolkit with many 'hand it on a plate' tools for implementing a whole-school ethos and practice of promoting emotional intelligence. This book touches on theory but also offers many tried-and-tested practical tools.

Within this book, you will find:

- an explanation of some of the key issues relating to emotional intelligence to help adults further develop their understanding;
- many activities that can be used with children to help develop their emotional intelligence – with extra focus given to anger and anxiety, as well as the impact emotions can have on learning and relationships;
- material covering the beneficial impact of emotional intelligence on supporting behaviour that challenges;
- ideas for developing a whole-school approach to putting emotional intelligence on a school's agenda; and
- the outline of a straightforward emotional intelligence curriculum (linked to the personal, social, health and economic education (PSHE) schemes of work).

## How to use this book

This book can be used as a dip-in resource to enhance your existing PSHE schemes of work relating to emotional intelligence; but it is more effectively used as a platform from which you can start to develop emotional intelligence throughout the whole school – a school which understands that emotions play a key role in how we react, interact, learn and behave, and that becoming more emotionally intelligent as a school will impact beneficially on all of these.

# Chapter 1

# UNDERSTANDING EMOTIONS – INFORMATION FOR ADULTS

## What's in this chapter?

This chapter includes explanations I have refined over the years to help adults understand what emotional intelligence is, what its benefits are and how we might go about developing it further. Additionally, it includes some general guidance for adults on how to help children boost their emotional intelligence.

This chapter has been included because, in order to support children with regulating their emotions, it helps if adults understand the messages children need to hear, what we are trying to achieve and why. This chapter also seeks to persuade any doubters of the importance of being able to manage our emotions.

## What are emotions?

If you ask children what emotions are, they will often answer, 'They are how you feel.' This is as good an answer as any – we all know what emotions are, but they can be quite difficult to define. In a biological sense, they are simply a reaction to external stimuli that triggers various responses in our body that evolved to help us decide whether to approach or avoid something. Think of fear: it's a brilliant survival response, inducing reactions in our body that give us a burst of focus and energy with the sole aim of keeping us safe (flight, fight or freeze). However, this biological definition omits any appreciation of the fact that, even with the same stimuli, we all experience emotions differently – a key acknowledgement in developing emotional intelligence.

DOI: 10.4324/9781032690773-2

From my experience of working with children and adults exploring emotional intelligence, it is clear we are all wired slightly differently. How we react, what we are uniquely sensitive to and the thoughts that are triggered in different circumstances vary from person to person, and even in the same person at different times. For any definition of 'emotions' to be really useful in the realm of emotional intelligence, it must acknowledge that emotions are most often a subjective experience. Although not a child-friendly definition, I think Hoffman (2016) covers this well:

> an emotion is a multidimensional experience that is 1) characterised by difference levels of arousal and degrees of pleasure – displeasure 2) associated with subjective experiences, somatic sensations and motivational tendencies 3) coloured by contextual and cultural factors and 4) can be regulated to some degree through intra- and interpersonal processes.

Emotions are definitely complex!

My version of this definition, used to help children understand what emotions are, looks more simply at their effects:

- They can be comfortable or uncomfortable.
- They can be strong or weak/noticeable or not that noticeable.
- They have physical symptoms that affect different parts of the body.
- They can last a very short time or linger for much longer.
- They tend to make you full of energy or want to back or hide away.
- They can affect what and how we think.
- They can affect us differently at different times, depending on how tired, sensitive or comfortable we are, and our relationship with anyone else involved in the situation that triggers the emotion.

## The messages we receive about emotions

In a world that values rationality, emotions are often overlooked and ignored, even though they are a significant part of what it means to be human. We are emotional beings, yet we are often left with the idea that emotions need to be suppressed and feel we need to pretend they do not have the impact they do. Emotions can affect our thoughts, our behaviour, our competencies and our attitudes – and it's sometimes quite a tall order to pretend they don't!

Most of the time, many of us try hard not to express our emotions overtly, especially in public or in the workplace. When we do, we might induce comments such as, 'Stop making a fuss,' 'Be professional' or 'Cheer up'. It's quite easy to start thinking that emotions are irrelevant and inconvenient, and should be hidden away. For this reason, it's not surprising that emotions get as little attention as they do.

Another unhelpful idea children can believe is that we should be, or should appear to be, happy all the time. This is actually impossible. Likewise, when we express negative emotions such as anger or sadness, we are sometimes made to feel shame for feeling them. These value judgements add an extra layer of complication to what we end up feeling. For example, we may feel not only angry, but also ashamed – like we are a bad person for feeling anger. If we have received the message that anger is 'bad', simply feeling it can damage our self-worth. Healthy emotions don't have this extra baggage attached.

## Gender differences

The messages we hear about emotions as a child affect how we learn to express them – or not. Although the following are some sweeping generalisations (and I fully acknowledge there are always exceptions), awareness of these unwritten rules helps challenge unhelpful ideas about emotions some children might have received.

In generalised terms, boys tend to receive the message – either directly or by observing other males – that they should be self-reliant, 'strong' and in control, and should never show vulnerability. They frequently hear phrases such as, 'Man up' and 'Boys don't cry.' As a result, the only emotion that some males have learned to express openly is anger, because they think aggression seems stronger and more powerful than many other emotions. Many males manage to cope with this conditioning, but it can often leave them feeling incredibly pressured to avoid appearing vulnerable or out of control, and that it's inappropriate to ask for help. These messages can leave men feeling isolated and likely contribute to the fact that the leading cause of death for males under 50 is suicide (Sutherland 2018).

## Aggression as a cover-up

As a teacher in a pupil referral unit, I taught many boys who frequently behaved aggressively. This was their go-to expression of emotion, regardless of what they were actually feeling. A little curiosity soon made it apparent that the aggression was almost always covering up feelings of vulnerability, shame, anxiety and/or overwhelm.

During the time they spent with me, I aimed to help them connect their behaviour with their underlying feelings and understand that all emotions are acceptable (and can be expressed in better ways).

Likewise, females also receive unhelpful messages about emotions. Although talking about feelings and showing vulnerability are usually considered acceptable in females, they are generally expected to be more 'contained' and express emotions more modestly.

For example, it is very countercultural for a woman to express anger through aggression. Instead, she might respond indirectly by complaining about someone out of earshot or, more passively, simply by accepting that she must put up with whatever happened – even if boundaries have clearly been overstepped. This can leave females feeling powerless and ineffective; and they may turn this anger inwards on themselves, which Busch (2009) suggests can sometimes lead to depression.

In reality, all genders would benefit from challenging these messages, so that males are comfortable expressing all emotions without aggression and females can express their emotions in a way that means their needs are more frequently met. One practical illustration of this is the benefit of both males and females expressing anger assertively, rather than passively, indirectly or aggressively.

# Gender and the expression of anger

In the case of many children I have worked with who struggled to self-regulate, there was a clear difference between how girls and boys expressed anger. When boys were angry, you would know this very quicky: their escalation swiftly led to acts of verbal and/or physical aggression. Girls tended to be far less obvious but might start clawing at their lower arms or making much quieter declarations of self-hatred. The difference is often described as either 'acting out' (predominantly boys) or 'acting in' (predominantly girls). It was often the case that because boys' anger was expressed in a far more noticeable way, they were more likely to get support with managing their emotions. However, both expressions are potentially harmful.

## What is emotional intelligence?

Most people have some awareness of what emotional intelligence is; but in my experience, ideas about and attitudes towards it can vary considerably. I have found that when I am presenting information about emotional intelligence, a degree of persuasion that it's worth focusing on is usually needed. Part of this persuasion comes from helping people understand what it is, so they can fully see its benefits at a personal level as well as its potential impact on children.

## *Linking emotional intelligence to our reactions*

Over the years, I have described what emotional intelligence is and how to develop it in a number of different ways. Here, I will share my most distilled and efficient version initially, and then expand upon it.

Consider this:

**Something happens...**                                    **...and we react.**

- a car rushes towards us

- Someone snaps at us

- We make a mistake

- We lose our phone

- We win some money

- We meet someone for the first time

- We think an angry thought

a mere
human

Reaction
(what we do)

Our responses to something that happens are varied: on occasion, they are optimal; sometimes they have little or no impact; and sometimes they make the situation worse. Our emotions don't always guide us to the best possible response in any situation.

Quite often, our reactions to stimuli can:

- be damaging;
- 'add fuel to the fire';
- fail to consider the best outcome;
- cause us unnecessary or prolonged distress;
- fail to prioritise or help preserve relationships with others; and
- rarely take into account all of the relevant information about the situation in an unbiased and rational way.

Our reactions not only often overlook many relevant considerations and details, but also depend on a lot of other factors. At a basic level, our reactions are linked to our thoughts (how we interpret the situation), emotions and physical sensations.

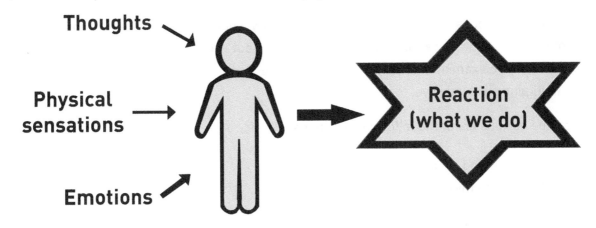

**Thoughts**

**Physical sensations**

**Emotions**

**Reaction (what we do)**

The thoughts, emotions and physical sensations that we end up experiencing are also dependent on a variety of factors, such as:

- how comfortable we are (are we tired/hungry/too hot?);
- what kind of day we've had so far;
- whether there's something on our mind troubling us;
- how stressed we generally feel;
- what our relationship with anyone else involved in the situation is like and what we think of them;
- what has happened to us in similar circumstances in the past;
- our personality – the thoughts, behaviours and attitudes unique to us;
- our propensity towards neuroticism – that is, our predisposition to experience negative emotions (Goldberg 1990);
- any automatic avoidance of situations we are not comfortable with that we might engage in; and
- whether any particular sensitivities have been touched upon.

Thus, upon more detailed examination, something seemingly as simple as 'something happens and we react' actually turns out to be more complex. There are many factors that influence how we react in any given circumstance and often we are not consciously aware of their effects.

This is where my simple explanation of developing emotional intelligence comes in: we gain emotional intelligence by being curious about the backstory of our reactions. It's an explanation that also gives us an obvious inroad to developing more emotional intelligence, as the starting point is to look out for our reactions. At first, we notice our reactions and become curious about what triggered them. Eventually, we become good at noticing emotions as they arrive and become more of a detached observer of them before our reaction kicks in. This means we are much less likely to react outwardly and impulsively, and our responses are far more considered. This takes a degree of determined focus but becomes easier with practice.

In starting this process, it is helpful to consider exactly what we can be curious about when we notice a reaction. There's plenty to be inquisitive about – and the greater our curiosity and the more we examine what is going on for us, the more quickly our emotional awareness and intelligence will improve.

We can be curious about the following questions:

- What am I feeling exactly?
- What triggered my reaction?

- Would it trigger the same response in everyone?
- Have I made any assumptions about what anyone meant?
- Have I considered what might be going on for anyone else involved?
- What did I think and how did it contribute to how I ended up feeling? Am I engaging in any unhelpful or unnecessary thinking? Can these thoughts be challenged?
- Was my reaction exaggerated by other factors (eg, how tired or stressed I am)?
- Is there an underlying need that is being ignored, dismissed or overlooked?
- Has someone touched on something I am particularly sensitive about?
- Am I feeling a need to protect myself and if so, from what?
- What would be the best outcome and what could I do to try to make this happen?

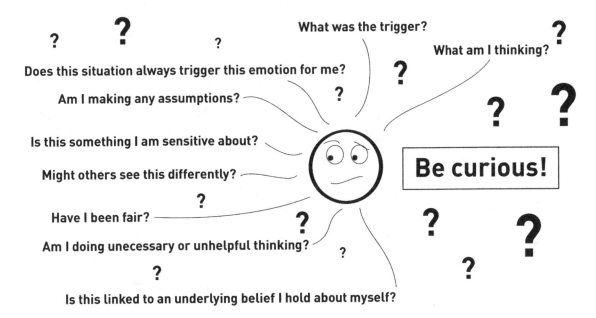

If, each time we feel an emotional response, we begin to focus inwardly and explore with curiosity what is going on for us, we have a better chance of reacting optimally and resourcefully. With this curiosity, we can start to:

- appreciate that our reactions depend on a lot of factors;
- resist the urge to react in the same self-protective way we always have and become more flexible in our responses;
- free ourselves from automatic thoughts that can be unhelpful;
- link our emotions directly to what has triggered them (so we don't carry the emotion elsewhere and take it out on someone else);
- question the appropriateness of our reaction;
- be more empathetic towards others involved and wonder what might be going on for them;

- make more objective decisions and problem solve, based on what is actually in front of us in any moment and not on any exaggerations, assumptions, misinterpretations or hasty conclusions we might have made; and
- become more self-aware.

In short, we become more emotionally intelligent and start to master our emotions and reactions, rather than letting them control us.

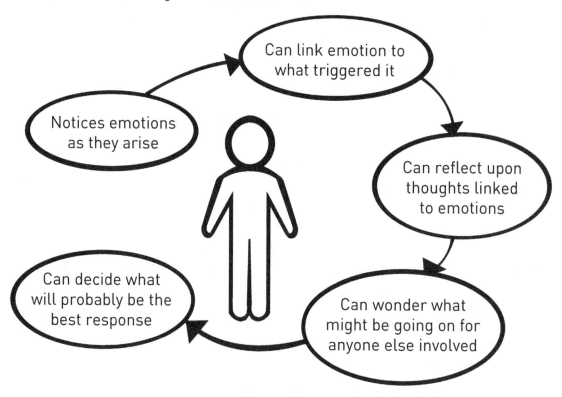

## What does poor emotional intelligence look like?

When we have poor emotional intelligence, we tend to have less flexibility in how we react to different situations and will often be 'on repeat' in how we react. We can also sometimes be highly 'dysregulated' (ie, have little control over how we react to our emotions) and respond in ways that make situations worse.

Poor emotional intelligence tends to mean we rely on what may have worked in the past to keep us feeling safe and protected (eg, being hypervigilant in a new situation; exhibiting controlling behaviours when things feel more uncertain or chaotic than we think we can cope with; or becoming aggressive if we perceive we are being criticised). Unfortunately, these reactions may no longer serve us well – and certainly not in every situation. Quite often, when we are unaware of our emotions and their resulting reactions, we revert to our default reactions so rigidly that we are blind to the possibility of responding in other ways.

This need to feel safe and protected can also mean we struggle to take risks and can go to great lengths to avoid situations where we think we might experience uncomfortable emotions (so we stay well and truly in our 'comfort zone'). Anyone who has ever tried to help a child who believes they are rubbish at maths, for example, will know how carefully they need to tread to keep the child in their comfort zone and not trigger their shame by coaxing them gently towards challenge.

## Comfort zones

I have taught many children whom I would describe as easily 'spooked' by any kind of challenge to their comfort zone. With dysregulated children, this comfort zone was metaphorically tiny. They would need very careful support, for example, when there was a change in routine, when they made a mistake, when there was a new person in the classroom or even when they changed from one lesson to the next – all of these were perceived as too great a risk for them. These children's intense need to feel safe meant that uncertainty, change and any risk of feeling shame were perceived as threats. They were always happier staying with what they knew.

These children's trauma and resulting poor emotional intelligence meant that negative emotions were triggered easily and felt intensely, and their defensive or controlling reactions could be extreme. They could only be encouraged and expected to take one tiny risk at a time if their threat system was not going to sabotage learning. Each success, though – however small – helped them start trusting in their ability to cope.

There are many behaviours we engage in because of poor emotional intelligence – whether because we are totally unaware of our emotions and automatic reactions; we are avoiding the risk of unenjoyable emotions; or we are allowing exaggerated, biased, single-minded thoughts to consume us. Behaviours I have heard people relate to their poor emotional intelligence on exploring these aspects of emotional responses have included:

- aggressive outbursts;
- passive aggression;
- ruminating and catastrophising;
- paranoia;
- avoiding and/or ignoring someone who triggered upset;
- inability to take criticism;
- taking things out on someone else;
- distracting or playing the clown;
- inability to be assertive;
- poor motivation;
- refusing to leave a comfort zone;
- giving up easily;
- withdrawing from situations or participation;
- trying unrealistically to control everything;
- sulking;

- becoming unable to do anything;
- always blaming others;
- being defensive, or even offensive;
- inability to see someone else's point of view; and
- being closed-minded.

Becoming aware of, focusing on and being curious about our emotional responses help to challenge these responses as our minds open up to other interpretations and possibilities.

## Considering our responses

When I talk to adults about their behaviours, their reflections can make them aware of many generalised responses, such as attempting to dodge uncomfortable emotions by avoiding situations; trying to control situations to avoid feeling powerless; or becoming defensive and pushing people away so they don't have to face the difficulties of whatever happened and the emotions it triggered. Understanding that these behaviours are the result of emotional responses can make us curious as to how our feelings trigger some repetitive reactions.

## How do we develop more emotional intelligence?

In an ideal world, we would all have been helped to make sense of our emotions from a very young age by a trusted adult who made us feel safe and secure enough to accept, understand and process all of our emotions – including the uncomfortable ones. When a young child receives this support, they will eventually become able to manage their emotions and self-regulate effectively. If this doesn't happen, their emotions will usually be more complicated and they will need to learn to connect with their emotions, accept them, understand what they might be indicating and learn how best to respond to them. This starts, as already stated, with noticing our reactions and being curious about them; but there are further helpful tools and ideas that can also help on the journey towards greater emotional intelligence.

### Emotion check-ins

One helpful tool for developing greater emotional intelligence is to regularly complete what I call an 'emotion check-in'. I often start training sessions with one. I simply ask participants to focus inwardly and consider what they might be feeling. Do they notice any physical sensations? Any enjoyable or unenjoyable emotions? If so, are these strong or weak? Do they feel able to be truly present in the here and now or is something agitating them and taking their thoughts elsewhere? Do they feel any trace of guardedness or need to protect themselves or are they totally comfortable in this space? Are they leaning towards feeling more energised or withdrawn? Can they put a name to what they are feeling?

Do they know what might have triggered any emotion they might be feeling? If they are feeling a background mood instead, how would they describe it?

As we get used to checking in with what we are feeling, we increase our awareness of emotions. The aim is eventually to reach the stage where we notice our emotions arrive as and when they do, as this is the make-or-break moment in preventing potentially damaging, impulsive reactions. If we get to this point, we can resist automatic reactions, slow things down and – by being curious about what is going on for us – consider and possibly challenge our interpretation of what has happened (see below), reflect upon what the best outcome would be and identify the most effective way of working towards it. The more we engage in this process, the more control we start to gain over our emotions.

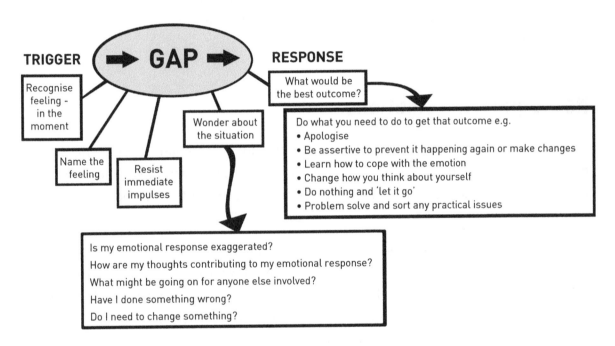

## Understand that emotions send us messages

Another aspect of developing emotional intelligence is to increase our consideration of what any emotion might be trying to tell us.

Many emotions can deliver quite clear messages, as in the following examples:

- You are feeling **angry and indignant** because someone has disregarded a boundary and you need to protect it, or has overlooked or dismissed your needs.
  **Message:** You need to assertively explain what you need.
- You are feeling **confused and agitated** because you are unsure of how to move forward as you don't have all the information you need.

**Message:** You need to find out more information.

- You are feeling *overwhelmed and powerless* because someone is bullying you.

  **Message:** You need to find support to help make the bullying stop.

- You are feeling *guilty and awkward* because you've done something you know was wrong.

  **Message:** You need to make amends and try not to do what you did again.

- You are feeling *scared and panicked* because you're in danger.

  **Message:** You need to make yourself safe.

- You are feeling *anxious and nervous* because you need to get on and do something that you don't think you will cope with well.

  **Message:** You need to prepare as best as you can and remind yourself of all the times you have coped before (and develop coping strategies for managing anxiety).

- You are feeling *sad and withdrawn* because you have experienced loss.

  **Message:** You need time to recover from that loss.

## Messages from emotions

When children have started to become more aware of their emotions, I ask them, 'What do you think the emotion is telling you?' This is another way of developing introspection and it often works to stop a child in their tracks as they consider the question.

When emotions send us straightforward messages, it's helpful to be inquisitive about those messages and see whether a clear way forward and what we need to do become apparent. It's also important to remember that in some situations, simply 'letting it go' might be the optimal choice. To 'let things go', we often need to use coping strategies to soothe ourselves and/or reframe how we think about a situation (see below).

It's also important to realise that the messages emotions send us are sometimes unhelpful. Fear – as a 'better safe than sorry' emotion – might tell us that the dark is dangerous when it is extremely unlikely to harm us. Anxiety might tell us to avoid doing something that would actually be good for us in the long run. If we are curious about our emotions, we can also start to work out when they are misleading us.

## *Considering different interpretations*

Another important factor in gaining more emotional intelligence involves increasing our awareness of how we interpret different situations where our emotions have been triggered.

When we experience an emotion, there are always associated thoughts. Sometimes these thoughts are straightforward. Other times they include distortions, denials, assumptions and exaggerations that can prevent us from finding an effective solution for dealing with the situation and extend our experience of an unenjoyable emotion. At these times, our thinking would benefit from some close scrutiny.

How we interpret situations has an impact on how we end up feeling. As we are (only) human, our interpretations can be fallible – even when we have convinced ourselves that they are the absolute truth!

Here's an example of how our interpretations impact on what we end up feeling. Think of a time when somebody didn't listen to you. There are a number of different interpretations you could have and what you end up feeling will depend upon your interpretation.

If someone did not listen to you, here are some possible interpretations you could find yourself adopting, along with the likely resulting emotions and responses:

| Trigger | Possible interpretation | Possible emotion | Possible response |
|---|---|---|---|
| Someone doesn't listen to you | • Nobody listens to me<br>• I am unimportant<br>• I have lost control<br>• They hate me<br>• They don't respect me | • Anger<br>• Shame<br>• Vulnerability<br>• Rejection<br>• Humiliation | • Aggressive outburst<br>• Withdrawal and inaction<br>• Attempting to control everything<br>• Wallowing<br>• Moaning |

Quite often, our negative interpretation is incorrect – born of tiredness, sensitivity, misunderstanding, jumping to conclusions, making assumptions, etc. It's more likely that the person who ignored you is stressed, upset or overwhelmed and simply does not have the capacity to listen to you. If someone does not listen to you, it is not usually as a result of what they think of you – and certainly not a reflection of what everyone else might think of you. If we feel we have been affronted, it's always wise to make it less about ourselves by asking, 'Under what circumstance might I do what they just did?'

## Understanding how emotions impact on thoughts

Another way to improve our emotional intelligence involves increasing our awareness of how our emotions impact on our thinking. When we are experiencing different emotions, the way we think is also affected. It's helpful to remind ourselves of this when we are in the grip of an emotion.

The following table lists some emotions and the impact they can have on our thinking:

| Emotion | The [insert emotion] brain |
|---|---|
| Anger | • Is usually only interested in meeting their own needs.<br>• Tends not to be able to 'receive' anyone else's side of the story.<br>• Has a narrow fixation on whatever triggered the anger.<br>• Might add unnecessary 'fuel' to the anger by looking for more reasons to be indignant or demonise someone. |
| Anxiety | • Ruminates – has unhelpful and sometimes obsessive thoughts going round and round their head.<br>• Catastrophises – starts to assume that everything that can go wrong will go wrong.<br>• Struggles to concentrate on things other than what is triggering the anxiety.<br>• Is unlikely to take any risks – even those which could prove beneficial. |
| Fear | • Only concern is reaching immediate safety from real (or perceived) danger or threat.<br>• Has a narrow focus on the danger or perceived threat.<br>• Cannot discern between what is truly harmful (eg, a car heading towards them) and what just makes them fearful (eg, going into a room of strangers).<br>• Is on high alert, looking out for other potential threats or dangers. |
| Sadness | • Struggles to get motivated to do anything.<br>• Is withdrawn and does not want to interact.<br>• Is uninterested and hard to engage.<br>• Can be numb, 'empty' and have little going on. |
| Happiness | • Can make people want to connect with others more.<br>• Is creative and explorative.<br>• Is likely to put a positive spin on things.<br>• Can be more agreeable and open to suggestion. |
| Disgust | • Judges quickly to avoid something.<br>• Sends a clear and rigid message not to try something again.<br>• Can 'close down' further thinking about the topic or thing (which can be unhelpful – for example, in the case of social disgust triggered by prejudice). |
| Surprise | • Brings a sharp focus on what is in front of them.<br>• Can warn you to stay alert.<br>• Is guarded and poised on the lookout for any further possible risks.<br>• Is unlikely to hang about to consider nuance. |

## Coping strategies

Another key aspect of emotional intelligence involves managing our emotions so that we become better at enduring all of them, including uncomfortable ones. Different emotions can require slightly different approaches to help us cope with them, but I tell children they generally fall into one of two categories – soothing ourselves and changing how we think about what happened – although some of the things that soothe us can also beneficially lead to a change in perspective.

Things that people rely upon to soothe themselves when experiencing uncomfortable emotions such as anxiety, sadness and overwhelm can be both healthy and unhealthy. Examples of beneficial coping strategies include:

- going for a walk – preferably outside and somewhere green;
- talking things through with someone;
- engaging in mindfulness and meditation;
- using online hypnosis;
- listening to music;
- having a good cry;
- doing something that takes up all of your focus (eg, watching a film);
- having a massage;
- finding a change of scene;
- stroking a pet;
- doing breathing exercises;
- visualising a beautiful place to relax in; and
- writing down what you're feeling and why.

Tools to help change how we think about a situation that might have caused uncomfortable emotions such as shame, anger or humiliation include:

- trying to find the funny side;
- thinking of any positives – even if it is that you have just learned a lesson;
- recognising and challenging any unhelpful thinking;
- reminding yourself of times when you coped before;
- visualising the triggering event and, in your head, changing the picture to black and white, making it smaller, turning down the volume and then playing a silly tune over it;
- wondering what might be going on for anyone else involved and imagining a situation where you can feel more forgiveness;
- allowing yourself some time to wallow and/or think intensely about what happened and then telling yourself to stop;
- reflecting on a time that will come when what happened no longer bothers you;
- telling yourself, 'This too will pass';
- finding comfort in the fact that others will have also experienced what you are experiencing;
- considering how things could be worse, to help you find some positives;
- thinking of many things you are grateful for;
- imagining the worst-case scenario and knowing you would ultimately cope with it; and
- making a plan to do something positive that you will enjoy.

## The benefits of emotional intelligence

When we master our emotions so they no longer control us, there are plenty of benefits. By learning to regulate our reactions, carefully considering what our emotions might be telling us, enduring uncomfortable emotions (rather than attempting to avoid them), releasing emotions without complication, learning to empathise and working out how to respond to our emotions resourcefully, our self-awareness increases and life definitely get easier!

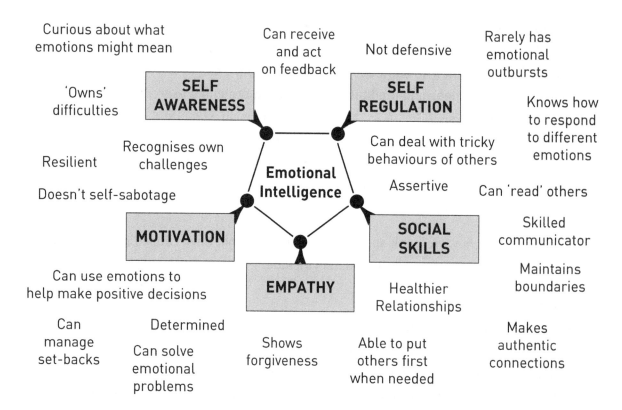

## Contrasting good and poor emotional intelligence

| Poor emotional Intelligence | A person with poor emotional intelligence: |
|---|---|
| | <ul><li>does not acknowledge their emotions consciously;</li><li>is unable to link their emotions to what triggered them;</li><li>has a limited emotion vocabulary;</li><li>can blame others for how they feel (eg, 'You made me angry');</li><li>is controlled by their emotions and may have unhelpful reactions;</li><li>has complex emotions (eg, they feel not just angry but also shame for being angry);</li><li>is 'on repeat', with similar situations always triggering the same emotions and reactions;</li><li>is unaware that how they interpret events can be challenged;</li><li>has emotional responses that can be excessive or under-expressed in relation to situations; and</li><li>tends to believe that their reactions are always justified.</li></ul> |

| Good emotional Intelligence | A person with good emotional intelligence: |
| --- | --- |
| | • notices emotions in the moment they arrive;<br>• has a large emotion vocabulary and can express how they feel accurately;<br>• can link emotions to their triggers;<br>• does not judge emotions as 'good' or 'bad';<br>• accepts that unenjoyable emotions are part of life and has worked out how to endure them;<br>• is detached enough to be curious about their emotions so that impulses can be resisted, thoughts can be challenged and the best outcome for each situation can be considered;<br>• understands that emotions send messages, and that some of these are helpful and some less so;<br>• never blames others for how they feel and takes responsibility for their own emotions and addressing them (eg, 'I feel angry when ...');<br>• objectively and immediately assesses triggers of emotions for genuine threats and any need to address them;<br>• is in control of how they express their emotions;<br>• has emotions that arrive and leave with relative simplicity and no secondary emotion responses (eg, feeling shame for being angry); and<br>• can empathise with others (ie, imagine what it must be like for others in their situation). |

## Guidance for helping children to develop emotional intelligence

Here are some key considerations that should serve as the foundation of an adult's approach to helping develop children's emotional intelligence. All of these (and more) are embedded in the activities within this book.

## *Have regular emotion check-ins*

A regular emotion check-in puts emotions on the agenda and helps children to develop greater awareness of their emotions. It demonstrates that expressing how you feel is totally acceptable and normalises all feelings. It also helps because when we express how we feel, we feel better heard and understood.

## *Increase children's emotion vocabulary*

Research (eg, Feldmen Barrett 2007) has shown that having more words to express how we feel in itself increases our understanding of our emotions. Start young children with 'happy', 'sad', 'angry' and 'scared', and slowly add to this list when talking about emotions. English is rich with words that describe how we feel.

## *Validate children's emotions*

Always validate children's emotions, even if you feel they seem exaggerated or over the top. Whatever a child is feeling is real for them. Use phrases like, 'I would feel angry too if ...' or, 'I can see why you're worried.' This prevents children from bottling up or hiding negative emotions and helps them feel it is acceptable to express and be curious about their emotions. As an added bonus, when you notice children's feelings, they feel cared about and you send them a message that all of these emotions – including the negative ones – are accepted.

## *Help children accept both enjoyable and unenjoyable emotions*

Help children to understand that it is normal to feel both enjoyable and unenjoyable emotions. It is completely unrealistic to think that we can feel happy all of the time – even if the world of advertisements and social media gives us this impression. Help children to accept unenjoyable emotions as a normal part of being human by being a supportive and soothing presence when they are experiencing these feelings. Many worthwhile things in life require us to endure uncomfortable emotions.

## *Never place judgement on emotions*

Never describe enjoyable emotions as 'good' and unenjoyable emotions as 'bad'. If we tell a child they are wrong or 'bad' for feeling angry, for example, they will not only feel angry, but also feel some shame for feeling it. Negative judgements of emotions can incentivise a child to bottle up or hide negative emotions, which can make them less emotionally aware. Likewise, do not put a value judgement on positive emotions or children will start to believe that they are 'good' only when they are experiencing – or look like they are experiencing – enjoyable emotions such as happiness.

## *Help children to link physical symptoms to each emotion*

Some children struggle to identify what they are feeling because they do not know how to link their physical reactions to different emotions. Discuss the physical symptoms of different emotions to help children recognise each emotion more fully (eg, when a person feels angry, their heartbeat tends to speed up; they get a surge of energy; their face might become hot; and they might clench their teeth and fists). Exploring the physical symptoms of different emotions also increases the chance of children noticing emotions as they arise.

## Explore the triggers of different emotions with children

Help children to link their emotions to what triggered them. Triggers can be explored by asking children how they would feel in different situations – for example, if you lost your favourite toy or if you were really hungry and about to eat your favourite food. Alternatively, you could ask children what triggers them to feel different emotions such as anger, excitement or sadness. Triggers can also be explored as emotions arise by speculating about what a child might be feeling (eg, 'I wonder if you're feeling disappointed because we can't go swimming now?') This will also help children to notice their emotions as they arise.

## Autism and understanding emotions

I find some autistic children need a little extra help in understanding what they might be feeling. Exploring the physical symptoms of different emotions can really help with this.

## Help children to see the effect of emotions on their thinking

Talk to children about 'the angry brain', 'the worried brain', the 'happy brain' etc to consider how emotions affect our thinking. For example, when we are angry, we are likely to think about our own needs and what made us angry; when we are worried, we tend to focus only on what we're worried about; and when we are happy, we often feel more adventurous and interested in other people.

## Teach children to take a pause

Some children often react impulsively to their emotions. Emotions can have a powerful impact on our behaviour. Because we rarely make good choices when we are in the grip of a powerful emotion, it's always a good idea to take time out before reacting. Once children have started to recognise emotions as they arise, teach them strategies for taking a pause before reacting. For example, when they become angry, they might need to learn to count down from ten, take deep breaths or walk away until the intensity of their anger subsides. This can take only a few seconds but can make the difference between a reaction that triggers destructive responses and one that helps to sort a situation out. Remember, we can't always help what we feel, but we can learn to choose how we behave, whatever we are feeling. Common emotions that may need a pause before reacting include anger, shame, humiliation, feeling misunderstood, panic (if not in danger), embarrassment, excitement, hurt and frustration.

## Discuss coping strategies

Help children to develop coping strategies that work for them when they are experiencing strong, unenjoyable emotions. These will be different for different individuals and different emotions. Here are some examples:

- **Worry:**
  - Learn why humans worry.
  - Practise relaxation techniques.
  - Face the fear by breaking down possible approaches into small steps.
  - Try visualisation exercises.
- **Anger:**
  - Take time out to pause when angry.
  - Explore and challenge the thoughts that arose when you were angry and decide whether they were helpful or not.
  - Consider what made you angry and what can be done about it (if anything).
- **Sadness:**
  - Understand that sadness is a normal reaction to loss.
  - Take time out to allow yourself to be sad.
  - Find things that comfort you, such as a hug or stroking a pet.
  - Know that there will be a time when you will no longer feel sad.

## Help children to empathise

Help children to empathise when others are having an emotional reaction – even if that other person's emotional upset is making them uncomfortable (but obviously not if it's unsafe). If a child can imagine how another person is feeling in any situation that arises, they are more likely to be able to help and address emotional problems which will enhance their friendship skills. You can help develop children's empathy by discussing how different characters might feel in stories or films, and discussing situations their friends might be struggling with and how people are feeling.

## Always describe the 'cause' of an emotion as 'what has been triggered' (in us)

This is a subtlety that needs explaining. Attributing the cause of an emotion to something external can take away our part in, and responsibility for, the emotions that arise within us. We can say, 'You made me angry' if we believe that the cause of our emotion lies wholly down to another person or external events. Acknowledging that an event triggered an emotion within us helps us to 'own' our emotions and understand that not everyone will respond to the same stimuli in exactly the same way. Our emotional triggers are personal to us.

## Teach children to use 'I' messages

To help children avoid blaming others for their emotional responses (as this is rarely helpful), teach them to use 'I' messages. Using 'I' messages to express how you feel is less blaming and less disputable than accusing others of triggering your emotions – for example, 'I feel angry when people tease me,' instead of 'You made me angry.'

It's a good idea to encourage children to look inwards and be curious and interested in their emotions and the messages – both helpful and unhelpful – that these might be sending them, rather than looking for someone to blame for how they feel.

## Teach children about our negativity bias

Our brains evolved to notice the negative more than the positive. This is because it was more important for our survival to notice the snake in the grass than the beautiful flower. An example of this is that the sole critical comment amid a barrage of praise is the one that grabs our attention most and lingers. This negativity bias has an impact on how frequently negative emotions are triggered. Being aware of this bias can help children challenge it.

## Model emotional intelligence

As we know, much of what children learn comes from what is modelled to them. Even if – as for most of us – your emotional intelligence is a 'work in progress', you can still make a conscious effort to talk more openly about your feelings. The easiest way to do this is to use 'I' messages that link how you feel to what has happened – for example, 'I feel flustered when I can't find something.'

# Chapter 2

# ACTIVITIES TO USE WITH CHILDREN TO SUPPORT THE DEVELOPMENT OF EMOTIONAL INTELLIGENCE

## What's in this chapter?

This chapter includes instructions and resources for a number of tried-and-tested activities that can be used with children to help develop their understanding of emotions and improve their emotional awareness and intelligence. This chapter focuses on a variety of emotions.

## *Activity notes*

- You will find a description of each of the activities in the first part of this chapter, followed by the relevant activity sheets. These can be either photocopied or downloaded for easy printing by following the access instructions at the beginning of this book.
- Activities are described with an objective, instructions, an indication of whether any further resources are needed (including printable resources from this book) and at least one suggested extension idea.
- The activities involve a variety of teaching and learning techniques, including discussion prompts, quizzes, agreement spectrums, sorting activities, drama activities, games and lessons that use printable worksheets.
- The activities at the start of this chapter are appropriate for younger children and progress to those suitable for older children, roughly in developmental order – although

DOI: 10.4324/9781032690773-3

many activities could easily be simplified for younger children or made more challenging for older children. Some activities include suggestions for such adaptation. Also, some generic activities – such as the 'emotion check-in' – could be repeated as children move up the school.

- Some activities can be used as lessons, while others are suitable for regular use in smaller time slots – such as a quick game at the end of a school day.
- Differentiated emotions lists/cards (Sheets A to C) that can be used for more than one activity are found at the end of this chapter.

## Emotional intelligence: what to teach and why

| Aspect of emotional intelligence that can be taught (and learned) | How learning this helps |
|---|---|
| Identify and name what you are feeling | • Makes emotions more conscious.<br>• Helps the thinking/labelling part of the brain engage with an emotional situation. |
| Have a large emotion vocabulary. | • Gives you the words to express exactly how you feel, which can help you feel better and self-regulate.<br>• Increases your awareness of the scope of different feelings. |
| Recognise the physical symptoms of different emotions. | • Makes you more conscious of your emotions.<br>• Helps you recognise emotions as they arise.<br>• Helps you focus inwards rather than react automatically or impulsively. |
| Understand that how we react to an emotion can depend upon a variety of factors. | • Helps you consider what might be contributing to your reactions.<br>• Helps you learn to 'own' your individual responses.<br>• Elicits curiosity about emotional responses.<br>• Increases self-awareness. |
| Understand that our emotional reactions can be unique to us. | • Helps you understand that the same situation will trigger different emotions in different people.<br>• Enables you to start taking responsibility for how you react to different emotions. |
| Notice emotions at the moment they arrive. | • Increases the chance of avoiding potentially damaging responses that make situations worse and gives you greater flexibility in how you respond.<br>• Increases the chance of noticing any automatic, unhelpful responses and thinking associated with emotions.<br>• Increases self-awareness.<br>• Contributes towards becoming more conscious of reactions which help and those which make situations worse. |
| Recognise what triggers different emotions. | • Helps you link triggers to your emotional responses.<br>• Helps you consider whether a situation that triggered an emotion has an issue that needs addressing or whether your emotion just needs managing. |

| Aspect of emotional intelligence that can be taught (and learned) | How learning this helps |
|---|---|
| Expect to feel, and learn to accept and endure, both enjoyable and unenjoyable emotions. | • Helps you become more accepting of all emotions, including unenjoyable emotions, as part of human existence.<br>• Helps prevent you from thinking you are 'bad' for experiencing negative emotions (eg, 'I am "bad" for feeling angry'; 'I am "good" when I am happy'). |
| Learn coping strategies for managing uncomfortable emotions. | • Helps build resilience – the ability to cope with and recover from testing situations.<br>• Expands your comfort zone and enables you to be more motivated, determined and better able to manage change. |
| Understand that emotions send us messages that are sometimes helpful and sometimes unhelpful. | • Increases awareness of when and how to act on an emotion.<br>• Helps you consider whether a situation that triggered an emotion has an issue that needs addressing, whether it can teach you something about yourself or whether your emotion just needs to be endured. |
| Express what you are feeling in a resourceful way – for example, being assertive by using 'I' messages (eg, 'I feel angry when people insult me'). | • Reduces the chance of making a situation worse when reacting to an emotion.<br>• Increases confidence, agency and wellbeing, and improves relationship skills.<br>• Helps you manage situations more proactively and directly, increasing the likelihood of difficult situations being addressed more quickly and effectively. |
| Be able to empathise with others. | • Develops acceptance and tolerance of different reactions.<br>• Enhances compassion.<br>• Helps you develop an awareness that your behaviour impacts on others.<br>• Enhances interactions and relationships – as you can 'read' people. |

## Activities

### Teddy's day

 *Objective*

To help children link enjoyable and unenjoyable emotions to their triggers.

### ✓ *What's needed?*

Access to the story *Teddy's day* (page 76) for you to read; a teddy (not essential).

##  Instructions

- Explain to the children that you're going to read them a story about Teddy. The story describes what Teddy got up to yesterday.
- Also explain that at some points in the story Teddy felt sad; at other points he felt happy; and sometimes he felt something in between the two.
- Next, explain that when you read the story, you're going to stop to ask everyone whether they think Teddy is happy or sad. They can do this with a beaming smile for 'happy' and a frowning face for 'sad'. If they think Teddy probably felt something in between, they can indicate this with a straight face.
- Read the story and pause at the places indicated by a star for the children to respond.
- At each pause, look to see whether there is agreement. There will be times when some children are smiling and others are not. Use these to explain that we don't all feel the same, even when the same things happen to us. Also ask the children whether there are any other feeling words that could describe how Teddy might be feeling.
- You can also ask the children why they think Teddy feels the way he does and what they think he might be thinking at the different points in the story.

##  Extension ideas

- The children could make statements about the things Teddy got up to and ask the class to respond with a smiley face or a frowning face to indicate how they think Teddy might feel – for example, 'Teddy was handed an ice cream.'
- You could use the 'smiley face' or 'frowning face' indication to ask the children how they think particular characters in any story might be feeling. You could add 'angry', 'worried' and then additional feelings as the children get older.

## Note

Teddy can be a teddy bear for very young children or a child called Teddy for older children.

## Emotion hunt

### Objective

To start noticing how the expression on a person's face can indicate what they are feeling.

*Instructions*

- Tell the children that they are about to go on an emotion hunt. By this, you mean that they are going to look in the classroom (school, playground etc) for pictures of faces that show different feelings. For example, they might find a picture of a smile on a mug or a sad face in a book etc.
- Explain that each time a child finds a face expressing an emotion, they should bring it to you if they can. (You could provide a camera to capture those examples that can't be moved. With this, some children cleverly take pictures of each other making the expressions of different emotions!)
- Once several emotions have been collected, look at them one by one and ask the children the following questions:
  - Can you make the same expression?
  - What emotion are you probably feeling when you look this way?
  - What could have made a person feel this way?
  - Which of these faces looks the happiest – and which the least happy? Can we sort them in order and imagine what might have just happened to them?

 *Extension ideas*

- Ask the children to look for different emotions at home and report back to you what they find. If the class only find happy and sad faces, ask them if they can find an angry face or a scared face at home.
- With older children, you can ask them to find evidence of emotions in stories and pull out the text from the story indicating that an emotion is being experienced.

 *Note*

Invariably – especially in spaces used by younger children – the smile is most frequently found and expressions of other emotions are harder to find. Sometimes just a happiness hunt can be fun!

# Emotion whispers

## 🚀 *Objective*

To 'read' the emotional expressions on the faces of others.

 ## What's needed?

Most children find it quite easy to copy another's expression; the value here lies in helping them to focus carefully on another's expression and 'read' their face.

 ## Instructions

- Ask some of the children to volunteer and get into a line of four facing the rest of the group or class.
- Whisper an emotion into the ear of the child at one end of the line or let them choose one.
- This person starts 'passing on the emotion' along the line. They do this by making the facial expression they think matches the emotion and turning to the person next to them in the line so they can see it. Explain they must try to make no noise at all. Also encourage the children to do this secretly, so the others in the line can't see it before their turn (it doesn't really matter too much if they do, however!).
- The second person in the line does the same to the third person in the line.
- Once the emotion has been passed to the fourth person at the end of the line, ask them what they think the emotion is, to see whether it has been successfully passed along the line.
- You can eventually make the lines longer.

 ## Extension ideas

- Once the emotion has been passed along the line, ask the children in the line to make the expression they made in the game, but this time look forward to show it to the rest of the class. Ask the class to sort the children in a row from the child who looks the most [whatever the emotion is] to the least.
- The children can also speculate as to what might have happened to each child in the line and share their ideas with the rest of the group.

 ## Note

This is a fun, quick game to play at the end of the day.

# Happy or sad?

## Objective

To start linking experiences to the emotions they are likely to trigger.

## ✅ What's needed?

One copy of the sheet *Happy or sad?* (page 77) per child.

## 🔍 Instructions

- Explain to the children that everyone feels happy sometimes and sad other times. Feeling enjoyable emotions such as happiness and unenjoyable emotions such as sadness is just a normal part of being human.
- Give the children a copy of the sheet *Happy or sad?* and ask them to complete the task outlined on it.
- You could ask the children to share further personal triggers for or memories of feeling happy and sad and create a list from their responses.
- Explain that life is full of things that happen that can trigger different emotions in us. Ask the children to think of something that happened to them recently and share how they felt about it.
- The children could draw two different life events and write the emotions they triggered underneath – preferably one enjoyable emotion and one unenjoyable emotion, so both are acknowledged.

##  Extension ideas

- Ask the children to think of other things that could make one person happy and another sad – for example, eating tomatoes, being given cake instead of sweets, tidying up, doing a jigsaw puzzle, playing on swings, singing, going for a walk in the rain, using scissors, watching football, listening to a story, climbing a tree, colouring in, running – to illustrate further that we can have different responses to the same thing.

##  Note

What can be interestingly pointed out to children when they do this task is that we can't always make assumptions about how others feel based on what we feel ourselves. Snow might not make all children happy, for example. You can use this to illustrate how the same things do not trigger the same emotions in different people and that many of our responses are unique to us.

# Is this a 'yes' or 'no' moment?

 **Objective**

To get children to reflect upon and assess how they feel in any moment.

 **Instructions**

- Describe a 'yes moment': when you're feeling an enjoyable emotion, such as happiness, excitement, eagerness, interest in seeing what will happen, curiosity, liveliness, enthusiasm etc.

- Then describe a 'no moment': when you're feeling an unenjoyable emotion – you feel hesitant; you don't really feel like getting on with things; you feel a bit sluggish or withdrawn; you don't really feel like taking part or joining in; you're doubtful; you feel a bit delicate, sensitive or quiet etc.

- Use this as a check-in at various times. The children can simply use a thumbs up or down, arms up in the air or not, or some other visual means to indicate how they are feeling.

- Explain that nobody ever only feels 'yes moments', and that 'no moments' are a normal part of being human. Some of our best achievements require us to tackle things we might feel doubtful about (ie, feeling a 'no' moment), so it's a good idea to have a go, even if we're unsure about what we're about to do. It can also help us to feel better simply when we are asked, and think about, how we feel.

- Discuss with the children what can help us to cope with and/or get motivated during 'no' moments'.

 **Extension ideas**

- You could assess how the children feel at the start of a day by asking, 'Right now, does this feel like a "yes day" or a "no day" for you?'

 **Note**

Once the children understand what you mean by a 'yes moment' and a 'no moment', this can be used as a regular check-in. You can start using it during lessons or playtime, or at other times.

# Emotion check-in

 *Objective*

To get the children to reflect upon what they are feeling and start linking their feelings to physical sensations, thoughts and triggers.

 *Instructions*

- Ask the children to close their eyes, if they are happy to, and take three deep breaths.
- Explain that you will ask them to focus on how they feel. Next proceed to ask the following questions, pausing for a short while after each one to allow the children time to reflect. Make it clear that they need to answer the questions inside their heads and not share out loud.

  *Younger children:*
  - Do you feel happy, calm or is something bothering you?
  - Are you just thinking about sitting here right now or is your mind thinking about another time or place?
  - Would you say you are feeling an enjoyable or unenjoyable feeling?
  - Is what you're feeling weak or strong?
  - Where in your body are you feeling something?

  *Older children:*
  - Are you breathing at a normal rate?
  - Can you hear your heartbeat? If so, does it seem loud or quiet? Fast or slow?
  - Would you say you feel comfortable or uncomfortable, or somewhere in between?
  - Does your mind feel quite calm or do you have thoughts racing around inside it?
  - Are you thinking about sitting right here in this room or has your mind wandered off to think about something else?
  - Is what you're thinking about bothering you?
  - Does any part of your body feel tense or do you feel completely relaxed?
  - If how you are feeling was a colour, what colour would it be and where would the colour be in your body?
  - If you could put a word to how you are feeling, what would that word be?
  - Is there a reason you can think of for why you feel like you do?

- Invite the children to open their eyes and ask the class whether anyone would like to share how they feel and, if they can, explain what might have triggered them to feel that way.

- Make a point of validating the children's feelings – for example, 'Yes, I would feel like that too' or, 'I can understand why you feel that way.'

 ## Extension ideas

- Ask the children to make the expression that illustrates how they feel inside and ask others to guess what they might be feeling.
- For the duration of a morning or day (for example), ask the children to note down on a piece of paper (or an emotion tracker – see page 246) how they are feeling when you declare it's time to 'check in'. This helps children become more aware of their emotions as they arise. Younger children can draw smiley, neutral or sad faces; older children could use an emotion word from a given selection to describe how they feel.

 ## Note

The more you do this, the better the children will become at tuning in to their emotions. This activity can be completed with questions that require greater reflection as children get older.

# Emotion diary

 ## Objective

To reflect on the emotions of the day and what triggered them.

 ## What's needed?

One copy of the *Emotion diary* (page 78) per child.

 ## Instructions

- Instruct the children to reflect on their day and consider three times when they remembered feeling an emotion.
- Ask the children to draw or write down what happened on these three occasions in the left-hand side of the table and then indicate, by colouring in one of the faces in the column on the right, whether the emotions they felt were enjoyable, unenjoyable or something in between.

- Next, ask the children one at a time to share what happened and encourage everyone to try to name what emotion they probably felt.

 **Extension idea:**

- You could try to find whether there was something that happened during the day that made the whole group experience an enjoyable emotion.

 **Note**

I find younger children often need some reminders of what they have done in their day!

# I am a potato

 **Objective**

To increase emotion vocabulary and start to 'read' people's expressions, tone of voice and body language to work out the emotions they are likely to be experiencing.

 **What's needed?**

It can be helpful if a variety of emotion words or an emotion poster is on display to help the children guess the emotions.

 **Instructions**

- Choose a volunteer.
- Either whisper an emotion to them or let them choose one from a list you're holding or from a display.
- Tell the volunteer that the only words they can say are, 'I am a potato'; they must try to convey their selected emotion as they speak these words through their tone of voice, facial expressions and body language.
- Invite the other children to guess the emotion.
- Once the emotion has been guessed correctly, ask the children whether the emotion is enjoyable or unenjoyable; and/or ask them to think of a time when someone might be triggered to feel that way.
- Give the child who guesses correctly the next emotion to demonstrate in the same way.

Here are some emotions that could be used for 'I'm a potato', getting progressively more sophisticated.

| Easy | > | Getting more difficult | > | Difficult |
|------|---|------------------------|---|-----------|
| • Happy | • Jealous | • Grateful | • Tense | • Perplexed |
| • Sad | • Guilty | • Content | • Concerned | • Impressed |
| • Scared | • Embarrassed | • Proud | • Astonished | • Vulnerable |
| • Angry | • Furious | • Amused | • Ecstatic | • Regretful |
| • Con-fused | • Cheerful | • Amazed | • Contempt | • Distressed |
| • Worried | • Nervous | • Stressed | • Distractible | • Intimidated |
| • Excited | • Lonely | • Satisfied | • Offended | • Overwhelmed |
| • Shy | • Delighted | • Adoring | • Withdrawn | • Preoccupied |
| • Bored | • Irritated | • Pleased | • Flustered | • Insecure |
| • Relaxed | • Curious | • Hopeful | • Awed | • Humiliated |
| • Disgust-ed | • Shocked | • Enthusiastic | • Rejected | • Motivated |
| • Miser-able | • Thrilled | • Mischievous | • Relieved | • Agitated |
| • Panicked | • Disappointed | • Blissful | • Cautious | • Exasperated |
| • Upset | • Confident | • Cruel | • Hesitant | • Accepted |
| • Tired | • Exhausted | • Appalled | • Timid | • Triumphant |
| | • Terrified | • Flustered | • Passionate | • Self-conscious |
| | • Distressed | • Alert | • Disbelieving | • Fulfilled |
| | • Brave | • Awkward | • Disapproving | • Resigned |
| | • Determined | • Doubtful | • Dread | • Pensive |
| | • Playful | • Selfish | • Uneasy | • Forlorn |
| | • Hopeless | • Thoughtful | • Ashamed | • Flabbergasted |
| | • Interested | • Baffled | • Humiliated | • Sceptical |
| | | • Affection | • Tentative | • Tempted |
| | | • Suspicious | • Anticipatory | • Unmotivated |
| | | | • Euphoric | • Apprehensive |
| | | | • Impatient | • Expectant |
| | | | • Outraged | • Remorseful |
| | | | | • Discouraged |
| | | | | • Resentful |

## Extension ideas

• Play the game without the voice so the child mimes saying, 'I am a potato'. This means guesses are based on facial expressions and body language only.

- Play the game with the child's back turned to the other children, so their guesses are based on tone of voice only.
- The children can play a guessing game where one child attempts to describe an emotion using only three words.
- Play a game where a volunteer stands in front of the class and everyone except the volunteer is shown an emotion word. The volunteer then has to ask the other children questions to try to find out what the emotion is, using yes/no/depends questions only.

##  Note

Children love how silly this guessing game is. I use this activity with very young children but Year 6 children also love it!

# Enjoyable and unenjoyable

## *Objective*

To increase emotion vocabulary; to understand that emotions can be enjoyable and unenjoyable.

## *What's needed?*

*Feeling Cards Sheet A* (page 104) cut out; a paper sign saying 'Enjoyable' displayed on one side of the room and another saying 'Unenjoyable' on the other. Use *Feeling Cards Sheets B* and/or *C* (pages 105 and 106) for older children.

## *Instructions*

- Invite individual children to pick an emotion card, read it aloud and indicate whether they think the emotion is enjoyable or unenjoyable by standing on the side of the classroom with the appropriate sign: 'Enjoyable' or 'Unenjoyable'.
- Invite the child to try to explain what the emotion they have selected feels like and where in the body they feel it. Invite the class to help. Don't be scared to use words or phrases that might not normally be used to describe emotions, such as 'a sinking feeling', 'fuzzy', 'heavy', 'makes you want to scream', 'makes you want to move', 'whizzy', 'fast', 'slow', 'makes you want to hide', 'fidgety', 'loud', 'flat', 'wobbly', 'shaky', 'makes your tummy fizzy', 'spiky', 'peaceful', 'jagged' etc.
- Explain to the children that nobody can expect to feel happy all the time. Everyone feels enjoyable and unenjoyable emotions and this is completely normal.

*Extension ideas*

- Create a class poster with an 'enjoyable-unenjoyable' spectrum drawn across the top of a large, landscape-positioned piece of paper. Each time the class learns a new emotion word, write it on a piece of paper, discuss it and its possible triggers, and stick it on the spectrum where the children think it should go. This can also indicate how enjoyable or unenjoyable an emotion is by using the extremes of the spectrum to represent 'extremely enjoyable' and 'extremely unenjoyable', with the lesser intensities closer to the centre.
- Discuss the idea of emotions also being comfortable and uncomfortable to help children consider different emotions further. Sometimes children will declare that some enjoyable emotions – such as excitement – can be a bit uncomfortable!

 *Note*

This activity can be completed by different age groups and adapted simply by using fewer words for younger children and more words for older children.

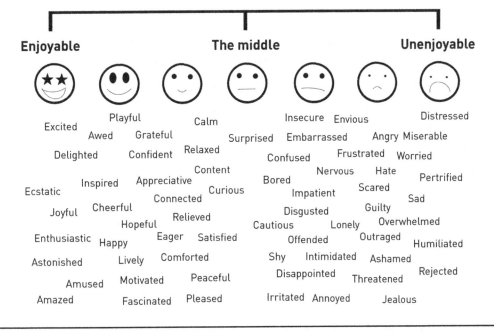

# What might she be feeling?

## 🚀 Objective

To link expressions and body language to what a person might be feeling.

## What's needed?

All children should be able to see the pictures on the sheet *What's she feeling?* (page 79).

 ## Instructions

- Working in pairs, the children should look at the sheet and decide which picture shows which emotion. Possible answers could include: 1) relaxed; 2) sad; 3) worried; 4) disgusted; 5) scared; 6) embarrassed; 7) excited; 8) angry. However, remember that the children may see different emotions in each expression – rarely does an expression represent one single emotion and we have many different words for similar emotions. Encourage the children by saying it's okay to disagree slightly.
- Ask the children to suggest what might have triggered each emotion.

 ## Extension ideas

- The children could make an emotion poster by taking photos of each other making the expressions they think match different emotions.
- Play 'Statue', where one child stands 'frozen' in a position they think represents a particular emotion and the other children guess the emotion. Once the children have guessed correctly, ask the child who is the statue to describe how they think the statue would be painted; and then ask them to suggest a soundtrack that would be played non-stop from the statue. You could also ask the children to suggest what they think might have happened just before the statue froze.

 ## Note

Some children find 'reading' emotional expressions easy, while others struggle. I have sometimes pretended to find this difficult myself, to help those who struggle feel more confident to participate.

# Where in the body do we feel it?

 ## Objective

To help children focus inwardly and consider the physical sensations of different emotions.

# ✅ *What's needed?*

Four large 'blob people' drawn on separate pieces of sugar paper/wallpaper; a copy of the sheet *Where in the body do we feel it?* (page 80); colouring pencils.

# 🔍 *Instructions*

- Ask the children to think of something that makes them happy and share some of their triggers for happiness.
- Next, ask them to remember a time when they felt happy and think about and/or visualise that time in their heads.
- Then ask the following questions:
  - How would you describe the feeling? (To help, you can suggest some describing words, such as: 'Hot, warm or cold?' 'Fuzzy or Sharp?' 'Calm or lively?' 'Jiggly or still?' 'Encouraging or discouraging?' 'Enjoyable or unenjoyable?' 'Comfortable or uncomfortable?')
  - Where inside your body do you feel it? Is it all over or just in certain places?
  - How does it make your head feel?
  - Do you think of the feeling as having a colour and if so, what colour is it?
  - Does it make you feel like being still or jumping about?
  - What kinds of thoughts does it make you feel like having?
- As a class, take a large sheet of sugar paper/wallpaper with a blob person outline drawn on it. Use a colour you all agree on (for happiness, it's often yellow, pink or light blue – or lots of colours!) to mark on the body (where there is some consensus about) where happiness is felt and any words or phrases that have been used to describe these sensations.
- Repeat the exercise for sadness, anger and fear.
- Explain to the children that we all feel emotions slightly differently and give them a copy of the sheet *Where in the body do we feel it?* to indicate where in the body they think they feel each emotion. Encourage them to add describing words too.
- Explain further that when we feel an emotion, it's a good idea to notice the effect it has on our body, as this gives us a clue that we're starting to feel it. Getting good at noticing the moment emotions arrive is part of being clever with emotions. When we notice an emotion, rather than reacting straight away, we have a better chance of slowing things down and working out the best thing to do next.

*Extension ideas*

- The children can share the blob people they have coloured and labelled on the sheet *Where in the body do we feel it?* with a partner and discuss what they experience in the same way and what they experience differently with each emotion.
- Ask the children to become 'emotion detectives' when they go home. Tell them to watch out for any emotions they have, where they feel them in the body and what might have triggered them. They can then 'report back' their findings the next day.

 *Note*

Focusing inwardly on the physical sensations of an emotion can be useful for noticing and identifying what we're feeling, as well as putting a pause between the trigger of an emotion and our reaction.

# What does it feel like?

 *Objective*

To focus inwardly on the sensations that emotions can trigger in us; to try to explain emotions using describing words.

 *What's needed?*

One copy of the sheet *What does it feel like?* (page 81) per child.

 *Instructions*

- Explain to the children that although we all know what anger, sadness, happiness and other emotions are, it is quite hard to describe how they feel.
- Ask the children to answer questions such as the following so they start to understand how abstract adjectives can be used to describe different emotions. Make it very clear that there is no right or wrong answer – just ask them to share what feels like the right choice to them:
    - Does anger seem hot or cold?
    - Does excitement seem smooth or spiky?
    - Does fear seem quick or slow?
    - Does happiness seem round or square?

- o Does worry seem noisy or quiet?
- o Does boredom seem fuzzy or clear?
- Give each child a copy of the sheet *What does it feel like?* and ask them to choose an emotion to explore by completing the sheet for that emotion.
- The children can then draw an abstract picture on the back of their sheet that they think represents the emotion.

 *Extension ideas*

- Discuss the idea that art and emotion are often linked, and that many artists are trying to trigger emotions in you with what they create. You could look at some well-known pieces of art and ask the children how they make them feel.
- As a creative exercise, ask the children to choose between two different concepts that could each be used to characterise an emotion and then discuss their ideas with them. Here are some examples:
  - o Does anger feel more like a hard rock inside you or a fire?
  - o Does happiness feel more like floating or jumping?
  - o Does sadness feel more like a heavy weight or a foggy day?
  - o Does fear feel more like something is gripping you or like you want to run really fast?
  - o Does happiness make you feel more like you're enjoying a warm, sunny day or like you have just walked into a sweetshop?
  - o Does excitement feel more like tasting sherbet or watching fireworks?
  - o Does boredom seem more like grey or brown?
  - o Does impatience feel more solid or fluid?
  - o Does loneliness look more like a single tree on a hill or an abandoned teddy bear?

 *Note*

This activity can produce some quite creative pictures as children really start to tune in to different emotions.

# Trigger runaround

 *Objective*

To help children start to link emotions to their potential triggers.

## ✅ What's needed?

One copy of the sheet *Trigger runaround* (page 82) for you to read from.

## 🔍 Instructions

- Ask for three volunteers to join you at the front of the room.
- Whisper three 'runaround' triggers to the three volunteers from across the top row of the sheet.
- Ask the three volunteers to stand where the rest of the class can see them and make the expression they think they would have made if they had just experienced the trigger whispered to them.
- Ask the rest of the class, 'Who do you think has just ...?' and read one of the three triggers.
- The children can demonstrate their answer by standing near the person they believe is the 'answer'. (If space is tight, you can just ask one child at a time to come up and guess which of the three children they think just experienced the trigger you stated.)
- Do the same for the remaining two triggers.
- Children nearly always make the correct choice in this activity, so explore the triggers further by asking the following questions after each round:
  - What word would you use to describe how they might be feeling?
  - Are there any other words that could be used to describe how they are feeling?
  - What else could trigger you to feel that way?
  - How would you feel if that happened to you?
  - Do you think everyone would feel exactly the same after these things happened to them?
  - What kinds of things could make us react differently to the same trigger on different days (eg, how tired we were, how we felt about anyone else involved, what had happened to us so far that day, what mood we are in)?

## 🌀 Extension ideas

- The children can eventually make up their own triggers – events, interactions, situations or circumstances – with which to play this game. Emotions can become less contrasting to make the game more challenging (eg, sad, disappointed and frustrated; happy, excited and surprised; worried, scared and confused).

## 📝 Note

These triggers can be used in a variety of ways and this is just one example. For example, you could ask the children to draw an emoji (on a piece of scrap paper) of the person who has just experienced one of the triggers.

# Max's day

 **Objective**

To link emotions to their triggers; to start realising that our emotional responses can be unique to us; to pay close attention to expressions as a clue to what someone might be feeling.

 **What's needed?**

Access to a copy of *Max's day* (page 83) to read aloud.

 **Instructions**

- Ask for two volunteers and have them stand on either side of you, so you are all in a line facing everyone else and the two volunteers cannot see each other.
- Explain that you are going to read a story about Max and that the two volunteers will pretend to be Max. The volunteers will make an expression to show how they think Max would respond at each stage of the story.
- Read the story one line at a time and pause for the volunteers to make the expression they think Max would have at each stage of the story.
- Ask those watching to shout 'Snap!' if the two volunteers' faces look similar and 'Not snap!' if the volunteers' expressions don't appear to be the same.
- When the faces are 'Not snap!', use this as an opportunity to discuss how two people can react quite differently when the same thing happens (or might happen) to them.

 **Extension ideas**

- When the children say, 'Not snap!', ask both volunteers what they think Max would be feeling at that moment and why.
- The children can make up statements or scenarios to continue the game – for example, Max realised he was walking home from school that evening rather than getting a lift.
- Eventually, the children can suggest things that have happened to them that they believe others might react to differently – for example, 'I got moved near to the teacher's desk' – and see whether they get a 'Snap!' or a 'Not snap!' from the volunteers on either side of them.

- You could give each child a copy of *Max's day* and have them draw a smiley, neutral or sad face in the squares at the end of each statement to indicate how they think they would feel if they were Max and compare their answers with a partner.

 **Note**

Make sure the children on either side of you can't see each other when you do this activity.

# A simple question

 *Objective*

To start realising that emotions can affect how we behave, which in turn can affect how others treat us.

 *Instructions*

- Ask the children to pair up.
- Introduce the simple question, 'What are you doing?' and explain that they will be using this question to explore something.
- Ask each person in the pair to ask the question in the 'tone' of a different emotion (eg, happy, sad, angry, scared, confused, excited, bored, enthusiastic), or as if they were feeling each emotion they are exploring.
- After each question, ask their partner to explain what the different 'tones' triggered them to feel and think.
- Discuss with the children how this shows how our feelings can impact on our behaviour if we let them, and how our behaviour in turn can impact on others.
- Also stress that we can't help what we feel, but we can always choose how we behave (eg, it's okay to feel grumpy but it's not usually a good idea to take it out on others).

 *Extension ideas*

- Make a pretend 'playground' at the front of the class and ask the children to join in with the play while obviously and exaggeratedly expressing a particular emotion (eg, happy, sad, angry, scared, confused, excited, bored, enthusiastic). You can ask the children who they ended up wanting to avoid and who they felt drawn to.

- Ask the children to mime everyday activities – such as brushing their teeth, being a teacher, eating toast or kicking a football – while pretending to feel different emotions for the rest of the class to guess.

 **Note**

This activity can be quite humorous! It's important that young children remember it's a game.

# Very happy to very sad

 **Objective**

To increase emotion vocabulary; to appreciate that emotions can be different strengths.

 **What's needed?**

One copy of the sheet *Very happy to very sad* (page 84), cut into its nine sections.

 **Instructions**

- Ask for nine volunteers (with younger children, start with fewer children).
- Hand out one of the nine happy/sad cards from the sheet *Very happy to very sad* to each volunteer and ask them to read privately what's on their card. With younger children, you can read the card quietly to each child as you hand it over.
- Ask the children to pretend that what's on the card has just happened to them and to practise making the expression they think they would have in that situation.
- Arrange the children in order from 'Overjoyed' to 'Distressed' and see whether this creates a visual spectrum from really happy at one end to really sad at the other. Then ask the rest of the class who looks overjoyed, happy, cheerful, pleased, showing no emotion, sorry, sad, miserable, distressed etc.
- Alternatively, with older children, ask them to arrange themselves in a line from who they think is the happiest to the saddest, using the cards to guide them.
- The rest of the class can then be invited to join the spectrum by thinking of something that happened to them that triggered them to be sad or happy and joining the line at the point which represents how they felt.
- Remember to de-role everyone at the end of the game by asking a frivolous question like, 'Did you notice what the weather was doing when you travelled to school this morning?'

**Extension ideas**

- Discuss the question: 'Do you think you can be happy all the time?'
- Add words and phrases to the happiness and sadness spectrum, such as 'ecstatic', 'thrilled', 'euphoric', 'overjoyed', 'exhilarated', 'over the moon', 'jubilant', 'joyous', 'elated', 'cheerful', 'glad', 'content', 'satisfied', 'gloomy', 'heavy-hearted', 'down in the dumps', 'sorrowful', 'wistful', 'depressed', 'disappointed', 'doleful', 'melancholic', 'dejected', 'glum', 'forlorn', 'low-spirited'.
- Complete this activity with the following spectra:
  - **Anger:** Calm, bothered, irritated, annoyed, cross, angry, furious.
  - **Fear:** Feeling safe, uneasy, suspicious, alarmed, scared, terrified, petrified.

 **Note**

This activity provides an excellent photographing opportunity once the children have created the spectrum!

# Symptom checker

 **Objective**

To link different emotions to the physical symptoms and sensations they can cause.

 **What's needed?**

Access to the information on the sheet *Symptom checker* (page 85) for all children; a large sheet of paper for each group of three children.

 **Instructions**

- Ask the children to tell you the ways in which feeling happy differs from feeling sad. Ask them to give as much detail as they can.
- Next, ask the children how feeling angry differs from feeling sad. Likewise, ask for as much detail as possible. Some of their answers will relate to physical symptoms and some will be more about triggers.
- Show the children the sheet *Symptom tracker* and explain that this focuses on the symptoms of unenjoyable emotions, such as anger, fear, worry and sadness.
- Give groups of three children a large sheet of paper and ask them to draw a blob person on the sheet. Next, allocate either anger, fear, worry or sadness to different

groups and ask them to use the sheet *Symptom tracker* to draw what they think the physical symptoms and urges are when someone experiences the emotion they have been allocated.

- Ask the groups to discuss their findings. Compare and contrast groups who have been allocated the same emotion and see whether they have noted similar or different ideas.

 ## Extension ideas

- The children could discuss what they think might help people cope with these emotions and the sensations they can cause.
- The children could explore the symptoms of additional emotions – including some positive emotions – such as surprise, disgust, disappointment, excitement and happiness.

 ## Note

Linking physical symptoms will be really easy for some children, but others may need help to make these links – particularly some of those with autism. With children who struggle to identify the symptoms of emotions, you can make this activity easier by giving a choice of two symptoms to choose from (eg, 'Does anger make your eyebrows go up or down?' 'Does sadness make you feel lively or like you don't want to move much?' 'Does fear makes you breathe more quickly or slowly?').

# What faces can tell us

 ## Objective

To be able to link the emotional expression on a face to what might have triggered it; to increase empathy.

 ## What's needed?

Access for all children to the pictures on the sheet *What faces can tell us* (page 86).

## Instructions

- Ask three volunteers to come and stand where everyone can see their faces. You could change these three volunteers every two rounds or so.

- Next, read out each of the following events one at a time and ask all three volunteers to demonstrate what their face would probably look like if it happened to them:
  - They have just been told they have won a bucket of sweets.
  - They have just looked out of the window and seen it was snowing.
  - They have just been grabbed by a bony arm on a ghost train.
  - Someone has just tripped them up deliberately.
  - Someone has just given them an ice cream.
  - They have just eaten something that tastes horrible.
  - They have just been told to tidy their bedroom.
  - They are lost in the park and can't find the adult they came with.
  - Someone has just laughed at a picture they painted.
  - They have just found a book they really like that they thought they had lost forever.
  - They have just learned how to ice skate.
  - They have just realised they have lost their coat.
  - They have just been pushed really high on the swings.
  - They have just dropped their ice cream on their foot.
  - Someone is bossing them around and trying to get them to play a game they don't want to play.
  - They have just walked into a room full of people they don't know.
  - They have just scored a goal.
  - Their friend has just gone off to play with someone else.
  - They have just dropped their lunch on the floor in front of lots of people.
  - They have just been told to do three different things at the same time.
- After each round of expressions:
  - check to see whether all three children are making similar expressions and if not, investigate why (eg, one child might love tidying their bedroom); and
  - ask the children what they think each child is feeling. Encourage the use of different words to describe similar feelings to increase the children's emotion vocabulary.
- Next, show the children the pictures on the sheet *What faces can tell us* and ask them to say which picture shows a person who:
  - has just trodden in dog poo (disgusted);
  - has just been given a present they really wanted (excited/happy);
  - thinks they are about to be hit by a cricket ball (panicked/scared);
  - has just been told their party has been cancelled (sad/disappointed)
  - is watching a scary part in a horror movie (scared/shocked); and
  - has just been called a nasty name by someone (upset/angry/furious).

Also ask the children how they think the person is feeling in each photo (see brackets above).

- Explain that we can all be feelings detectives. When we look at a person's face, there are sometimes clues that can tell us how they might be feeling. We won't always guess correctly, but it's good to try to be aware of what others might be feeling so we can offer help or change how we behave to avoid triggering them to feel worse. You could explore how the behaviour in the following situations is probably not helpful:
  - Oliver is clearly grumpy but Poppy keeps pestering him to play a game she knows he doesn't really like.
  - Charlie looks sad but George hasn't noticed and is really chatty and telling Charlie all about how excited he is about his birthday party.
  - Sophie is furious but her friend Emily hasn't noticed and has just teased her about her messy hair.
  - Mia is really worried about something but Ali hasn't noticed and is telling her all about the art competition he won.
- Explain to the children that noticing how someone is feeling is kind and can be a way of showing we care.

 ## Extension ideas

- The children could make up their own situations and matching expressions and then photograph them.
- The children could discuss how best to comfort someone when they are feeling sad, angry or scared by considering what they think they need themselves when they feel that way.

 ## Note

The most important aim of this activity is to help children be curious about what others might be feeling. Some children naturally do this more proficiently than others, but everyone can learn to be better at empathising.

# Happy, angry, sad or scared?

 ## Objective

To increase emotion vocabulary

**What's needed?**

A copy of the sheet *Happy, angry, sad or scared?* (page 87).

 **Instructions**

- Give groups of four children the sheet *Happy, angry, sad or scared?* and ask them to sort the words as described on the sheet. They could colour code the emotions at the top of the sheet and circle the words below with the corresponding colours. Check through the answers once the children have completed them:
  - **Happy:** Ecstatic, jubilant, gleeful, on cloud nine, tickled pink, thrilled, overjoyed, euphoric, buoyant, elated, pleased, over the moon, on top of the world.
  - **Angry:** Livid, blown a fuse, outraged, infuriated, exasperated, vexed, boiling mad.
  - **Sad:** Glum, sorrowful, down in the dumps, downcast, discouraged, forlorn, down in the mouth.
  - **Scared:** Afraid, terrified, panicked, petrified, intimidated, cautious, trembling like a leaf.
- You could ask the children to find further synonyms for each of these emotions.
- Explain that having more words to describe how you feel can actually help you become more aware of your emotions and help you to express exactly how you feel.

 **Extension ideas**

- The children could try to find idioms that relate to ways of feeling. Children usually enjoy exploring idioms for different ways of feelings by considering the literal meanings – which are often quite funny! Examples might include 'It's driving me up the wall,' 'I've got my knickers in a twist,' 'I have butterflies in my tummy.'

 **Note**

Words offered as synonyms for emotion words don't always have exactly the same meaning as the original word. Be sure to discuss these differences.

# Emotions as visitors

 **Objective**

To understand that emotions come and go, like visitors; to consider the effects different emotions have on us when they visit.

# ✓ What's needed?

Enough string (or wool) to make the outline of a person so each group or four can create a person outline (the outlines need not be neat or realistic!).

# 🔍 Instructions

- Use wool to make a large body outline on the floor – one per group of four. You can ask the children to do this, which can be an entertaining activity in itself!
- Choose one emotion to explore – anger or excitement are good ones to start with.
- Explain to the children that you are going to ask some questions about the emotion and one person at a time in each four is going to answer. They should all take turns to be the person who answers.
- Explain that everyone will step inside the body shape to answer each question in a certain way, explained below. Initially, the children will direct their answers to the others in their group; but add that you might ask some children to repeat their responses to the whole group.
- Ask the children, 'When this emotion visits ...':
  - *'What might your face look like?'* Ask them to stand in the head and make the expression they think they would have when this emotion visits. Children could also be given string to make the face (eg, one piece for the mouth, two pieces for the eyes and two more for the eyebrows). They can have fun trying to make these faces and that can be an activity in itself.
  - *'How might this visitor make you sit or stand?'* Ask them to get inside the body shape and sit or stand how they think they would when they feel this emotion.
  - *'Where in the body might you feel this emotion?'* Ask them to jump to the relevant places and say what they might feel there.
  - *'What might your voice sound like when this emotion visits?'* Ask them to stand where the mouth would be and say, 'I am [insert emotion].'
  - *'Is this emotion enjoyable or unenjoyable?'* Ask them to smile and cheer in the head if enjoyable; frown and boo if not.
  - *'How long do you think the emotion will stay?'* A long time or a short time? Ask them to stand inside and indicate the length of time with their arms – wide apart means a long time.
  - *'How noticeable is the emotion?'* Ask them to stand inside the body shape and make themselves noticeable and big or small and not.
  - *'How might the emotion make you want to behave?'* Ask them to jump inside the shape and mime that behaviour.

- ○ *'Why might the emotion have visited?'* Ask them to stand inside the body and say, 'I feel this emotion when ...'
- ○ *'What does it feel like when the emotion has gone?'* Ask them to stand inside the body and say, after the emotion has gone, 'Now I feel....'
- ○ *'What might help this visitor to leave?'* As them to talk to the emotion to help it find a way to leave. Sometimes you just have to wait for it to leave.
- Discuss the children's answers.
- Choose more emotions to explore in the same way.

 ## Extension ideas

- The children could draw different emojis to place at the head of the body before an emotion is explored.
- The children could describe the impact of visits from different emotions by completing the sentence, 'When [insert emotion] visits, I tend to ...' and answer with as much as they can remember from the main activity.
- The children could draw these visitors by personifying different emotions.

 ## Note

Helping children to think of emotions as visitors can help them start to observe their arrival and departure, which can lead to more control over them.

# 'I' messages

 ## Objective

To understand why 'I' messages are useful and learn how to use them.

 ## What's needed?

Access for all children to the information on the sheet *'I' messages* (page 88).

 ## Instructions

- Place a chair at the front of the room and give it a name. I find 'Colin Chair' works just fine!

- Ask the children to imagine the chair is a person (or if you have something you can substitute in here that could work better, please do). However, be careful if you use a child or adult for this purpose, as it can be triggering.

- Tell the children Colin Chair did something to upset you. You could ask them to make up things a chair could do to upset a person – for example, wobble; not be behind you when you sit down; insult your bottom!

- Now demonstrate being angry with the chair by saying, 'You made me angry' and ask the children how this would make Colin feel.

- Next demonstrate how to use an 'I' message to inform Colin of how you feel by saying: 'When you insulted my bottom, I felt angry.'

- Ask the children which statement is more likely to make Colin think about what he did and say sorry. They (nearly always) choose the 'I' message.

- Explain that if we use 'I' messages to let someone know we're angry or upset:
  - they are more likely to listen;
  - they are less likely to become really upset;
  - they can't deny what you feel (although a small number of people might try);
  - you're not blaming them for how you feel – you're just letting them know how you feel about what happened;
  - you're taking responsibility for how you feel; and
  - they are more likely to want to make things better or apologise.

- Tell the children that 'I' messages are about explaining your needs without upsetting the person you are explaining them to. 'You made me angry' is more likely to annoy someone than an 'I' message.

- Let the children see the information on the sheet and practise creating 'I' messages.

 ## Extension ideas

- Tell the children you are going to use 'I' messages over the next few weeks and if someone notices, they should put both their arms up to show that they noticed.

- Explain that you will also be listening out for the children using them.

 ## Note

Modelling 'I messages' is crucial if these are to become an established way in which the children express their emotions. To get 'buy-in' from children, I find they have to believe that their emotions are their own responsibility.

# How would you feel?

 **Objective**

To help match emotions to triggers; to increase emotion vocabulary; to enhance empathy and understanding that we don't all react in the same way to the same event.

 **What's needed?**

A copy of the sheet *How would you feel?* (page 89).

 **Instructions**

- Give the children a copy of the sheet *How would you feel?* and ask them to consider what they think each of the scenarios might trigger them to feel. Explain that they can use more than one word, as we sometimes feel a mixture of emotions in any situation.
- Ask pairs of children to share how they think they might feel in each situation with each other, to explore different reactions.
- Next, ask pairs of children to sort each scenario on a spectrum from the things that would trigger the most enjoyable emotions to those that would trigger the least enjoyable emotions. Pairs may find they disagree on where to place some of the scenarios.
- Discuss with the children the idea that we don't all react in the same way to the same thing, as we have different values, hopes, things that annoy us, sensitivities etc.

 **Extension ideas**

- The children can use a thesaurus, tablet or computer to find more words that could be used to describe how they might feel in each of these situations.

 **Note**

It's always good to describe emotions as having been 'triggered', so children understand the idea that the emotion has been awoken in them and was not completely caused by external events.

# Name that feeling!

 **Objective**

To help children further develop their understanding of different feelings.

## ✓ What's needed?

One copy of the sheet *Name that feeling!* (page 90) per pair.

## 🔍 Instructions

- Give pairs of children a copy of the sheet *Name that feeling* and ask them to match up each emotion with its description.
- Go through the answers as a group and ask the children whether they think they could add to any of the descriptions given. Generally, children agree on the following:
  - **Happy:** It's a smiley feeling! It can make you feel all light and lively, and like nothing will bother you. It can also make you feel like being kind to others.
  - **Excited:** It's a lively emotion that often means you can't sit still. You often feel it when you are really looking forward to or really enjoying something.
  - **Sad:** You feel like this when something upsets you, such as losing something you love. It can make you feel like you want to hide away and be quiet.
  - **Angry:** It's a feeling that can make you feel powerful, but not in a helpful way. When you feel it, you can usually only think about the thing that triggered it.
  - **Worried:** It's how you feel when you're really bothered about something and find it hard to think about anything else. It makes you feel wobbly.
  - **Bored:** It's how you feel when you can't be bothered to do anything – but because you can't be bothered to do anything, you stay feeling this way!
  - **Grumpy:** It's a feeling that can last a while and make you want to stomp about. When you feel it, it can be hard to convince you that you will enjoy anything!
- Next, ask pairs of children to look at the emotions listed at the bottom of the sheet and jointly create similar descriptions for one or more of those emotions, as instructed on the sheet. Allow some time for them to do this.
- When the children have created some descriptions, ask them to share them with the class and see whether anyone can guess which emotion they are describing.

## 🌀 Extension ideas

- The children can look at emotions not listed on the sheet and create descriptions for those.

## ✍ Note

Notice that the emotions on the sheet are described in generic terms without using a specific trigger to describe them (eg, a specific trigger for sadness would be, 'It's what you feel when your pet dies'). Encouraging children to try to describe emotions in this way can be a creative activity in itself.

# Can we find emotions to name?

 *Objective*

To help the children become more introspective about what they feel.

 *Instructions*

- Explain to the children that other languages have names for emotions that we don't and share these examples with them:

| Emotion | Language | Meaning |
| --- | --- | --- |
| *Commuovere* | Italian | What you feel when someone tells you a story that moves you to tears. |
| *Meraki* | Greek | What you feel when you put your heart and soul into doing something. |
| *Resfeber* | Swedish | The jittery feeling that you experience leading up to taking a journey – part nerves, part excitement. |
| *Duende* | Spanish | An emotional response triggered by art. |
| *Pena ajena* | Mexican Spanish | The awkward, cringing feeling you get when you watch someone being humiliated or doing something embarrassing. |
| *Tarab* | Arabic | The feeling you get when music is incredibly uplifting and you're lost in it. |
| *Gilgil* | Tagalog | The urge to pinch or squeeze someone because they are so loveable or cute. |
| *Yuan bei* | Chinese | What you feel when you complete a task and believe it is a brilliant – possibly perfect – achievement. |
| *Iktsuarpok* | Inuit | The slightly restless feeling you get when you know someone is about to visit and you want to keep checking if they've arrived. |

- Give pairs of children the following feeling descriptions and ask them to make up a name for them. Obviously, there is no right answer, but encourage the children to try to create words that sound a bit like the emotion they are describing:
  - The pleasant feeling you get when you pick up an old toy that you forgot you had and it brings back happy memories.
  - The fleeting irritation you feel when you cause yourself slight pain by accident – for example, by stubbing your toe.
  - The agitated feeling of having lots of things to do and being confused about where to start.

- o   The satisfying feeling when you finish tidying something up really well.
- o   The complicated excitement you feel when you really want something to happen but you can't be certain it will happen.
- Put the children into groups of four and ask them to try to think of triggers, situations and descriptions of emotions that we don't have specific words for and give each one a name. Ask them to write a list of as many as they can think of.
- Ask each group to share their favourite two or three ideas.

##  Extension ideas

- The children could continue this activity as informal homework: thinking about what they feel that evening and seeing whether they can bring any ideas for invented emotions and their names to school the next day.
- The children can make up emotion equations that attempt to describe the emotions in the table above – for example: *Pena ajena* = embarrassment + sympathy + squirming!

##  Note

If you keep this activity ongoing so that children can add further emotions, it encourages them to tune into what they are feeling more regularly.

# A park full of feelings

##  Objective

To increase understanding between emotions and likely triggers; to help the children understand that many of the things we do trigger emotions and it's a rare moment that we are feeling nothing at all.

##  What's needed?

A sheet of paper for each child to draw on; possibly a list of emotions on display.

##  Instructions

- Explain to the children that they are going to draw a picture of a park and that everyone in the park will be experiencing a different emotion. They can choose the emotions to include in their picture, but they need at least seven.
- Emotions that work well include the following:

- ○ **Easier:** Happy, excited, scared, lonely, bored, relaxed, shy, angry, frustrated.
- ○ **Difficult:** Confused, satisfied, distracted, delighted, content, worried, disappointed, impatient, curious.
- ○ **More difficult:** Insecure, humiliated, amazed, determined, nervous, cautious, tempted, fascinated.
- Explain that because it's a park, lots of different things can happen in it – and they don't all have to be things you'd usually see in a park! Examples might include a picnic; someone on a unicycle; someone walking a flamingo!
- Ask the children to choose their emotions and think of a situation in which someone might feel each of them. For example, for 'cautious', someone could be walking on a tightrope; for 'tempted', someone could be walking past with an ice cream; or for 'confused', someone could be looking at a signpost that says the swings are in two opposite directions.
- Share some thoughts as a group so that anyone struggling has more ideas to choose from.
- Let the children draw their park full of feelings and label each person with what they are feeling.
- When the children have finished, ask some volunteers to describe their pictures, what's happening and what the different people in the park are feeling.

 ## Extension ideas

- You could take one emotion (eg, happy) and list what the people in the children's parks are doing to trigger that emotion, to explore the variety of triggers.
- You could create a park backdrop as a display (eg, grass, tree, flowers, sky) and ask the children to add characters feeling different emotions to the display.

 ## Note

This activity can result in some children explaining in greater detail what is going on for each person in their park and can give you some insights into how they see the world.

# An emotion profile

 ## Objective

To explore and understand individual emotions in greater detail.

**What's needed?**

One copy of the sheet *An emotion profile* (page 91) per child; a list of emotions.

 **Instructions**

- Give each child a copy of *An emotion profile* and ask them to choose an emotion and complete the sheet for that emotion.
- If time allows, either you or the child can discuss what they thought about when they considered the emotion they chose.

 **Extension idea:**

- The profiles that the children produce can be stapled together to make a class emotion book.

 **Note**

An emotion profile can be completed in spare moments during the day if you have copies of *An emotion profile* available for the children.

# Which emotions might make you want to ...?

 **Objective**

To consider some of the behaviours that different emotions can make us want to do; to consider which reactions are helpful and which are not; to understand that we can't help how we feel, but we have a choice as to how we behave

 **What's needed?**

One copy of the sheet *Which emotions might make you want to ...?* (page 92) per pair. One large sheet of paper per pair.

 **Instructions**

- Explain to the children that different emotions can make us want to behave in different ways. Sometimes these are helpful and other times they're not.
- Give pairs of children the sheet *Which emotions might make you want to ...?* and ask them to use different colours to colour in the emotions in the boxes at the top of the sheet.

- Next, ask pairs of children to decide which emotion a person is most likely to be feeling if they are behaving or responding in each of the ways listed. Some of the responses could be the result of feeling more than one emotion.
- When they have considered all the responses, ask the children to complete the task at the bottom of the sheet.
- Explain to the children that all feelings are acceptable, but some behaviours are helpful and others are unhelpful or even harmful and definitely make the situation worse.
- Give each pair of children a large sheet of paper and ask them to write the five emotions on the sheet, so that there is space to write things around each emotion.
- Ask the children to write helpful things a person could do when they feel each of these emotions next to each emotion on the sheet. They might struggle at first with the enjoyable emotions – to help them, you could ask questions such as the following:
  - When you're happy, what kinds of things could you do to enjoy your happiness even more?
  - Other than the things on the sheet, what else might you feel like doing when you're happy? How could you make these things even more fun?
  - When you're happy, how could you spread your happiness to others?
  - Are there thoughts that would be fun to have when you're feeling excited?
  - How could you use up your energy when you're excited?
  - When you're excited, are there things you could do that might annoy other people?
  - If you were really happy or excited and you stood next to a friend who was upset, what might be difficult about you each feeling such different emotions?
- You can also encourage the children think of helpful things they could do when they feel negative emotions by asking the following questions:
  - What would be a good way of getting help when you feel this way?
  - Does something need to change and if so, how can you make it change?
  - Do you just need time to recover and what might be the best way of doing this?

## Extension ideas

- The children could make posters illustrating helpful things to do when they are experiencing different emotions.
- The children could keep an emotion diary for the week and, each time they feel a strong emotion, write down what they felt like doing, what they actually did (and whether it was helpful or unhelpful) and what else they could have done.

## Note

This activity is a good starting place for considering the extreme behaviours some children engage in, especially those who really struggle to self-regulate.

# Can we work out what they might be feeling?

 **Objective**

To deduce what a person might be feeling from clues within a text; to link actions to emotions; to develop more empathy.

 **What's needed?**

One copy of the sheet *Can we work out what they might be feeling?* (page 93) per pair.

 **Instructions**

- Ask each pair to discuss and decide what they think each of the main characters in each section of the sheet *Can we work out what they might be feeling?* is probably feeling and which clues led them to their answers. Possible answers include: 1) angry; 2) embarrassed; 3) scared; 4) excited; 5) bored; 6) happy/joyful; 7) surprised; 8) worried/anxious. However, as most emotion words have synonyms, the children might come up with other answers.
- Ask pairs of children to create their own paragraphs as described on the last part of the sheet.
- Invite the children to share their paragraphs and see whether others can guess the emotions that are implied.

 **Extension idea**

- The children could search for implied emotions through text in their reading books.

 **Note**

This can double up as an English lesson on inference.

# Emotions affect how we think

 **Objective**

To understand how emotions can affect how we think.

# ✅ *What's needed?*

One copy of the sheet *Emotions affect how we think* (page 94) per group of four children; scissors.

# 🔍 *Instructions*

- Ask the children to cut out the emotions and the ways of thinking on the sheet *Emotions affect how we think* and work in groups of four to match the emotions with the tendencies of how they can make you think. When the children have sorted the emotions and the effects they have on thinking, go through the following answers:

  - **Anger:** This emotion can make you think only about protecting yourself and not consider others much. It can narrow your focus so you only think about the thing that triggered the emotion. The thoughts you have when you experience this emotion can sometimes make you feel the emotion even more!

  - **Anxiety:** When you feel this emotion, the same troubling thought may keep going round and round in your head. It can also tend to make you think everything that can go wrong will go wrong. This can leave you little space to concentrate on anything else and can make you too cautious to try out anything new.

  - **Fear:** This emotion will make you think only about getting you to safety. It will override all other emotions. Unfortunately, it sometimes makes you think that some things are dangerous when they're not, as it wants to be 'better safe than sorry'.

  - **Sadness:** This emotion can make you think less and your brain can feel numb. It tells you that you don't really want to do anything and you just want to recover from what has happened.

  - **Happiness.** This emotion helps you to think the best of everyone so that you want to connect with them and be friendly. It also helps you be explorative, creative and open to new ideas.

  - **Disgust:** When you feel this emotion, your brain makes really quick judgements so you can avoid something. This could be a substance or something someone did that you didn't like. It's sometimes hard to change your mind once you feel this emotion.

  - **Surprise:** This emotion makes you alert and very focused on what is in front of you, so you can quickly see whether it's unsafe or not. This focus usually only lasts a short while.

- Explain that our emotions evolved thousands of years ago to help us survive – either by keeping us safe or by ensuring we were not kicked out of our tribe. Ask the children to discuss how these emotions helped us to survive. Answers might include the following:

- o **Anger:** Protected us from threats.
- o **Anxiety:** Kept us on high alert if a threat seemed imminent.
- o **Fear:** Helped us escape from immediate danger.
- o **Sadness:** While this is not conclusive, it is thought that sadness indicated to the tribe we needed 'time out' and ensured they would not resent us if we took this for ourselves.
- o **Happiness:** Helped us connect with others and seek out things that were good for us.
- o **Disgust:** Helped us avoid things that might harm us, like rotting meat or poo. We can also have social disgust for behaviours that might or we might perceive could cause harm.
- o **Surprise:** Kick-started our alertness in case something unusual turned out to be dangerous.
- Extend the discussion by asking the following questions:
  - o Is 'surviving' the same today as it was thousands of years ago when these emotions evolved? (Ask the children to explain their answers.)
  - o Do you think these emotions are always suited to how we live now?
  - o How can some of the thinking that results from these emotions be unhelpful?

 ## *Extension idea*

- The children could make posters raising awareness of the tendencies of the different brains (eg, the angry brain, the anxious brain).

 ## *Note*

Understanding why our emotions evolved and the effects they can have on us can help children realise that the messages our emotions send us are not always adapted or suitable for today's world.

# Lots of words for emotions!

 ## *Objective*

To increase emotion vocabulary; to empathise; to understand that the same situation can trigger different emotions in different people.

## ✅ *What's needed?*

For younger children, a copy of *Lots of words for emotions! Sheet A* (page 95); for older children, *Lots of words for emotions! Sheet B* (page 96).

## 🔍 *Instructions*

- Let the children see the information on the sheet *Lots of words for emotions!* (*Sheet A* and/or *Sheet B*), and explain that all the words surrounding each scenario are possible ways that a person could end up feeling in each situation. Also explain that it is very unlikely that one person will feel all of them. How we end up feeling about something that has just happened can depend on a lot of things, such as:
  - how tired we are feeling;
  - how we feel about anyone else involved;
  - who was there to witness what happened;
  - how our day has been so far;
  - any misunderstandings we might have had about what happened; and
  - how easily our uncomfortable emotions are triggered.
- Ask groups of four children to consider one scenario at a time and discuss which words could be used to describe how they think they might feel in that situation.
- Ask the children to look up any words they don't know the meaning of.
- Ask the children to use a tablet, computer or thesaurus to see whether they can find any more emotion words that could be used to describe how someone might feel in each situation.
- Ask each group to present an emotion word that they have learned the meaning of, explain what it means and suggest a situation that could trigger it.

## 🌀 *Extension ideas*

- The children could think of another scenario and surround it with emotion words that could describe how someone might feel in the situation – for example, a teacher you really like has just told everyone they are leaving; you are going to be in a play tomorrow and you don't feel confident about how well you will perform; you are starting secondary school tomorrow.
- The children could categorise new emotion words as either enjoyable or unenjoyable, or try to find another way of categorising them (eg, intensely positive, mildly positive, intensely negative, mildly negative).

**Note**

I have found this is a great way for increasing vocabulary for different emotions, as it creates intrigue about whether each emotion is a possible reaction or not.

# We sometimes jump to conclusions!

##  Objective

To understand how our interpretations of events can affect how we end up feeling.

## ✓ What's needed?

A copy of the sheet *We sometimes jump to conclusions!* (page 97).

##  Instructions

- Explain to the children that when something happens to us, our interpretation of what has happened affects what we end up feeling.
- Give pairs of children the sheet *We sometimes jump to conclusions!* and read through the start of the sheet.
- Ensure that the children understand that we all interpret the things that happen to us differently, depending on factors such as:
  - how tired we are feeling;
  - how we feel about anyone else involved;
  - who was there to witness what happened;
  - how our day has been so far;
  - any misunderstandings we might have had about what happened; and
  - how easily our uncomfortable emotions are triggered.

Take the example of someone being called stupid: look at the different interpretations and ask the children whether they can think of any other possible thoughts someone might have in response to being called stupid.

- Ask pairs of children to complete the sheet, using the prompts underneath the table to help them.
- Once the children have completed the task, ask them to share anything they noticed as they completed it. Hopefully they will see how different interpretations affect our feelings, and that we can work on changing our interpretation of a situation so that our emotional response is not so unenjoyable.

- Ask the children to complete the same task, this time using as an example someone not listening to them in a situation where they really wanted to be listened to.
- Emphasise further that quite often, when someone does something that upsets us, we are often not very forgiving – even if they have done something we have also done in the past ourselves. When someone upsets us, it's always a good idea to:
  - ask yourself to think of a time when you behaved like the person who upset you;
  - wonder what might be going on for the other person – for example, they might be really stressed, upset or annoyed with you for some reason; and
  - not assume that the person who upset you had any intention of causing upset. They probably were not really thinking about you when they did what they did, and they might be really surprised and sorry to realise they upset you.

 ## Extension ideas

- The children could look up any of the emotion words at the bottom of the sheet that they don't know the meaning of and find further synonyms for them.
- The children could write their top tips for when someone upsets you.

 ## Note

Using the phrase, 'Under what circumstances might I do something like that?' when someone upsets you is always a good aid for forgiveness. However, in my experience, a small number of children will insist that they would never do what someone just did to upset them!

# Accepting uncomfortable emotions

 ### Objective

To appreciate that many unavoidable but also worthwhile things that we do require us to endure uncomfortable emotions.

 ### What's needed?

One copy of the sheet *Accepting uncomfortable emotions* (page 98) per pair. A variety of ways of feeling written and on display, such as 'worried', 'nervous', 'insecure', 'unconfident', 'doubtful', 'ashamed', 'cynical', 'embarrassed', 'half-hearted', 'pessimistic', 'uncomfortable', 'reticent', 'wobbly', 'humiliated', 'self-conscious', 'jumpy', 'anxious', 'easily put-off', 'uncertain', 'hesitant', 'indecisive', 'unconvinced' (as well as some positive emotions, such as 'determined', 'ambitious', 'resolute').

# Instructions

- Give the children a copy of the sheet *Accepting uncomfortable emotions*, read through it and ask pairs of children to complete the task described on the sheet.

- Once the children have completed the task, discuss what was considered further by talking about our comfort zone. Having a 'comfort zone' means we that often try to avoid experiencing uncomfortable emotions (which is impossible) by doing only things we are comfortable doing. Some people's comfort zones are smaller than others. When we leave our comfort zone, we usually grow and learn more than when we stay within our comfort zone. (Be sure to delineate the difference between what's comfortable and what's safe!)

- Extend the discussion further by asking the following questions and discussing the answers:
  - Why does learning new things sometimes trigger uncomfortable emotions and which emotions are they?
  - Why might we sometimes avoid sorting out problems we have with friends and just choose to complain about them behind their backs?
  - What is your attitude to solving problems – do you see them as a threat or an opportunity?
  - When we explain to someone that they have upset us, they don't always respond well. What uncomfortable feelings might be triggered when someone tells us we've upset them?
  - Why does change sometimes trigger unenjoyable emotions?
  - What emotions are triggered when we feel uncertain and cannot be sure how something is going to turn out?

#  Extension ideas

- Acknowledge that sometimes it takes bravery to admit what's outside our comfort zone! Then ask the children to draw their comfort zone as a circle and write some things they are comfortable doing inside it and anything they currently find too challenging outside it. They could choose from things such as: standing up in front of a lot of people to speak; running really fast; walking into a room of people you don't know; answering questions in class; using a pogo stick; climbing a tree; meeting a new person; staying several nights away from home; eating a new food; changing where you sit in class; telling someone why they have upset you; being told you need to improve the work you have done; riding on a rollercoaster; going for an all-day walk; going to the doctor; camping in a tent.

**Note**

Once you have done this activity, you can refer to the uncomfortable emotions we regularly feel in everyday situations, such as those we feel when learning something new; having a slightly tricky but necessary conversation with someone; getting used to a change; accepting a disappointing change of plan etc.

# What messages can emotions send us?

 **Objective**

To consider any messages that different emotions might send us.

 **What's needed?**

A copy of the sheet *What messages can emotions send us?* (page 99); scissors.

 **Instructions**

- Explain to the children that our emotions evolved to help us survive, so they tend to keep us safe (eg, fear gives us a burst of energy to run away from danger) or help us find things that are good for us (eg, love and happiness can make us connect with and look after each other). So although emotions can sometimes be a bit tricky, they exist for good reasons and they can often indicate something needs addressing.

- Give each pair of children a copy of the sheet *What messages can emotions give us?* and ask them to cut out each section so that they can match up each emotion with the message it can send us. Here are the answers:
  - **Anger:** That someone has done something we think they should not have done. It usually means we need to talk to that person assertively and explain how we feel.
  - **Sadness:** That we need to take some time out to recover and look after ourselves until we feel better.
  - **Guilt:** That we have done something we know is wrong and we need to put it right or apologise.
  - **Overwhelm:** That we are not coping very well. It usually means we need to pause and take a deep breath. Then we need to make a plan that breaks down what we need to do into smaller steps.
  - **Worry:** Often this means there is something niggling at us that we might be trying hard to ignore. It can mean we need to get on with something we would rather put off.

- o **Fear:** This usually means that something is making us feel unsafe and we need to make ourselves safe again quickly. Sometimes we need the help of trusted adults to help us feel safe again.
- Consider these emotions and messages further by asking the following questions:
  - o Is it usually things other people do that more often trigger our anger or do we often become angry about things that involve nobody else?
  - o Is it always a good idea to tell someone if they trigger our anger?
  - o Why do you think some people get angry and others don't in the same situation?
  - o Is sadness an emotion that tends to last a long time or a short time?
  - o How do we know when sadness has left us?
  - o Do you think it's good that we feel guilt?
  - o How does guilt encourage us to say sorry and try to make amends?
  - o When we're overwhelmed, how do we tend to think and behave?
  - o What helpful message does overwhelm send us?
  - o Think about something you have worried about. Was it something you could do something about or was it just your head running away with itself?
  - o Can worry sometimes drive us to do useful things?
  - o Fear is an emotion that can override anything else we are feeling – why do you think this is?
  - o Fear gives us a burst of energy – why do you think this is?
  - o Are we sometimes scared of things that are not actually dangerous?
- Emphasise that our emotions evolved at a time when we lived quite differently, so although emotions send us messages, these are not always helpful (eg, when we're scared because we have walked into a room of people we don't know – it's not actually dangerous, but our body reacts as if it is). It's always a good idea to consider whether an emotion's message is helpful or not.

 *Extension ideas*

- The children could consider the messages that other emotions might be sending (eg, happiness, surprise, disgust).

*Note*

I always stress to the children that we should notice our feelings first, consider what they might be telling us and then work out what we might need to do. Even if we end up doing nothing, we should try not to ignore our emotions.

# What could they do?

 **Objective**

To realise that emotions are sometimes telling us that we need to do something.

 **What's needed?**

A copy of the sheet *What could they do?* (page 100).

 **Instructions**

- Explain to the children that emotions are often sending us a message that we need to do something. When we get good at considering those messages, they can help us decide what we need to do.
- Give children access to the sheet *What could they do?* and read through it as a class.
- Ask pairs of children to discuss the four situations outlined on the sheet and ask them to consider in greater detail what is triggering the emotion in each of these people. Encourage the children to explore further by asking them to explain how each person has ended up feeling what they have – for example:
  - Joe knows he probably hasn't done enough revision but is conflicted because revision isn't as enjoyable and is more challenging than playing on a games console.
  - Dylan probably didn't mean to upset his friend but feels guilty when he realises that he has.
  - Archie has too much to do and he doesn't believe he can do it all.
  - Arya feels humiliated and let down by her friend. She's now angry because she doesn't think her friend should have called her useless.
- Ask the children to discuss the following questions:
  - What would be the best thing for each of these children to do?
  - What might stop each of these children from doing that 'best thing'?
  - How might anyone else in each situation respond when each child does this 'best thing'?
- Reiterate that it's always good to be curious about what our emotions might be telling us and whether there's anything we can do to help the situation. There are never any guarantees that solutions can be found; but if something is bothering us for a while, this usually means we're ignoring a situation when it would be better to try to address it (Note: There are some occasions, however, when 'letting something go' is the best response – to do this, we usually have to reframe how we think about what happened or is happening.)

*Extension ideas*

- The children could come up some advice for each of the children on the *What could they do?* sheet as if they were an agony aunt.
- The children could share situations they have experienced in which they felt an unenjoyable emotion, what they did and whether they could have done something better.

 *Note*

As children become more emotionally intelligent, they eventually get to a place where they can automatically investigate what an emotion might be telling them. It's delightful when this happens!

# Feeling better

 *Objective*

To consider different coping strategies for different emotions.

 *What's needed?*

A copy of the sheet *Feeling better* (page 101).

 *Instructions*

- Explain to the children that sometimes we just have to put up with unenjoyable emotions, but there are nearly always things that can help us cope with them. It's also true that different emotions sometimes need different strategies or plans to help us manage them well.
- Ask the children to think of a time when they experienced an unenjoyable emotion, such as anxiety (worry), sadness, anger, overwhelm, dread, guilt, embarrassment, disappointment, shame, hurt or feeling misunderstood. Ask them what kinds of things they did when they felt this way and compile a list of their answers. You might need to give a few examples from the sheet *Feeling better* to start the children off.
- Give the children access to the information on the sheet *Feeling better*. This sheet contains a lot of information which could be explored over several sessions (see the extension ideas below). Go through the sheet and check for understanding.
- Explain that this list includes some things you can do to soothe or distract yourself when you are experiencing an unenjoyable emotion, and other things that can help

you change your thinking so you have a better chance of being less bothered by what has happened.

- Ask each child to select the six ideas on this sheet (and those listed earlier) that they think would work best for them.
- Ask the children to share their top six ideas and see whether some ideas are much more popular than others.
- Finally, ask the children to create a personal poster/leaflet/reminder to remind themselves to use these strategies.

 ## Extension ideas

- The children could consider the emotions of anger, anxiety and sadness; what might help someone cope with each of these emotions; and how what helps might be different for different emotions. Pairs of children could produce spider diagrams of different things that could help for each emotion.
- Tell the story of Akeno, who stood up in class and gave a really silly answer to a question and felt painfully embarrassed. He went home and thought about what had happened over and over again. What advice could the children give Akeno to help change how he is thinking about what happened?
- Ask the children to draw a happy place that they can go to in their heads when they are experiencing an unenjoyable emotion. This can be real or imaginary.
- Explain that exercise nearly always helps people feel better. Ask the children to consider what exercises they could do indoors if they can't get outside for a walk.
- Explain that people usually feel better after a good cry. Discuss what sometimes stops us from crying.
- Ask the children to list kind things they could do for others when they are experiencing an unenjoyable emotion. Being kind often helps us to feel better. Sometimes children need help to believe this.
- Smiling and laughing nearly always help. Tell the children to start with a false laugh by saying, 'Ha ha! Hee hee!' over and over and see whether they eventually start laughing for real!
- Watch online videos about different relaxation breathing techniques.
- The children could create a collection of ideas for when they are feeling unenjoyable emotions that can be made available for everyone. The ideas could be written on cards, painted on pebbles, made into a book, etc.
- The children could create the details of a magical, imaginary journey that they can recount in their minds at night if they are struggling to go to sleep. The journey could start with a weather report; breakfast; a friend joining them; a journey down a hill by

some means; a fairground ride; a choice of transport for the rest of the journey; a character who tells them which way to go at a crossroads; lunch; a nice place to relax after lunch; finding something exciting that fits in their pocket; a lesson where they quickly learn to do something that's amazing; going into the sky somehow to cross some hills; a magical forest; a snack shack that serves anything they want; a game; and a place to sleep at the end. Once the journey has been designed, the children can recall it again and again. The repetition can eventually make it boring enough to induce sleep!

##  Note

If the children struggle to come up with suggestions for Part 2 of the sheet, give them scenarios of 'pretend characters' – for example, 'Tom is really dreading school tomorrow'; 'Kate is really embarrassed about what happened at school yesterday.' It helps if you state that these characters are younger than the children taking part, as this seems to help the children with volunteering suggestions.

# If emotions could talk

###  Objective

To explore and develop a greater understanding of different emotions.

###  What's needed?

Access for all children to the text on the sheet *If emotions could talk* (page 102).

###  Instructions

- Read the sheet *If emotions could talk* together.
- Explain to the children that they will be working in pairs to choose two emotions to bring to life by working out what they might say.
- You can help the children with the following prompts:
  - Are there other words for this emotion?
  - What kinds of situations can trigger this emotion?
  - What are the physical symptoms of this emotion?
  - How might this emotion affect how people think or behave?
  - Is this emotion enjoyable or unenjoyable? Comfortable or uncomfortable?
- Ask the children to create speech bubbles and then ask some volunteers to share what they have created so others can guess which emotion is talking.

 *Extension idea:*

- The children could create sentences that each emotion might say linked to similes and metaphors –for example:
  - If I was a weather, I would be …
  - If I was a sound, I would be …
  - If I was an animal, I would be …
  - If I was a way of walking, I would be …
  - If I was a taste, I would be …

 *Note*

Children love reading out their sentences in a voice that they think each emotion would probably have!

# Low-mood menu

 *Objective*

To create a menu of activities that the children can do when they are feeling low.

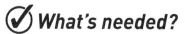 *What's needed?*

Access to the information on the sheet *Low-mood menu* (page 103); a folded sheet of A4 or A3 for the children to create their menus.

*Instructions*

- Ask the children what they think moods are (my favourite answer ever was, 'Like less noisy, less powerful background emotions').
- Explain that everyone experiences low moods and that nobody can feel upbeat and happy all the time. Explain that part of the problem with a low mood is that because we feel low, we sometimes can't be bothered to find things that could make our day feel a little more enjoyable. That's where the low-mood menu comes in: it can be used to remind us of simple things we can do when we are experiencing a low mood.
- Show the children the information on the sheet *Low-mood menu*. Invite groups of four to brainstorm more ideas for the low-mood menu and write them down. Collate a list of their ideas.

- Invite the children to make and decorate their own low-mood menus (these often end up doubling up as a menu for when children are bored).

 ## Extension ideas

- The children could make a 'things that soothe me' menu for when they feel anxious or unsettled.

 ## Note

This activity works just as well with adults as it does with children!

# Teddy's day

Teddy arrived at the park. * He climbed to the top of the slide. It was really high. * Teddy slid down to the bottom and decided to run to the roundabout. Just as he got going, he tripped. * Teddy looked down and saw that he had cut his knee. *

Teddy's dad rushed over to help him. * His dad cleaned up his knee, put a plaster on it and gave him a cuddle. *

To cheer Teddy up, his dad suggested they go and get an ice cream. * There was a long queue for ice cream. * Teddy and his dad stood in the queue and eventually got to the front. * Teddy could not decide which ice cream to have. * In the end, he quickly chose an orange-flavoured ice lolly because the queue was building up behind him. *

Teddy had licked his lolly twice when someone bumped into him, making him drop his lolly on the ground. * Someone laughed at what had happened. *

At this point, Teddy saw his friend Dak. Dak saw Teddy and smiled at him. * Dak came straight over and said, 'Shall we go and climb that tree over there?' * Teddy was a bit scared of climbing trees but agreed to go with Dak anyway. * Dak quickly climbed really high up in the tree (she is an excellent tree climber), but Teddy didn't go any higher than the lowest branch. * Dak shouted for Teddy to follow her, but he really didn't want to. *

Eventually Dak climbed down and Teddy suggested they go to the swings. Dak said, 'Yes, I love the swings!' * At the swings, Dak pushed Teddy as hard as she could so that he went really high. * But Dak soon got bored and wandered off, leaving Teddy on the swings on his own. * Teddy found his dad and said, 'I want to go home now.' *

# Happy or sad?

Draw the following things and decide which would make you happy and which might make you sad.

| | |
|---|---|
| Snow | A pet kitten |
| Ice cream | Losing a toy you like (draw your favourite toy) |
| The beach | Being ill |

# Emotion diary

| Three things you did today | How you felt |
|---|---|
|  |  |
|  |  |
|  |  |

# What might she be feeling?

In which picture do you think this girl is feeling...

- angry
- excited
- disgusted

- sad
- worried
- scared

- relaxed
- embarrassed

1

2

3

4

5

6

7

8

# Where in the body do we feel it?

| | |
|---|---|
| **Happiness** | **Sadness** |
| **Anger** | **Worry** |

# What does it feel like?

I choose to think about feeling:

**happy**     **sad**     **angry**     **worried**     **excited**     **bored**

(Circle one)

**I think feeling** _____ **is:**

(Write the emotion you chose on this line)

**enjoyable     or     unenjoyable**

(Circle one)

**I think feeling** _____ **feels...**

(Write the emotion you chose on this line)

(Choose a few words)

**fizzy**     **spiky**     **still**     **wobbly**     **flat**

**sore**     **quiet**     **calm**     **wonky**     **sizzling**

**dull**     **colourful**     **sparkly**     **loud**     **bubbly**

**shaky**     **blasting**     **lively**     **soft**     **blank**

**gloomy**     **plain**     **exploding**     **sleepy**     **simple**

# Trigger runaround

| | | |
|---|---|---|
| Has just been given a bag of their favourite sweets. | Has just been told off for something they didn't do. | Has just seen a spider and really doesn't like spiders. |
| Has just been called a nasty name by someone. | Has just realised their favourite toy is broken. | Has just been given a present and told they can open it. |
| Has just dropped their ice cream. | Has just had someone push in front of them in the queue. | Has just been asked to do something they don't understand. |
| Can't find their coat to go out and play. | Has just said goodbye to someone they are really going to miss. | Has just had a car drive past and honk its horn really loudly. |
| Is on a rollercoaster. | Has just learned how to ride a bike for the first time. | Has just been teased for making a mistake. |
| Is being given a cuddle by someone they love. | Has just came first in a race. | Has just been told that nobody wants to play with them. |
| Has just realised they have not been invited to a friend's party. | Is holding a really cute baby chick. | Is trying to listen to a story but keeps being poked by the person sitting behind them. |
| Has just learned they have won an art competition. | Had just learned their party has to be cancelled. | Is being interrupted by someone every time they go to speak. |
| Has just accidentally dropped their sandwich in a really smelly bin. | Has just realised they have been walking around with their jumper on inside out. | Has just got a test back and found out they got a really bad mark. |

# Max's day

| What happened | How would you feel if you were Max? |
|---|---|
| Max was woken up by his mum calling his name. | |
| He remembered it was a school day. | |
| He looked out of the window and saw that it had snowed overnight. | |
| He went downstairs and realised there was none of his favourite cereal left. | |
| He had to have toast and peanut butter instead. | |
| His mum got a phone call saying school was cancelled because of the snow. | |
| Later that day Max went to the park with his mum. | |
| He made a huge snowman but his fingers got really cold. | |
| Then he saw some older kids he knew a bit. | |
| He had a snowball fight with these older children. | |
| One snowball landed right on the side of his head. | |
| Max's mum said it was time to go home. | |
| On his way home he slipped over. | |

# Very happy to very sad

## Overjoyed

You just won the best prize ever!

## Happy

Some of your favourite friends are coming round for tea soon.

## Cheerful

It's a lovely sunny day.

## Pleased

The next lesson is something you really like.

## Neutral

You feel neither happy or sad.

## Sorry

You upset your friend.

## Sad

You have no one to play with.

## Miserable

It's your favourite teacher's last day at your school.

## Distressed

You are lost in a big city and cannot find anyone you know.

# Symptom checker

When you feel an unenjoyable emotion ...

---

### Your head!

- What shape does your mouth make?
- What position do your eyebrows get into?
- Do your eyes become narrower, wider or stay the same?
- Does your voice become higher or lower, faster or slower, louder or quieter or stay the same?
- Does your face feel hot?
- Do you tend to look downwards or upwards?

---

### Your body

- Do you breathe quicker or slower?
- Does your heartbeat speed up, slow down or stay the same?
- Does it affect how your tummy feels?
- Do you have tense or tight muscles anywhere?
- What position do you hold your body in?

---

### Other sensations

- Does it make you feel more energetic, fidgety or like you want to be still and quiet?
- Does it make it hard to concentrate?
- Does it tend to make you feel like you want to hide or does it make you want to seek out other people to be with?
- Do you feel like you want to cry?
- Do you tend to find yourself only thinking about one thing?

---

# What faces can tell us

Our faces can give away a lot about what we are thinking and feeling.

# Happy, angry, sad or scared?

| happy | angry | sad | scared |
|-------|-------|-----|--------|

Sort these words and phrases into those that are closest in meaning to 'happy', 'angry', 'sad' or 'scared'. You will know some of these words but you might need a computer or dictionary to help you with others.

Cautious     Discouraged     Panicked     Jubilant

Petrified     Forlorn     Tickled pink     Outraged

Euphoric     Buoyant     Glum     Pleased     Fearful

Terrified     Over the moon     On top of the world

Livid     On cloud nine     Blown a fuse     Infuriated

Fuming     Exasperated     Boiling mad     Morose

Panicked     Ecstatic     Down in the dumps

Overjoyed     Downcast     Down in the mouth

Afraid     Thrilled     Petrified     Gleeful     Intimidated

Trembling like a leaf     Sorrowful     Vexed     Elated

# 'I' messages

'I' messages are a great way to tell someone how we feel when they do something that affects us. We can use 'I' messages when we need to be assertive. Being assertive is about saying what you want or need in a respectful and calm way.

With 'I' messages, instead of saying, 'You made me angry,' we say:

> I feel angry when
> people don't listen to me.
> I need you to listen.

Here's how to create an 'I' message

- **'When you ...'**          say what happened that affected you
- **'I feel ...'**            say what you felt
- **'Because ...'**          say how you are affected or
          what you need to happen to feel better.

Create 'I' messages for the following situations:

| You are getting annoyed because someone is talking loudly so you can't hear what you want to listen to. | You feel upset because your friend has deliberately left you out of a game. |
|---|---|
| What do you say to the person talking? | What do you say to your friend? |
| Someone has just pushed in front of you in the dinner queue. | A friend has just snatched your felt-tipped pens and used them without asking. |
| What do you say to them? | What do you say to this person? |

# How would you feel?

Imagine each of the following things happened to you. How do you think you would feel? You might feel more than one thing. You can use the feeling words listed below to help you.

| | | |
|---|---|---|
| You have lost your homework on the way to school and you're about to be called up to hand it in. | You told a lie last week about being able to juggle. Now your teacher is asking you to show everyone how to juggle. | Your friend let you copy their work in the last maths lesson but the teacher has just asked both of you to explain why your work is exactly the same. |
| You bought some new trainers that you love but someone has just teased you and said they look awful. | When you get home from school, your dad says there's a surprise waiting for you in your bedroom. | You have just found out that a close friend has been telling everyone they don't like you as much as they used to. |
| You arrange to meet your friend at the park but when you get there, they don't turn up. | You are told off for something you did not do and when you try to explain that you did not do it, no one believes you. | You won a prize in a writing competition that someone in your class told you you'd never win. |
| Art is the next lesson and you hate art. The friend you sit next to loves it. | It is your birthday tomorrow and you suspect that you have not been bought the only present that you really, really wanted. | You don't understand a question in a science test but everyone around you looks like they know exactly what they're doing. |
| You are the only person in your school who has been selected to go to an event where you have been asked to talk to lots of people about what your school is like. | You want to be on the school hockey team and you played really well in the last match. | You lost your hamster yesterday when you let it roam around in your bedroom. You have just seen him in your drawer! |

| | | | | |
|---|---|---|---|---|
| Proud | Excited | Surprised | Concerned | Overwhelmed |
| Grateful | Sad | Agitated | Awkward | Satisfied |
| Disgusted | Embarrassed | Happy | Confused | Tense |
| Desperate | Hopeful | Ashamed | Angry | Doubtful |
| Scared | Disappointed | Regretful | Nervous | Relieved |
| Worried | Annoyed | Tempted | Bored | Guilty |
| Frustrated | Jealous | Alarmed | Panicked | Bewildered |

# Name that feeling!

Here are some ways children have described different emotions. Match up each emotion to its description.

| | | |
|---|---|---|
| Happy | | It's how you feel when you can't be bothered to do anything, but because you can't be bothered to do anything, you stay feeling this way! |
| Excited | | It's a smiley feeling! It can make you feel all light and lively and like nothing will bother you. It can also make you feel like being kind to others. |
| Sad | | It's a feeling that can make you feel powerful, but not in a helpful way. When you feel it, you can usually only think about the thing that triggered it. |
| Angry | | It's a feeling that can last a while and make you want to stomp about. When you feel it, it can be hard to convince you that you will enjoy anything! |
| Worried | | You feel like this when something upsets you, such as losing something you love. It can make you feel like you want to hide away and be quiet. |
| Bored | | It's a lively emotion that often means you can't sit still. You often feel it when you are really looking forward to or really enjoying something! |
| Grumpy | | It's how you feel when you're really bothered about something and find it hard to think about anything else. It makes you feel wobbly. |

Can you describe any of the following emotions in a similar way?

Shy    Frustrated    Scared    Disappointed    Lonely    Embarrassed    Guilty

# An emotion profile

The emotion I chose to explore is:

(Write the emotion in bubble writing in this box, in the style and colour you think suit it)

What does a person's face look like when they feel it? >>>

Is it an **enjoyable** or **unenjoyable** emotion?

(circle one)

Does this emotion usually hang about for a long time? YES/NO

Label where a person might
feel the emotion in their body
when they feel this way.

Describe something that could happen that might
trigger this emotion for someone:

Describe something someone might feel like doing
when they feel it.

What could someone do to enjoy the emotion more or what might help them if
it's unenjoyable?

# Which emotions might make you want to ...

Match each emotion to what a person might do when they feel it. Each emotion could make someone feel like doing more than one of these things.

When someone feels ...

| happy | angry | worried | excited | sad |
|-------|-------|---------|---------|-----|

They might ...

sit quietly      insult someone      jiggle about      smile

talk to someone      bite their nails      shout at someone

cry      have a burst of energy      find it hard to concentrate

hide their face      hit something      be lively      frown

talk a lot about what happened      fidget      be impatient

think the same thought over and over      be kind to someone

stop taking part in something      talk a lot      tell someone off

want a hug      stomp about      not feel like doing anything

Circle any of the things you think are helpful to do and cross out any you think are unhelpful. If you think they are neither, leave them as they are.

# Can we work out what they might be feeling?

| 1 | 2 |
|---|---|
| Katy stomped over to Ben. She assumed he was her friend but she wasn't so sure after what he'd done. She had one or two things she was going to say to him, that was for sure. | Marley wasn't sure he'd ever be able to show his face again. Every time he thought about what had happened and how many people were staring at him, he felt sure he'd never be able to live it down. |
| **3** | **4** |
| Ali couldn't look. He could hear his heart pounding in his head. He gripped the rail as tightly as he could and forced himself to put one foot in front of the other. | It wasn't that long to wait now but it still seemed like ages to Amara. Every time it popped into her head, she got a fizzy feeling in her stomach and couldn't sit still! |
| **5** | **6** |
| Leo rolled his eyes, yawned and stretched. The afternoon had gone on forever. He couldn't believe he'd been made to come here. He'd searched everywhere but there was nothing he could find worth paying any attention to. | Nothing could ruin today. It was impossible. Yasmine actually skipped to school, the beaming smile on her face making it clear to everyone exactly how she felt. She wanted to give everyone a big hug! |
| **7** | **8** |
| Jimmy really hadn't expected that to happen at all. The shock of it was still lingering and his eyes remained wide open. | Aizen couldn't focus on his work. All he could think about was what was going to happen tomorrow. He just couldn't be sure how it would pan out or if he would cope. The thoughts in his head went round and round. It felt like torture. |

Write your own paragraph that implies Fred is experiencing an emotion, without using the word for the emotion Fred is feeling.

You could try the following emotions:

**Frustrated   Guilty   Proud   Disappointed   Jealous   Relieved   Determined**

# Emotions affect how we think

| Emotion | How this emotion might affect your thinking |
|---|---|
| Anger | This emotion will make you think only about getting you to safety. It will override all other emotions. Unfortunately, it sometimes makes you think that some things are dangerous when they're not, as it wants to be 'better safe than sorry'. |
| Anxiety | This emotion helps you to think the best of everyone so that you want to connect with them and be friendly. It also helps you be explorative, creative and open to new ideas. |
| Fear | This emotion can sort of make you think less and your brain can feel numb. It tells you that you don't really want to do anything and you just want to recover from what has happened. |
| Sadness | When you feel this emotion, your brain makes really quick judgements so you can avoid something. This could be a substance or something someone did that you didn't like. Sometimes it's hard to change your mind once you have felt this emotion. |
| Happiness | This emotion can make you think only about protecting yourself and not consider others much. It can narrow your focus so you only think about the thing that triggered the emotion. The thoughts you have when you experience this emotion can sometimes make you feel the emotion even more! |
| Disgust | This emotion makes you alert and very focused on what is in front of you so you can quickly see whether it's unsafe or not. This focus usually only lasts a short while. |
| Surprise | When you feel this emotion, the same troubling thought may keep going round and round in your head. It can also tend to make you think that everything that can go wrong will go wrong. This can leave you with little space to concentrate on anything else and can make you too cautious to try out anything new. |

# Lots of words for emotions! Sheet A

Delighted   Curious   Thrilled   Special   Embarrassed

Excited

Proud

Awkward   Touched   Amused

Thankful                                  Enthusiastic

Affection

Somebody surprised you
with a box of chocolates
for being such a good friend.

Suspicious

Pleased                                    Coy

Love

Appreciative   Charmed   Indebted   Confused

Grateful   Cheerful   Upbeat   Anything else?

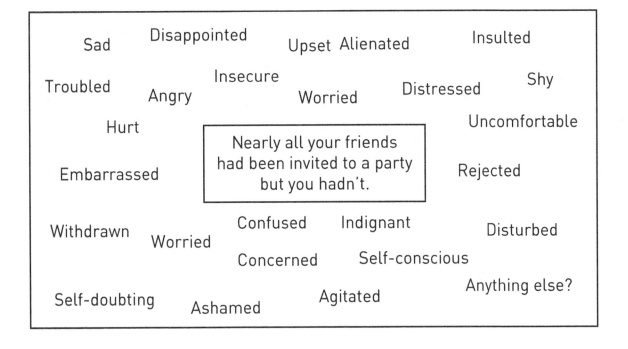

Sad   Disappointed   Upset  Alienated   Insulted

Troubled   Angry   Insecure   Worried   Distressed   Shy

Hurt                                       Uncomfortable

Embarrassed   Nearly all your friends
had been invited to a party
but you hadn't.   Rejected

Withdrawn   Worried   Confused   Indignant   Disturbed

Concerned   Self-conscious

Self-doubting   Ashamed   Agitated   Anything else?

# Lots of words for emotions! Sheet B

Angry  Helpless  Agitated  Hatred  Indignant  Stressed

Disgusted  Dejected  Tormented  Vengeful  Embarrassed

Irritated  Insulted  Puzzled  Alarmed  Annoyed  Nervous

Shocked  Discombobulated

Hurt

You're told off by a strict, scary teacher for something you did not do.

Astonished

Surprised

Infuriated

Perplexed  Worried  Baffled  Shamed

Frustrated

Overwhelmed  Powerless

Ashamed  Contempt

Undermined  Horrified

Offended  Panicked

Anxious  Misunderstood  Anything else?

---

Embarrassed  Humilated  Pitiful  Not-bothered

Cool  Awkward  Entertained

Surprised  Worried

Shocked  Preoccupied  Disappointed  Flustered

Foolish  You stood up in front of lots of people and forgot the one line you had in a play you were performing in.  Frustrated

Self-conscious  Resigned

Fragile  Anxious  Mortified  Amused  Regretful

Ashamed  Angry with yourself  Nonchalent

Disgraced  Pathetic

Forgiving  Exasperated  Anything else?

# We sometimes jump to conclusions!

Imagine you are in a room with just one other person, who calls you stupid. In the left-hand column of this table are some thoughts you could end up having because of this.

| Possible thoughts | What might this trigger you to feel? | How might you react? |
|---|---|---|
| They're really nasty to say that. How dare they! | | |
| They're right – I am stupid. | | |
| They must dislike me to say that. | | |
| I'm not stupid. | | |
| I wonder if they are having a bad day? | | |

**Some emotion words to help you consider what you might feel:**

Curious   Indignant   Angry   Sympathetic   Worthless   Self-doubting   Unconfident

Contempt   Rejected   Dismissive   Vengeful   Forgiving   Irritated   Sad   Hopeless

**Some responses to help you consider how you might react:**

- Insult them back
- Lose your temper
- Assertively declare, 'I'm not stupid'
- Ask them if they're okay
- Go and moan about them to someone
- Sulk

- Avoid them
- Give them an angry look
- Say something nasty under your breath
- Cry
- Ignore them
- Feel sorry for yourself

# Accepting uncomfortable emotions

It's good to accept that we all experience uncomfortable emotions at times. In fact, many things that worth doing need us to endure unenjoyable emotions.

- Decide why the things on each card could be helpful or worth doing.
- List which unenjoyable emotions might be triggered when doing each of them.

| | |
|---|---|
| Learning to type on a keyboard without having to look at the keys, even though you find it really difficult. | Asking someone what they think about the story you just wrote, so you can get feedback that could improve it. |
| Asking for help from a stranger in a public space because you're lost. | Joining a club you've been really keen to join, even though you don't know anyone there. |
| Spending lots of time learning your lines in a school play that you have big role in. | Assertively telling a friend that what they did yesterday upset you. |
| Doing something for the first time, like catching a train on your own. | Joining an enormous queue to get tickets for something you really want to go to. |
| Honestly sharing how you feel about something that's worrying you. | Talking to someone who isn't usually very friendly towards you. |
| A friend telling you that you upset them yesterday so you decide to sit down and talk about it. | Committing to running a marathon. |
| Deciding to ask the teacher if you can sit somewhere else in class because you enjoy chatting to your friend too much and this stops you concentrating. | Deciding to tell your mum that from now on you would like her to knock before she comes into your room. |

# What messages can emotions send us?

| Emotion | What could this emotion be telling us? |
|---|---|
| Anger | That we are not coping very well. It usually means we need to pause and take a deep breath. Then we need to make a plan that breaks down what we need to do into smaller steps. |
| Sadness | This usually means something is making us feel unsafe and we need to make ourselves safe again quickly. Sometimes we need the help of trusted adults to help us feel safe again. |
| Guilt | That someone has done something we think they should not have done. It usually means we need to talk to that person assertively and explain how we feel. |
| Overwhelm | That we need to take some time out to recover and look after ourselves until we feel better. |
| Worry | That we have done something we know is wrong and we need to put it right or apologise. |
| Fear | Often this means there is something niggling at us that we might be trying hard to ignore. It can mean we need to get on with something we would rather put off. |

# What could they do?

## Experiencing unenjoyable emotions

When we experience unenjoyable emotions, they are often sending us a message that we need to do something. If there's something we can do to help with a situation that's triggering an unenjoyable emotion, we need to work out what it is and how we're going to do it.

What could these children do to help sort out the situation they are in to help address their unenjoyable emotions?

| | |
|---|---|
| Joe has a maths test at school on Monday. He is trying hard to distract himself from thinking about it. He has done a little bit of revision. He'd rather play on his games console. If he's honest, he keeps feeling really anxious about the test.<br><br>What could Joe do? | Dylan grabbed Mo's snack at break time and ran off with it. He eventually gave it back but Mo looked really upset and walked off. Dylan didn't see him again that day. Dylan is feeling really guilty.<br><br>What could Dylan do? |
| Archie is going on a school trip tomorrow and has lost the list of things he needs to take. He's also got loads of homework to do to hand in tomorrow because he forgot to do what was set last week. His dad is also insisting he tidy his bedroom and his mum has asked him to help with the washing up. He is feeling overwhelmed.<br><br>What could Archie do? | Arya is really angry. Her close friend Nina laughed at her and called her useless because she completely missed the goal in a football match, despite being right in front of it. Every time Arya thinks about what happened, she feels angry.<br><br>What could Arya do? |

When we experience unenjoyable emotions, it's always good to ask ourselves whether there is something we could do that will help. This could include:

- apologising to someone
- finding out more information
- talking to someone and being honest about how we feel
- making a step-by-step plan
- practising something so we feel more confident
- being assertive to prevent something from happening again.
- forgiving someone and 'letting it go' – as we all make mistakes sometimes

# Feeling better

It is impossible to get through life without experiencing unenjoyable emotions and we shouldn't expect to be able to avoid them. However, when we are feeling uncomfortable emotions, there are things we can do that can help us cope better.

Which of these things do you think would help you cope with unenjoyable emotions such as anxiety, anger or sadness?

## Soothing ourselves

- Talk to someone.
- Go for a walk outside.
- Do some exercise.
- Have a good cry.
- Stroke a pet.
- Take some deep breaths.
- Sit calmly and quietly.
- Massage your feet.
- Find a change of scene.
- Visualise a wonderful place where you feel calm and happy.
- List all the things you are grateful for.
- Listen to some music.
- Have a cuddle with someone you love.
- Do something that uses up most of your mind – like watching a film.
- Do something kind for someone else.
- Make a plan to do something fun.
- Write it all down.
- Meditate or do something mindfully.
- Draw simple pictures (flowers, smiley faces, clouds) or write words ('calm', 'lullaby') over and over.

## Changing your thinking

- Remind yourself you won't feel like this forever.
- Think of any positives – have you learned anything?
- Recognise and challenge unhelpful thinking (eg, assuming you won't cope).
- Think of a time when you were fine and coped before.
- Forgive yourself for any mistakes or mess-ups you made – we all make them and you're probably the only person thinking about them!
- Remind yourself that it is very likely that you will cope and be fine.
- Know that others will have felt (or will be feeling) this too.
- Picture what's on your mind and then make it smaller, make the picture black and white, make it more distant in your mind and make any sounds quieter.
- Allow yourself some time to mull things over and then tell yourself to stop.
- See whether you can find a funny side.
- Consider how it could be worse, laugh and be grateful.
- Imagine the worst-case scenario – could you cope with that? Probably!
- Try to be more forgiving of anyone else involved and remember that we all have bad days and mess up sometimes.

# If emotions could talk

Hi, I'm anxiety. Some people call me 'worry'. I can give you a wobbly tummy feeling, make it hard for you to sleep, make you feel unsettled and fill you with a sense of dread. I often turn up when you've got something to do in the future that you don't believe you will cope with. I can fill you with doubt and negative thoughts. I bother some people more than others. I used to help people stay safe thousands of years ago by keeping them alert in case a threat came along. I am not often needed to keep you safe nowadays but that doesn't stop me hanging about.

Hi, I'm sadness. Because I am so well known, there are lots of words to describe me, such as 'miserable', 'down in the dumps' and 'dejected'. I arrive when someone experiences some kind of loss. That could be the loss when a pet dies or a loss when someone was hoping for something and it didn't happen. I sometimes make people cry. I can create a sinking feeling in the tummy. I also make people feel like they don't really want to do anything much other than mope around. I'm not really a lively emotion and I'm not enjoyable.

If these emotions could talk, what do you think they would say? Choose two emotions and decide what they might say if they could speak.

Anger    Embarrassment    Shame    Surprise    Jealousy

Disappointment    Irritation    Excitement    Relief

Pride    Overwhelm    Anticipation    Contempt

Affection    Gratitude    Envy    Suspicion    Boredom

Admiration    Hurt    Amusement    Guilt    Insecurity

# Low-mood menu

Some days we just wake up with a low mood. This happens to everyone and is a normal part of being human. When this happens, we often don't feel like doing anything much – which is a shame, because quite often when we do something, we feel better. This is where a low-mood menu comes in.

A low-mood menu includes activities that you could do when you feel low. The activities should be things you would not hate to do and that don't require too much effort. Create your own low-mood menu. Here are some ideas to help you:

- Tidy a messy drawer.
- Challenge someone you're comfortable with to a tickle fight.
- Look at old photos.
- Watch a film.
- Light a candle.
- Do a jigsaw.
- Listen to some music.
- Go for a walk.
- Sit still and listen to every sound for three minutes.
- Have a rummage in your room and see if anything needs to be thrown out.
- Create a giant doodle.
- Find as many different shades of green outside as you can.
- Hide some kind messages for people to find around your home.
- Turn your feet into two characters and have them talk to each other.
- Stare at the sky for five minutes.
- Make a birthday card for someone whose birthday is soon.
- Copy a picture from a book.
- Write a list of questions you'd like answered.
- Draw three ugly monsters, colour them in and decide which is the ugliest.
- Go on a sound scavenger hunt: go around your home and see how many different noises you can make. You could also go hunting for different notes.
- Go on a smell scavenger hunt and see how many different smells you can collect (try to avoid any stinky socks!).
- Look in a mirror and find the funniest face you can pull.
- Find a sorting job to lose yourself in (eg, throwing out felt-tipped pens that don't work).
- Look at a book and see if it can teach you anything
- From where you're sitting, see how many things you can see that start with the letter 'c' (or choose another letter, or try the alphabet).
- Make a plan for something to do tomorrow.
- Massage your face

# Feeling Cards – Sheet A

| Happy | Sad | Angry |
|---|---|---|
| Scared | Surprised | Excited |
| Bored | Guilty | Embarrassed |
| Playful | Lonely | Relaxed |

# Feeling Cards - Sheet B

| | | |
|---|---|---|
| Shy | Confused | Worried |
| Disgusted | Quiet | Panicked |
| Jealous | Shocked | Disappointed |
| Determined | Nervous | Furious |
| Thrilled | Confident | Interested |
| Delighted | Satisfied | Enthusiastic |
| Anxious | Pleased | Proud |
| Frustrated | Hopeful | Impatient |
| Irritated | Brave | Amazed |

# Feeling Cards – Sheet C

| | | |
|---|---|---|
| Flustered | Alert | Curious |
| Grateful | Amused | Withdrawn |
| Rejected | Ashamed | Tense |
| Astonished | Impressed | Agitated |
| Preoccupied | Vulnerable | Cautious |
| Triumphant | Exasperated | Accepted |
| Forlorn | Hesitant | Fulfilled |
| Flabbergasted | Sceptical | Insecure |
| Humiliated | Motivated | Overwhelmed |
| Intimidated | Elated | Full of dread |
| Admiration | Awe | Despair |
| Contempt | Envy | Pity |
| Defensive | Humble | Relieved |
| Impulsive | Encouraged | Perplexed |

# Chapter 3

# A CLOSER LOOK AT SOME INDIVIDUAL EMOTIONS

## What's in this chapter?

This chapter includes activities that look at ten emotions individually.

## *Activity notes*

- The activities are described with an objective, instructions, an indication of whether any further resources are needed (including printable resources from this book) and at least one suggested extension activity.
- The activities involve a variety of teaching and learning techniques, including discussion prompts, quizzes, agreement spectrums, drama activities, games and lessons that use printable worksheets.
- The age that each activity is suitable for has not been stipulated. Most activities could be simplified for younger children or adjusted to be more challenging for older children.

## Some information about the emotions in this chapter

| Emotion | Information |
|---------|-------------|
| Happiness | Happiness probably evolved so that we could connect with others, seek out things that soothe us so we could 'rest and digest' and be explorative and creative. Today we, tend to think of two types of happiness:<br><br>• joy – the instant pleasure that usually arrives because of what's just happened; and<br>• a broader sense of contentment, fulfilment and satisfaction with our lives. |

DOI: 10.4324/9781032690773-4

| Emotion | Information |
|---------|-------------|
| Fear | Fear evolved as a safety mechanism that gave us a boost of energy and intense focus to help us avoid danger. Unfortunately, it's not a finetuned mechanism and it functions in a 'better safe than sorry' way. This means it can misfire and be triggered by things that are not actually dangerous, such as the dark. |
| Sadness | We experience sadness when we experience loss. That loss could be a death (eg, of a pet), a friend moving away or losing something we value. We usually need time to recover from loss, so sadness tends to make us withdraw for a while. |
| Boredom | When we're bored, we often can't be bothered to find something interesting that would stop us from being bored. Boredom can be down to apathy and a lack of motivation to do anything, or finding ourselves in an under-stimulating situation that we cannot escape. |
| Embarrassment | We experience embarrassment when we have done something that we believe will make others think we are stupid or foolish. It is in the shame family of emotions. |
| Excitement | Excitement is an enjoyable emotion, although it can also be a little physically uncomfortable sometimes! |
| Guilt | Guilt evolved to help us want to make amends when we know we have done something wrong that could upset or cause difficulties for another person. |
| Disappointment | Disappointment is in the sadness family of emotions. We feel it when we were expecting something – to happen, to exist, to turn out a certain way – but the reality falls short of our expectations. |
| Gratitude | Feeling grateful helps to support our mental wellbeing. Gratitude can help us feel better and help put things into perspective. |
| Shame | Shame is an emotion that is not often acknowledged, although for some children its effects are extremely powerful. It can leave children feeling as if they are worthless and that everyone else believes this too. |

# Activities

## Happy!

 **Objective**

To consider what brings us joy.

 **What's needed?**

One copy of the sheet *Happy!* (page 122) per child.

 **Instructions**

- Introduce 'happiness' by asking the children what it feels like.
- State that happiness is an enjoyable emotion but also make it clear that nobody can expect to be happy all the time.

- Next, give the children a copy of the sheet *Feeling happy* and ask them to cut out the images one row at a time and put each row into the order from what would make them most happy to least happy.
- Ask pairs of children to list any more things they can think of that could trigger them to be happy.
- Next, explore the idea of what tends to bring happiness further by asking the children the following questions:
  - Do some of us like surprises more than others?
  - Does being with other people help us to feel happy?
  - Do treats always make us feel happy?
  - Do activities that we give lots of attention to tend to make us happy?
  - Do new things always trigger happiness?
  - Are there places that can make us happy?
  - Can music and/or dancing make us happy?
  - When we create or make something, can this bring us joy?
  - Does being noticed and people wanting to spend time with us make us happy?
  - When we are kind to someone else, does that make us happy?
  - Can successfully learning something new trigger happiness?
  - Do trips to places you know you like, or to new places, make you happy and is this different for different people?
  - Does having choice help us to feel happy?
- Lastly ask children to draw or write four completions to the following sentence: 'I feel happy when ...'

 ## Extension ideas

- The children could draw different acts of kindness to display around the classroom as reminders (eg, inviting someone to join in; asking how someone is; comforting someone who is upset; remembering someone's birthday; remembering details another person has shared with you; smiling as a greeting).
- Older children could discuss the broader definition of 'happiness' and consider what might make 'a happy life'. You could give them criteria to discuss or put in order from most impactful to least impactful (eg, lots of money; a job you enjoy; hobbies you love; good friends; being able to manage emotions well; adventure; being optimistic; being able to help others).

 ## Note

When I do this activity with children, they often choose to put things in different orders so it becomes an opportunity to celebrate and show respect for our differences.

# Being scared

 **Objective**

To consider fear and the times when it can be helpful and when it can be unhelpful.

 **What's needed?**

Access to the information on the sheet *Being scared* (page 123).

**Instructions**

- Ask the children what feeling scared is like and explore the physical and mental symptoms of fear (eg, your heart races; you can freeze or get a surge of energy that makes you want to move; you can only focus on what has scared you).

- Explain that fear can be really useful because it gives us a burst of energy when we suspect we might be in danger. Add that it's helpful but that it's not a very finetuned system, because we can be fearful of some things that are not actually likely to harm us. Fear is a 'better safe than sorry' emotion. Because of this, we sometimes feel the uncomfortableness of fear when it's not particularly helpful.

- Let children see the different things on the sheet *Being scared* and make it clear that not everyone will be scared of all of these things, but that they all things that some people might be scared of.

- Talk through the task as outlined on the sheet and ask pairs of children to complete the sorting activity. This usually induces lots of discussion, as you can find potential 'dangers' with many things; and some older children may argue that there is a danger of social disgrace/ostracism, which might not be physically dangerous but is psychologically harmful.

- Discuss each of the things on the sheet and explore the likelihood of each thing causing genuine harm to illustrate how the feeling of fear can sometimes be unhelpfully exaggerated.

- Ask pairs of children to create a helpful phrase that they can tell themselves when they are scared of something that is unlikely to harm them.

 **Extension ideas**

- The children could write a recipe for being brave.
- Older children could investigate the' flight, fight or freeze' response that adrenaline triggers and devise a way to teach others about it.

- The children could consider why we sometimes deliberately scare ourselves (eg, a thrilling ghost train) and why we do this (we trust we are not actually in real danger and we feel in control).

 **Note**

This activity quickly helps children to understand that not everything they fear can actually harm them.

# Sadness factsheet

 **Objective**

To learn about sadness; to identify some coping strategies for sadness; to develop some awareness of what depression is.

 **What's needed?**

Access to the information on the *Sadness factsheet* (page 124).

 **Instructions**

- There is a lot of information on the *Sadness factsheet*. This can simply be read through and discussed, or each section can be considered further by completing tasks relating to it. Some examples are outlined below.
- The physical symptoms of sadness and its triggers: The children can reflect upon which of these they experience when they are sad and draw them onto a 'blob person' that represents them. They can add triggers for sadness that they have personally experienced and the sad thoughts that went along with these tiggers.
- Some words in the sadness family: Some of these words:
  - quite straightforwardly mean 'sad' (**glum, miserable, unhappy, feeling down, dejected**);
  - have more meaning attached to them or give a clue about what might have triggered the sadness (**regret** – for something you wish you hadn't done; **disappointed** – over something that you hoped for not happening; **upset** – implies a sadness over something that happened recently, often triggered by what someone else did; **heartbroken** – implies someone has done something to let you down; **grief** – a sadness because of loss; **mournful** – also feeling sad because of a loss; **remorseful** – feeling sad about something you did that you knew was wrong); and

- ○ others give and idea of being really sad to the point of distress (**despair, distress, inconsolable, anguish, hopeless**).

  Younger children could look up the words they don't know; while older children could consider which of these words define more than straightforward sadness and in what way they do this.

- Normalising sadness and considering depression: It's helpful to explain that sadness is completely normal and we should expect to feel sad now and then in our lives. It's also helpful for children to understand the definition of 'depression' on the sheet and how it differs from sadness.

- The positives of sadness and what can help: We don't tend to think of sadness as having a positive side. However, sadness probably evolved to ensure we took time out to recover after loss and so that our peers were more lenient with us when we did. You could discuss with the children what they feel they need when they are sad and they could create a class collage of strategies that help when you feel sad.

 ## *Extension ideas*

- The children could carefully consider and create 'words of consolation' for someone who feels sad. They could then evaluate how comforting each phrase is and how much they would welcome them when they felt sad.

- Find a selection of sad pieces of music (which are often written in a minor key) and ask the children to consider what each piece of music or song triggers them to feel (eg, 'Eleanor Rigby' by the Beatles, 'Gnossienne No 1' by Erik Satie, 'Violin Concerto No 2' by Philip Glass, 'Nocturne in E Flat Major' by Chopin; and for older children, 'Both Sides Now' by Joni Mitchell', 'Strange' by Celeste, 'True Colors' by Cyndi Lauper, 'Trouble' by Cat Stevens, 'The Sound of Silence' by Simon and Garfunkel, 'Sour Times' by Portishead).

 ## *Note*

When I talk to children about sadness, it often becomes apparent that they think feeling sad is something that should be avoided. I send a very loud message that it's both unavoidable and a very normal part of being human!

# Boredom

 ## *Objective*

To consider boredom and its impact.

 **What's needed?**

Access to the statements on the sheet *Boredom* (page 125).

 **Instructions**

- Share the statements on the sheet *Boredom* and ask groups of three children to take each statement and decide how much they agree or disagree with it. Ask them to give a reason for their answer if they can.
- After they have discussed all the statements, ask the children to write a definition of 'boredom'. Ask each group to share their definitions and see what all definitions have in common.
- Next, ask the children to think of a time when they were bored and what they tend to do when they are bored. Listen to some of their answers.
- Ask groups of children to write a statement to tell themselves next time they are bored that will urge them to get on and do something about, or accept, their boredom.

 **Extension ideas**

- The children could create individual 'what to do when I am bored' menus, much like the low-mood menu described on page 74.

 **Note**

Children often say, 'I'm bored' and look to you as if it is your problem. After this lesson, I make it clear that our boredom is our own responsibility!

# Embarrassment – true or false?

**Objective**

To reflect on the emotion of embarrassment, what can trigger it, how it affects you and what you can do to feel better when it has been triggered.

**What's needed?**

Access to the true and false statements on the sheet *Embarrassment – true or false?* (page 126).

# 🔍 *Instructions*

- Share the following (or some embarrassing things that have happened to you in the past) and ask the children to sort them from the things they believe would embarrass them most to the least:
  - Slipping on some ice in a busy street.
  - Spilling your money in a shop so the coins go in every direction.
  - Answering 'Manchester' to the question, 'What is the capital of England'?' in front of the class.
  - Using the wrong name for someone you have known for a week.
  - Farting in front of three of your friends.
  - Turning up to school with your top on inside out.
  - Spilling your drink on your lap at dinner time.
- Ask pairs of children to discuss what embarrassment feels like and then invite them to share their answers.
- Give the children access to the statements on the sheet *Embarrassment – true or false?* and ask pairs of children to decide which statements are true and which are false. Then discuss their answers.

| | | |
|---|---|---|
| 1. | Embarrassment arrives really slowly. | **False** – embarrassment is nearly always an emotion that arrives very quickly as soon as you realise what you've done. |
| 2. | Embarrassment happens when we do something silly or daft that we believe others will laugh at us for (or decide we are stupid). | **True** – embarrassment is all about worrying that we have made a fool of ourselves and assuming that others will judge us harshly or laugh at us. |
| 3. | Embarrassment makes you feel like you want to hide away. | **Usually true** – especially when we feel it strongly. |
| 4. | Everyone feels embarrassed every time they do something silly, like fall over. | **False** – some people are more prone to embarrassment than others and how strongly we feel it can depend on who is watching us. |
| 5. | You tend not to stay embarrassed for long. | **True** – unless you ruminate on what happened ('rumination' is thinking an unhelpful thought over and over). |
| 6. | If you think about the silly thing you did, you will feel embarrassed all over again. | **True** – but you're probably the only person still thinking about what happened and the strength of embarrassment tends to weaken with time. |

| 7. | There has to be someone watching you for you to become embarrassed. | **True** – embarrassment nearly always needs an audience to be triggered in the first instance. |
|---|---|---|
| 8. | Laughing along with everyone else when you do something silly can help you to feel better. | **True** – it almost always helps to see the funny side. |
| 9. | How embarrassed you become depends on who is watching. | **True** – how embarrassed we feel would probably be different if family members saw you compared to people at school. |
| 10. | You will probably spend more time thinking about what triggered you to become embarrassed than anyone else will. | **True** – most people will stop thinking about what happened before you do as they were less affected by it. |

 *Extension ideas*

- Ask groups of children to create a short drama sketch called 'Embarrassment' that includes a running commentary of the thoughts of the person who ends up embarrassed. Invite the class to advise each embarrassed person about how to deal with their embarrassment.
- Ask the children to consider whether there are any positive aspects about feeling embarrassed (eg, it might prevent you from repeating what you did – although things we get embarrassed about are often accidental, they can make others warm to us, they can make us more careful etc).

 *Note*

As children get older and what their peers think of them becomes more important, their embarrassment can increase. Because of this, I find it's good to talk to children about embarrassment before it becomes such a big thing!

# Excitement

 *Objective*

To explore the emotion of excitement

## ✓ What's needed?

One copy of the sheet *Excitement* (page 127) per child.

## 🔍 Instructions

- Read through the questions on the sheet and ask the children to answer them individually in note form.
- Ask the children to get into pairs and share their answers with each other.
- After sharing, ask the children if they have had any new thoughts about excitement.
- Here are some thoughts you could share if the children have not already considered them:
  - We can feel different degrees of excitement.
  - Excitement tends to energise us.
  - Excitement and fear/worry/anxiety share some physical symptoms.
  - We can be excited about anticipating something we really want, as well as being excited during an activity we love. We tend not to be excited about things left in the past.
  - How we think about something affects how exciting we think it is. (We can get to something that we were excited about and it can turn out to be a disappointment.)
  - Excitement can make us focus on the thing triggering our excitement and return to thinking about it a lot.

## 🌀 Extension ideas

- The children could draw a picture of the word 'excitement', making it look at exciting as possible!
- The children could consider whether excitement is infectious or not.

## 📝 Note

I often find that children who struggle to regulate can struggle as much with excitement as they can emotion like anger. Although we think of excitement as enjoyable – and in the main, it is – it can sometimes be agitating!

# Guilty!

## 🚀 Objective

To consider guilt, what it tells us and what we can do when we feel it.

##  What's needed?

Access to the information on the sheet *Guilty!* (page 128).

##  Instructions

- Read through the sheet *Guilty!* and ask pairs of children to complete the first three questions for each situation. Generally, the best way to address feeling guilty is to:
  - work out exactly what it is you feel guilty for; and
  - work out what could make things better (eg, an apology; a kind gesture; working out how to prevent it from happening again; being really honest about what happened; acknowledging and accepting that you did something wrong; offering to replace or help repair anything that was damaged; making it up with or being extra kind to the person you feel guilty about).
- Ask pairs of children to compose some helpful guidance for what to do when you feel guilty.

##  Extension ideas

- The children could create a short play called 'Guilty'.
- The children could draw guilty emojis and decide whose looks guiltiest.
- The children could consider why sometimes people don't make things better – even when they feel guilty (eg, they don't feel guilty enough; they don't care enough about how the other person might feel; they assume it will all disappear; they are not sure how to go about making amends).

##  Note

I find that for a small number of children, their guilt triggers intense shame and/or they lack the capacity for empathy, so they can struggle to get to the point of realising they need to make amends. They could still engage with this lesson, however, as the 'stories' do not ask children to reflect directly on themselves.

# Feeling disappointed

## Objective

To consider disappointment and how to manage it.

##  What's needed?

Access to the information on the sheet *Feeling disappointed* (page 129).

## Instructions

- Ask the children to share situations in which they felt disappointed or make up a story where a child is likely to end up feeling disappointed.
- Ask the children to explain why disappointment can feel so unenjoyable (eg, we might suddenly have to do without something we were looking forward to and excited about; we can feel out of control; we can pine for what we're missing out on; our expectations may have to be adjusted; we can feel let down by others; what we hoped for hasn't happened).
- Give the children access to the sheet *Feeling disappointed* and ask them to work through the tasks outlined on it.
- Finally, ask the children to suggest what they think is the best advice that they could give to a friend who is feeling disappointed.

## Extension ideas

- The children could look out for times when they feel disappointed and report back on how they dealt with it.
- The children could draw a timeline showing the positive and negative emotional journey of the experience of feeling disappointed (depicting an ideal way of managing it).

## Note

Some children really struggle to let go of disappointment as they feel it so strongly. This activity helps children with acknowledging, soothing and reframing disappointment to make it easier to let go of.

# Gratitude

##  Objective

To remind ourselves of all the things we are grateful for and how positive gratitude is.

## 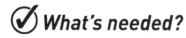 What's needed?

One piece of plain A4 paper per child.

 *Instructions*

- Ask the children what they think 'gratitude' or 'feeling grateful' means.
- Explain to them that reminding ourselves of what we are grateful for nearly always makes us feel better.
- Ask groups of four children to create the longest list they can of things they could be grateful for. Explain these can include things personal to them (eg, their family, a pet, a snuggly bed, a specific toy or game), as well as things everyone can be grateful for (eg, sunny days, beautiful trees).
- Give each child a piece of paper and ask them to draw the biggest heart on the sheet they can manage and then ask them to draw and colour the things they are grateful for inside that heart. (Alternatively, make space so you can roll some wallpaper along the floor, plain side up, and invite the children to draw what they are grateful for on it.) I guarantee the conversations while the children are drawing will be lively, interesting and generally upbeat!

 *Extension ideas*

- The children could create posters that remind people to be grateful, to be put up around the school.

 *Note*

Some children can struggle to think of things they are grateful for. When I experienced this, I would prompt them with a silly comment or gesture that I knew would make them laugh and then ask them if they were grateful for laughing!

## Shame

 *Objective*

To understand what shame is and how powerful it can be.

 *What's needed?*

Access to the information on the sheet *Shame* (page 130).

 *Instructions*

- Ask the children what they think is meant by 'shame' and listen to some of their answers.

- Explain that shame is not often spoken about, but it is a powerful emotion. It's the emotion we can feel when we don't feel good about ourselves because of something that has knocked our self-worth or triggered us to feel rejected by others. Some people feel shame more strongly and often than others.

- Give the children access to the multiple-choice questions on the sheet *Shame* and ask pairs of children to discuss them. All of the answers can be considered true of shame and this should give the children more insight into this emotion.

- Ask the children to try to become more aware of the emotion of shame and consider how they personally respond to it. You could ask the following questions:
  - Do you think you are aware of shame when it arrives?
  - Can you remember a time when you felt shame and what triggered it?
  - Do you think shame is a powerful emotion?
  - What kind of things can other people do that can trigger shame (eg, insulting us; pointing out an error we made; telling us off; excluding us; falling out with someone; laughing at something we've done)?
  - Does shame steal your confidence?
  - Does shame make you want to hide away?
  - Where do you feel shame in your body?
  - Do you sometimes get defensive and snap at people when you feel shame?
  - Does the voice in your head (everyone has one!) give you a very hard time when you feel shame?
  - Does shame make you believe everyone thinks you're rubbish and can you get carried away with thinking this?
    *Getting much more difficult ...*
  - Do you think you can feel shame in situations where nobody else is involved?
  - Do some places and companions make you more likely to feel shame?
  - Do you think shame causes you to make assumptions about what other people are thinking?
  - Are there some thoughts that can make shame worse and other thoughts that can help shame feel less strong and last less time?
  - What coping strategies for shame do you think you have?
  - Do you think perfectionists feel more shame?

## Extension ideas

- The children could create a social story about shame that could be used to explain the emotion to younger children and help them to cope with it.
- The children could list all the things they believe to be the opposite of shame.

- Read the following story, 'Tom's experience of shame', and ask the children to comment upon what it made them think.

## *Tom's experience of shame*

A boy called Tom boasted about what a fast runner he was in the week leading up to sports day. He declared often, 'I will definitely win the race!' He believed himself to be the best runner in the class. However, when sports day finally came, he came fifth in his race. This triggered shame in Tom.

He felt foolish for having boasted; he felt embarrassed for not winning; and he assumed that everyone else was finding it funny or ridiculous that after all of that boasting, he didn't win the race. When his friend laughed at him, Tom become defensive and told him to shut up and called him stupid.

The shame Tom felt affected his thinking and he started to give himself a hard time for not winning the race. He told himself over and over in his head that he was rubbish for not winning. The embarrassment part of shame made him want to hide away so he couldn't hear anyone saying any of the negative things he was thinking about himself. He didn't want anyone to notice him because when they noticed him, he assumed they were thinking about how he had not won the race. Tom felt really disappointed in himself for not being as fast as he liked to think he was.

In reality, a couple of people were pleased that he didn't win because he had been boasting so much; but most people didn't even think about it and certainly not as much as Tom had done himself. Most people didn't really care whether Tom won his race or not.

###  *Note*

I tend to look at shame with older children, as it is quite a complex emotion to fully understand. I often relate it to its close cousin, 'embarrassment', to help them understand what it feels like.

# Happy!

Put each of these rows of three into order from the thing that would make you most happy to the least.

# Being scared

We can be scared of lots of things. Some things we are scared of could actually harm us, but other things are very unlikely to harm us. Sort the following things into those that could be dangerous and those that can just trigger us to feel scared.

| | |
|---|---|
| Crossing a busy road with fast cars | Thunder and lightning |
| A non-poisonous spider | Standing up in front of lots of people to talk to them |
| Getting lost in a crowded street | Walking along a cliff top |
| A ride on a ghost train | Making a mistake in class |
| Watching something scary on TV | The dark |
| Coming across a tiger | Imagining a monster under the bed |
| Climbing a tree | Going to the dentist |
| Dogs | Fireworks |

# Sadness factsheet

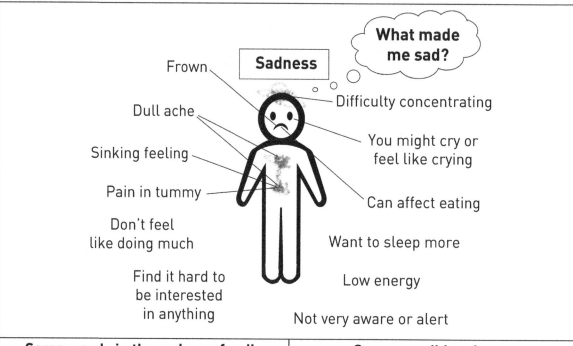

| Some words in the sadness family | Some possible triggers |
|---|---|
| upset glum miserable despair disappointed regret inconsolable unhappy feeling down unhappy grief distressed remorseful heartbroken dejected anguish hopeless mournful | • A friend moving away.<br>• A pet dying.<br>• A story of an earthquake on the news.<br>• Losing something you love.<br>• Not being invited to a party. |
| **Sadness is normal** | **Depression** |
| Although sadness is an unenjoyable emotion, it's perfectly normal. Everyone feels it and nobody can expect to feel happy all of the time. It's good to accept that sadness is a normal part of being human and not to panic when you feel it. | Depression is a constant feeling of sadness that lasts for weeks. When people are depressed, they show no interest in doing anything and don't want to do what they normally like to do. When people are depressed, they usually need help. |
| **The positives of sadness** | **To help with sadness we can...** |
| Sadness can:<br>• make us take time out or make us slow down<br>• let others know we need help<br>• give us time to recharge<br>• make us feel closer to those we love because we need them when we are sad<br>• make us think deeply about things and learn more about life<br>• tell us that something needs to change or that we need to try new things<br>• help us be more understanding towards others when they are sad | • not pretend we're happy and be sure to take time out to get on and feel sad until we recover<br>• find someone we love to talk to, have a cuddle with or be kind to us<br>• talk to others who have gone through the same thing<br>• find things that soothe us – go for a walk, listen to music, write our feelings down, find a comfortable place to have a good cry<br>• remember there will be a time in the future when we don't feel like this |

# Boredom...

- Is wanting someone or something to entertain you without you having to put any effort in.

- Can happen when you feel trapped doing something you don't want to do.

- Makes it hard to be interested in anything.

- Can happen when you can't find the effort to do anything.

- Is not taking responsibility for yourself.

- Makes you want to be somewhere else.

- Is like having a blank mind.

- Feels flat.

- Is being stuck.

- Is lazy.

- Makes you feel like you have no purpose.

- Happens when there's nothing to stimulate your thoughts.

- Is apathy.

- Is frustrating.

# Embarrassment - true or false?

| | |
|---|---|
| 1. Embarrassment arrives really slowly. | **True** or **false?** |
| 2. Embarrassment happens when we do something silly or daft that we believe others will laugh at us for (or decide we are stupid). | **True** or **false?** |
| 3. Embarrassment makes you feel like you want to hide away. | **True** or **false?** |
| 4. Everyone feels embarrassed every time they do something silly, like fall over. | **True** or **false?** |
| 5. You tend not to stay embarrassed for long. | **True** or **false?** |
| 6. If you think about the silly thing you did, you will feel embarrassed all over again. | **True** or **false?** |
| 7. There has to be someone watching you for you to become embarrassed. | **True** or **false?** |
| 8. Laughing along with everyone else when you do something silly can help you to feel better. | **True** or **false?** |
| 9. How embarrassed you become depends on who is watching. | **True** or **false?** |
| 10. You will probably spend more time thinking about what triggered you to become embarrassed than anyone else will! | **True** or **false?** |

# Excitement

1. Name two times when you have felt excited:


2. Were you more excited at one of these two times than the other? YES / NO


3. What effect can excitement have on how lively we feel?


4. Where in your body do you feel excitement?


5. In what way do you think excitement is different from being happy?


6. Describe what excitement feels like to you:


7. Can excitement ever be an uncomfortable feeling? YES / NO
   a. Explain your answer:


8. Can you be excited about things that are happening now as well as things that are going to happen in the future?


9. What effect can excitement have on your thinking?


10. Do you think we make some things more exciting because of the way we think about them?

# Guilty!

Feeling guilty might be very uncomfortable but it is an emotion that can nearly always teach us a lesson. We feel guilty when we have done something that was wrong, thoughtless or unkind and end up wishing we hadn't. It usually makes us want to make everything better.

Here are some guilty people. Can you work out:

- Who is guilty?
- What they feel guilty about?
- What they could do to feel better?

| | |
|---|---|
| Harriet forgot her mum's birthday. She usually makes her mum a card for her birthday. | When Jordan was really grumpy, he told Frankie that he hated her. |
| Maria took ages to paint a picture of a tiger and everyone thought it was amazing. Unfortunately, Elena spilled green paint all over it just as Maria was finishing. | Mackenzie copied Payton's maths. In the next lesson, the teacher made them both do the maths again at lunch time to teach them not to copy. |
| Charlie ate the last bit of cake. When his sister Maisie got home, he heard his mum saying, 'I've saved you some cake, Maisie, as I know you haven't had any yet.' | Hunter's friend Mateo was really upset about not being able to go on the school trip. Hunter rushed off to talk to other friends who were going on the trip and left Mateo feeling really left out. |

# Feeling disappointed

Imagine you're really excited because you're being taken to the beach with a really good friend and you've been looking forward to it all week …

… But then you're told that you can't go.

You are likely to feel a big dollop of **disappointment.**

1. Which of these emotions do you think are part of disappointment (circle them)?

   Sadness   Frustration   Calm   Grumpiness   Happiness   Anger
   Anything else?

2. Order these pieces of advice for coping with disappointment from what you think is most useful to the least useful.

| | |
|---|---|
| Tell someone how disappointed you feel. | Take time out for a quiet moment and cry if you feel you need to. |
| Once you feel less disappointed, make a plan to do something else you will enjoy. | Remember that disappointment does not usually last for long. |
| Give yourself five minutes to feel really disappointed and then tell yourself to stop. | Think of all the things in your life that you're pleased about. |
| Think about something else you are looking forward to. | Fully accept that what you were looking forward to or hoping for isn't going to happen, so you can stop thinking about it. |

# Shame

Imagine you put your hand up to answer a question because you felt sure you knew the answer but what comes out of your mouth is completely wrong. Not only that, everyone looks at you in class as if you're stupid. In a situation like this, many of us tend to feel shame.

Complete these multiple-choice questions about shame. More than one answer could be correct for each question.

1. Shame:
   a. makes you feel like you're not good enough.
   b. triggers you to believe everyone thinks you're rubbish.
   c. can make you feel disappointed in yourself.
   d. feels bit like embarrassment.
2. We can feel shame when we:
   a. feel we're not living up to our own or others' standards.
   b. make a mistake.
   c. feel rejected by someone.
   d. learn that we have been left out of something.
3. Shame can:
   a. make us really self-conscious.
   b. feel like the opposite of getting approval.
   c. make us judge ourselves really harshly.
   d. make us feel that nobody likes us.
4. We can respond to shame by:
   a. getting frustrated with ourselves.
   b. wanting to hide away.
   c. having a voice in our head that tells us off over and over again.
   d. snapping at someone.
5. To tackle shame, you need to:
   a. stop the thoughts that are telling you you're rubbish.
   b. remember all the times you've done well.
   c. remember your friends won't always judge you based on one thing you did.
   d. talk about how you feel and others are likely to reassure you.

If you were asked to describe what shame is, what would you say?

# Chapter 4
# A CLOSER LOOK AT ANGER

## What's in this chapter?

Anger is one of the emotions that parents/carers often state they have the greatest difficulty supporting their children with, and dysregulation and aggression can cause a lot of challenging behaviour in schools. This chapter includes a number of tried-and-tested activities about anger to proactively teach children how to better manage this potentially tricky emotion.

## *Activity notes*

- You will find a description of each of the activities in the first part of this chapter, followed by the relevant activity sheets.
- The activities are described with an objective, instructions, an indication of whether any further resources are needed (including printable resources from this book) and at least one suggested extension idea.
- The activities involve a variety of teaching and learning techniques, including discussion prompts, quizzes, agreement spectrums, drama activities, games and lessons that use printable worksheets.
- The age that each activity is suitable for has not been stipulated. Most activities could be simplified for younger children or adjusted to be more challenging for older children. Sometimes suggestions have been included for how adapt activities for different age groups.

## Key information about anger

| Topic | Further notes |
|---|---|
| Anger is a normal part of being human and everyone feels it | Try never to tell a child it's wrong to be angry. We all feel anger at times. If we shame a child by telling them it's bad or naughty to be angry, this complicates the emotion, as they will not only feel angry, but also feel like they are 'bad' for feeling it. Putting a negative value judgement on anger (or any emotion) can cause a child to try to suppress it, which means they will have less awareness of it and therefore less chance of managing it well. |

DOI: 10.4324/9781032690773-5

| Topic | Further notes |
|---|---|
| Anger is an emotion; aggression is a behaviour | We can't always control the emotions we feel but we can develop the ability to have conscious control over how we behave in response to an emotion. Aggression rarely sorts anything out and usually makes situations worse. Help children understand that anger (an emotion) is acceptable but that aggression (a behaviour) rarely is. |
| Anger is not often as useful or necessary today as it was for our ancestors | Anger evolved to give us a surge of aggression that could be used to protect ourselves physically. We very rarely have a validated need to be aggressive in this way nowadays. This is why anger can need a little focus in order to manage it resourcefully. |
| Anger words | There are many anger words because anger is such a normal part of human existence. Learning lots of emotion words helps us to become more aware of our emotions and be able to express them more accurately and appropriately. |
| The physical symptoms of anger | Some children struggle to recognise that they are becoming angry. Teaching them the physical symptoms of anger can help them identify that they are becoming angry and can help them focus inwardly – rather than reacting outwardly in a way that will probably make the situation worse. It's good to acknowledge that anger can be a tricky emotion because of the strong physical urges it can trigger. |
| Anger is usually triggered by things that irritate us, things that create a 'cost' to us or people doing something we think they should not do | It can be good to explore our triggers of anger and help children become aware of the kinds of things that trigger anger for them individually. Our triggers for anger are personal to us and not everyone is made angry by the same things. Awareness of this can help children 'own' their anger and acknowledge that what triggered their anger would not trigger everyone's. There is an individual interpretation and response to most potential triggers. |
| Our thoughts when we are angry can either help us or make us feel worse | When we are angry, we tend to put our self-interest above the interests of others. You can make children aware of this tendency and make it clear that this is part of the reason why decisions we make when angry can often make things worse and sometimes hurt others. |
| Expressing anger | When expressing anger, the aim is not to:<br><br>• be passive (ie, do nothing);<br>• respond indirectly (eg, complain to someone else); or<br>• be aggressive (ie, be verbally or physically abusive).<br><br>Instead, the aim is to be assertive (ie, explain how you feel, why and what you need to happen). Many adults struggle to be assertive. It is beneficial for children to understand that being assertive takes a lot of practice for most people. |
| Cooling-down techniques can help us manage how we express anger | If we struggle to express anger resourcefully, it's usually because we react impulsively, 'in the heat of the moment'. Learning methods that help us to 'cool down' when we're angry can help with this. |
| Empathising with someone who is angry | When someone is angry, it would be great if we could treat them how we would probably wish to be treated – which is usually to be heard, be understood, have the anger validated and be reassured that things have been acknowledged and will be addressed if that's appropriate. However, anger in someone else can trigger strong reactions in us: fear, embarrassment, shame and also anger. To empathise with someone who is angry, we can try to understand what their issue is rather than just reacting to their emotion – in other words, try to see the issue behind the emotion. You can also help children see anger as a 'cry for help', as it's often covering up more vulnerable feelings such as anxiety, overwhelm, stress etc. It's also helpful to acknowledge that we are more considerate about another's anger when we feel it is justified and not exaggerated. |

## Activities

## Angry Anira

 *Objective*

To understand the need to stop and pause before we react when we're angry.

 *Instructions*

- Read the children the following story.

---

**Angry Anira**

Anira was at infant school. She liked infant school but there was just one problem with it: lots of things happened there that caused Anira to become angry. Let's have a look at what happened yesterday.

When Anira first got to school and went to hang up her coat, she noticed someone else had put their coat on her peg. This made Anira angry. * So she grabbed the coat off the peg, threw it on the floor and put her own coat on the peg. The coat now on the floor was a purple coat that Anira knew belonged to Katy.

Next, she went into the classroom and wanted to sit next to Tom, but Alfie was already sitting next to him. This made Anira angry. * So she shoved Alfie off his seat and plonked herself next to Tom, who looked a bit upset.

At playtime, Anira wanted to use a skipping rope. When she got to the playground, she found that all the skipping ropes were already being used. This made Anira angry. * So she went up to Joseph and snatched the skipping rope off him. When he said, 'Give it back,' Anira become even angrier and told him he was stupid.

In a lesson after break, the teacher asked Anira to count the beanbags on the floor but she counted them incorrectly and said there were six when there were seven. Henry laughed at her for getting it wrong. This made Anira angry. * So she kicked Henry.

---

- Ask the children what they think of Anira and how they would feel if she was in their class.
- Explain that we all feel angry now and then, but if we don't get good at dealing with anger, it can mean we end up doing things that hurt others. Ask the children what they think could help Anira cope with her anger in a better way and listen to some of their suggestions.

- By exploring what Anira did, help the children understand the following:
  - If we take out our anger on other people, we always make things worse and hurt or upset other people.
  - Anger can be a strong emotion that can sometimes make us want to say something nasty, throw something or kick, punch or hurt other people, but this is never a good idea and hurting others is really unkind.
  - It is helpful to do something when we get angry that means we stop, slow down and take a pause. This will make it much less likely that we will hurt other people and more likely that we will work out how to sort out the situation in a better way.
- Ask the children what Anira could do to make sure she takes time to cool down when she becomes angry (eg, count to ten; take five deep breaths; turn away from the situation; put her hands on her head; fold her arms; curl her fingers around her thumb; say, 'Calm and cool' over and over again; look up at the ceiling).
- Now read each paragraph of Anira's story again and when you get to the star * in each paragraph, stop and let the children suggest something she could do to cool down and then create a different ending to the paragraph.

 *Extension ideas*

- You could read the story again with two children playing the part of Anira: one reacting to anger in an unhelpful or harmful way and the other using a cooling-down technique, to show the difference.
- The children could illustrate their favourite cooling-down plan for when they feel angry.

 *Note*

Young children tend to prefer very simple cooling-down strategies for anger. A young child finds it easier to manage physical actions such as folding their arms and taking deep breaths rather than thought processes.

# Where in the body do I feel anger?

 *Objective*

To learn to notice the physical symptoms of anger.

 *What's needed?*

One copy of the sheet *Where in the body do I feel anger?* (page 152) per child.

## 🔍 *Instructions*

- Ask the children to think of something that has triggered them to become angry.
- Ask three volunteers to come to the front of the room and share their triggers for anger.
- Explain that you're going to ask them one at a time to imagine being angry, to tune into the effects that anger has on their body.
- List the effects the volunteers share and ask the class to share any observations they make of the volunteers when they think about being angry (eg, they might notice that the volunteers are frowning).
- Invite the class to add any symptoms of anger they experience to the list you have created.
- Detach the volunteers from thinking about anger by asking a frivolous question such as, 'What would you like for tea tonight?'
- Next, either create a class poster of these symptoms or ask the children to label individual blob people on the sheet *Where in the body do I feel anger?* with the symptoms they experience when they are angry.

## 🗜️ *Extension ideas*

- The children could draw an angry face on the blob person after observing the effect anger has on the face.
- The children could see how many different ways they could finish the sentence starting: 'Anger feels like ...'

## 📝 *Note*

With younger children, this activity can be done as a whole class by labelling a 'blob person' on a large piece of paper with as many physical symptoms of anger as the children can think of.

# What can anger make us feel like doing?

## 🚀 *Objective*

To consider the impulses and behaviours that anger can trigger if we let it.

## ✅ *What's needed?*

Access to the information on the sheet *What can anger make us feel like doing?* (page 153).

 *Instructions*

- Explain to the children that when we're angry, unless we slow things down and take a pause, we can often react in a way that will make the situation worse. This is because anger's job is to protect us, so it can make us a bit selfish and therefore we don't think of how anyone else involved might be feeling or why they might have done what they did.
- Share the information on the sheet *What can anger make us feel like doing?* Read through the different responses and ask pairs of children to decide which would be good responses and which would probably make the situation worse.
- Explain that everyone feels angry at times and anger can't always be avoided. However, it's important to know that we can learn to choose how we behave when we feel angry – especially if we take a pause to slow things down and don't react straight away.

 *Extension ideas*

- The children could roleplay all of the possible responses they can think of to someone saying, 'You're stupid' to them and explore what they felt as a result of each response.
- The children could create advice for 'when someone triggers your anger' and share or display this advice somehow (eg, a poster, a story, top tips, matching questions to their answers, a labelled diagram, a multiple-choice quiz, a spider diagram, an interview, a radio or TV ad, an explanation to an alien, a mime!).

 *Note*

With children who struggle to regulate, I often acknowledge the urges that anger gives them to help make them more conscious (eg, 'I know your anger makes you want to throw things').

# Triggers of anger

 *Objective*

To consider what triggers our anger.

 *What's needed?*

Access to the information on the sheet *Triggers of anger* (page 154); an anger thermometer (page 159) for each child (for younger children) or each pair of children (for older children).

# 🔍 *Instructions*

*Younger children:*

- Ask the children to look at the triggers of anger on the sheet *Triggers of anger* and decide whether each thing is something that is a) irritating; b) something we think someone just should not do; or c) something that causes us upset or harm – or a mixture of these.
- Ask each child to stick (or write) each trigger on their anger thermometer at the place that represents how angry they think they would be if it happened to them.
- Ask pairs of children to compare their thermometers and ask whether we are all triggered to become equally angry by the same things. This will usually illustrate that different things can trigger different people to become angry.
- Ask pairs of children to discuss what could help someone deal with each of the triggers on the sheet and share their ideas with the whole group.

*Older children:*

- Explain to children that we usually get angry if:
  - someone irritates us;
  - someone does something we think and judge people should not do (eg, push in a queue); or
  - there is a 'cost' to us (eg, something of ours is broken or someone has made us look bad).
- Next, look at the triggers of anger on the sheet *Triggers of anger* and ask pairs of children to decide how angry each thing would trigger them to be.
- Ask the children to stick (or write) each trigger on their anger thermometer at the place that represents how angry they think they would feel if it happened to them. Ask them not to stick any of the triggers on the thermometer that they don't agree about and use these to explore why some people find some things more anger-inducing than others. This will illustrate that our personal triggers are all slightly different and some of us become more readily angry than others.
- Ask the children what might help in each of these situations and take some suggestions.
- Finally, extend the discussion by reading each of the following points and questions aloud, one at a time, and inviting children to answer:
  - Sometimes when we feel anger, it's an indication that a problem needs solving. Look at the triggers – can you find one that clearly has a problem that needs sorting and what is that problem?

- Sometimes, if we explain what we need clearly and assertively, we can prevent our anger from being triggered. Can you see a trigger that could be sorted by some-one explaining assertively what they need?
- When people are unkind to us, we often understandably become angry. The anger is justified; but rather than becoming aggressive, it's usually better if we can man-age to remain calm, explain how we feel and what we need. Can you find a trigger that this would be good advice for?
- Unfairness can often make us angry. Unfortunately, the world is unfair and some-times we have to just accept this and try not to waste anger on this reality. Can you see a trigger where it would be helpful to remember this?
- Sometimes we need to change how we think about a situation to help us feel less angry – for example, 'They were probably just having a bad day.' Find one of the triggers where this approach could help.
- Sometimes when we think we are angry, we are actually feeling other emotions that we might not want to admit to – for example, hurt, embarrassment, rejection, humiliation, disappointment. Can you name any emotions other than anger people might also feel with some of these triggers?
- We tend to be angrier if someone else has done something nasty to us deliberately than if they do it accidentally. Why might we be less angry about a baby getting chocolate all over us than a friend ignoring us?
- We might feel better able to express our anger to some people than others. Which people might we be most comfortable expressing anger to?
- 'If we learn to be more forgiving of other people's mistakes, our anger is triggered less often.' Do you think this statement is true?
- Irritations can make us angry, but they tend to be more likely to do so if we're feel-ing tired or hungry, or if we're having a bad day. What could we do if we realise we are angry because we're having a bad day?

## Extension ideas

- The children could 'collect' triggers for a week from TV, stories and their real-life experiences.
- Another way of thinking about triggers of anger is that we become angry when some-one has crossed one of our boundaries. 'Boundaries' are guidelines or unwritten rules that we have to protect ourselves from the behaviours of others that might upset us or make us feel unsafe. We expect others to follow these guidelines and we usually feel annoyed when they don't. For example, most people have a boundary that says

they don't like people shouting at them and they think it's wrong for them to do so. If someone does shout, they have crossed this boundary. With older children, you could explore crossing boundaries: the behaviours we tend to think of as unacceptable in our interactions with others (eg, hitting us; touching us without asking; getting really close to us; assuming it's okay to help themselves to our things; sharing our secrets without permission).

 **Note**

It's good to remember that sometimes anger is expressed when another emotion has really been triggered, such as shame, embarrassment, overwhelm or anxiety. For children who are reluctant to show any kind of vulnerability, anger makes them feels more in control and powerful than many other feelings. These children therefore need help admitting to and understanding that it is OK to experience emotions other than anger.

# Cooling things down

 **Objective**

To consider which 'cooling-down' strategies or plans might work for us.

 **What's needed?**

Access to the information on the sheet *Cooling things down* (page 155).

 **Instructions**

- Explain to the children that anger can trigger us to do things that can make situations worse, and can sometimes urge us to do damaging or hurtful things.
- Explain that in order to prevent destructive behaviours, we nearly always need to put a pause between our anger being triggered and our reaction, to slow things down. There are different ways of creating this 'cooling-down' gap between trigger and response, and some work better than others for different people.
- Ask the children whether anyone already uses a 'cooling-down' plan that they're happy to share.
- Next, show the children the information on the sheet *Cooling things down* and ask pairs of children to discuss each suggestion and decide on four that they think would work best for them individually.

- Once the children have chosen their four suggestions, ask them to choose one of the four and create a persuasive TV ad for it. Their ad could demonstrate the cooling-down plan, say why it's effective and include a slogan.

 ## *Extension ideas*

- Ask younger children to remember any times when they used their cooling-down plan, so they can report back to you what happened.
- Older children could discuss what makes a really good cooling-down plan by answering the following:
  - How does the plan engage the thinking part of your brain?
  - Is repetition good?
  - How distracting does the plan need to be?
  - Is it better if the plan has a start and end point or if it can go on and on?
  - Does the plan need to take the heat out of the anger and how can this be done?
  - Are some plans better in different situations?

 ## *Note*

I often tell children that you need at least six seconds between starting to feel angry and responding. This often works because it seems achievable to remain distracted for such a short amount of time! Usually if a child has caught their anger, this is long enough to prevent impulsive reactions.

# Angry thoughts

 ## *Objective*

To think about how anger can affect our thinking

 ## *What's needed?*

Access to the information on the sheet *Angry thoughts* (page 156).

 ## *Instructions*

- Explain to the children that when we are angry, we can get swept up in negative thinking, which can fuel our anger towards other people and be unhelpful. Also talk about how anger tends to make us think about our own needs only.

- Take a look at the information on the sheet *Angry thoughts* and talk through the first scenario on the sheet. Look at the angry thoughts and ask children to say how Finley would probably feel if he experienced each thought.
- Next, read the more helpful thoughts and ask the children how Finley might feel after each of those thoughts.
- Then ask pairs of children to complete the sheet for the two further scenarios.
- Share the ideas the children came up with and try to find the thoughts they think would most likely keep you angry and the three thoughts they think would be most helpful.

 ## Extension ideas

- The children could roleplay the situations on the sheet in groups of four. Two can act out the scenario, while the third and fourth can act out the thoughts and feelings that the first two might be having, to show how different thoughts can influence what happens and what people end up feeling.
- Older children can explore the idea of the 'angry mind': what its intentions are; what impulses it might drive; what thoughts it has; who and what it focuses on. They could draw the angry mind to increase their awareness of its tendencies.

 ## Note

After doing this activity, you can start to look at real-life situations in which someone has been angry and explore the angry thoughts that person had. (Obviously this is best done after everyone has cooled down and any conflicts have been resolved!)

# How do you react when you're angry?

 ## Objective

To consider passive, indirect, aggressive and assertive responses to anger.

 ## Instructions

- Explain to the children that we have choices about how we respond when someone upsets us.
- Ask the children to think about how they have responded in the past when they have ended up angry or upset because of what someone else has done or said.
- Describe the following four ways of responding to someone who did something that triggered our anger:

- ○ **Passively:** Do nothing.
- ○ **Indirectly:** Complain about the person to someone else.
- ○ **Aggressively:** Attack back – aim to emotionally or physically hurt the person (eg, an insult or punch).
- ○ **Assertively:** Use an 'I' message to explain how your felt when they did what they did.
- After describing the responses, consider each one at a time (you could roleplay all responses with a volunteer) and ask the children to think about what the advantages and disadvantages of each way of responding are. Examples are set out below.

| Response | Advantage | Disadvantage |
|---|---|---|
| Passive | • You don't have to take the brave step of talking to someone about how you felt. | • Nothing gets sorted.<br>• They might do it again.<br>• You don't feel great about pretending you were OK with what happened. |
| Indirect | • You don't have to take the brave step of talking directly to someone about how you felt.<br>• You can convince yourself that you feel better after a moan. | • Nothing gets sorted.<br>• They might do it again.<br>• You are unlikely to feel like anything has changed for the better. |
| Aggressive | • You don't have to think and you can just act on impulses.<br>• You 'get them back.' | • The situation could escalate and everyone end up feeling angry.<br>• You won't have sorted anything. |
| Assertive | • You try to tackle the situation directly, which could sort things quickly.<br>• You feel better for having shared how you felt.<br>• Sometimes it can solve problems and prevent the person from causing you upset again. | • It is not guaranteed to sort out the situation as some people respond to assertiveness defensively. (When someone does, it's usually a good idea to listen carefully to what they have to say and then when they have finished, make your assertive statement again.) |

- Revise composing 'I' messages (page 52).
- Ask children to roleplay using 'I' messages in the following situations:
  - ○ A friend laughs at you for not knowing something (eg, how to play 'Snap').

○ Your teacher tells you off for talking when they were telling the class what to do, but it wasn't you who spoke.

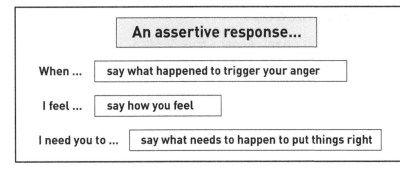

**An assertive response...**

When ... | say what happened to trigger your anger

I feel ... | say how you feel

I need you to ... | say what needs to happen to put things right

○ Your mum tells you that you haven't got time to go back indoors and grab your homework and you know your teacher will be really cross that you have forgotten it again.

○ Someone you know sits next to you at lunch time and talks non-stop at you about how good they are at something you're not that good at.

 *Extension ideas*

- You could discuss situations where it is a good idea to just 'let things go' and what can help you do this – for example, when a stranger who you're never likely to meet again does something inconsiderate; when a person has apologised because they realise they hadn't been very kind.

- Create a leaflet or story that could help younger children to understand the different ways you can respond when you're angry.

 *Note*

It's good to remember that it can take self-control and/or bravery to be assertive. Unfortunately, being assertive does not always sort out problems, but we have a better chance of finding helpful solutions by responding assertively – rather than aggressively, indirectly or passively – when our anger is triggered.

# Anger – true or false?

 *Objective*

To further understand anger.

# ✅ *What's needed?*

Access to the quiz sheet: *Anger – true or false?* (page 157).

# 🔍 *Instructions*

- Present the information on the sheet *Anger – true or false?* and ask groups of four to discuss their answers.
- Go through the answers and make the following additional points about each statement:

1. Anger is an emotion everyone feels now and then.

   **True:** Although we all experience it differently in terms of how often, how strongly, what triggers it, how well we manage it etc.

2. When we are angry, it's a good idea to react quickly.

   **False:** We don't usually make good decisions when we are in the grips of anger.

3. 'Exasperated' is one of many words that mean 'angry'.

   **True:** And there are many other words for 'angry' – particularly those that mean we're really, really angry!

4. When we are angry, it can affect how we think.

   **True:** Our 'angry mind' is only focused on protecting us (so it might urge us to attack others in trying to do this).

5. Anger makes some people aggressive.

   **True:** Although this is very rarely the best way of responding when we are angry.

6. When we are angry, we can struggle to make helpful choices.

   **True:** Our 'angry mind' can be impulsive, doesn't think forward to a future point when our current behaviour might seem silly to us and tends not to think things through carefully.

7. Anger is wrong.

   **False:** Anger is an emotion that everyone feels. It's how we respond to anger that can be 'wrong', if we end up harming someone or something.

8. Some people get angrier than others – even if they have just gone through exactly the same thing.

   **True:** Some people get angrier more often and for more reasons than others.

9. We might not be able to stop ourselves from becoming angry, but we can choose what we do about it.

   **True:** As with all emotions, we can't always control what we feel, but we can become good at choosing how we behave when we experience anger.

10. Anger tends to last for hours.

   **Depends:** The sensation of anger usually lasts a short time and it's hard to remain actively angry for a long time. However, our thoughts can re-trigger us to become angry long after the original event that triggered our anger if the situation remains unresolved.

11. Anger has brought about some big changes in society.

   **True:** Many social movements have been inspired by anger, such as the civil rights movement, women's suffrage, strikes over working conditions etc.

12. Anger causes problems.

   **Depends:** The emotion of anger itself, if managed well, need not cause problems; but aggressive responses can.

 ## Extension ideas

- Ask some of the children to mime one of the true statements (or possibly the opposite of a false statement) and see whether the others can guess which one they're miming.
- The children could read Aesop's fable 'The Man and the Serpent' and consider what it might teach us about anger.

 ## Note

This is a good activity to consolidate what has already been learned about anger.

# Anger freeze-frames

 ## Objective

To revise what has been learned about anger; to consider triggers of anger and the effect anger has on our thoughts and feelings; to understand what impulses it can trigger; to know how to cool down and what to do about anger.

 ## Instructions

- Ask pairs of children to create two 'anger freeze-frames' by getting into a 'frozen' moment – as if in a photograph – of a situation where one of you is angry. Ask the children to take it in turns to be the angry person.
- Give the children some time to do this. Ask them to practise so that they can recreate the 'photo' almost exactly the same each time they are asked to do it.
- Next, ask everyone to get into their freeze-frames on the count of three: '1, 2, 3 – freeze!'

- Choose one of the freeze-frames to remain frozen. 'Unfreeze' everyone else and ask them to observe the pair who are still frozen.
- Ask everyone to guess what they think might be happening in the freeze frame and take some suggestions.
- Un-freeze the pair being observed and ask the following questions:
  - How is it obvious who is angry in this freeze-frame?
  - What triggered your anger?
  - Aside from anger, are you feeling anything else (eg, humiliation, shame, embarrassment, fear, hurt)?
  - What does your anger make you feel like doing and what are you thinking?
  - What are the different ways you could respond to your anger in the moment immediately after this freeze-frame?
  - Which of those responses do you think would be the best?
- Freeze everyone again and choose another pair to explore in the same way and so on.

 ## Extension ideas

- The children could discuss why people sometimes end up doing things that trigger anger in others.

 ## Note

When I do this activity, I always take the children out of role at the end by asking an unrelated question (eg, 'If you had to be an animal, which one would you most like to be?'), so that they detach from any feelings of anger.

# Anger wisdom

 ## Objective

To consider any wisdom to be gained from quotations about anger.

 ## What's needed?

Access to the information on the sheet *Anger wisdom* (page 158).

 ## Instructions

- Share the quotations on the sheet *Anger wisdom* and ask pairs of children to discuss what each one may be telling us and whether they agree with its message or not.

- Ask pairs of children to consider all they have learned about anger and make up their own wise sayings about it. You could help them with the following prompts:
  - Being angry is okay – it's how you express it that is important.
  - It takes bravery to be assertive.
  - Anger once protected us well when we lived quite differently, but it is sometimes not suited to modern life.
  - Anger can drive some harmful reactions.
  - It's good to work out the message that anger might be sending you.
  - The same situation will trigger different amounts of anger in different people.
  - Anger is sometimes covering up more vulnerable feelings.
  - The angry brain is not very good at empathising with others.
  - If you don't address what triggered your anger, it's likely to return.
  - Sometimes the wisest thing to do is 'let it go'.

 ## Extension idea:

- The children could look for more sayings about anger on the internet.
- The children could create some questions about anger they could use to explore their parents/carers' thoughts about anger.

 ## Note

I find that some children love looking at sayings about any topic and searching for the wisdom within them.

# Words for 'anger'

 ## Objective

To normalise anger and increase emotion vocabulary.

 ## What's needed?

For younger children: some of the words on the sheet *Words for anger* (page 159), written on strips of paper; a large anger thermometer drawn on a piece of sugar paper. For older children: one copy of the sheet *Words for anger* (page 159) per pair; scissors; glue.

 ## Instructions

- Explain to the children that many different words can have the same or similar meanings.

- Show the children the anger thermometer and explain that it can be used to show how angry someone has become: the bottom of the thermometer represents being really calm and the top really angry.
- Look at the many words for 'angry' and explain that we have so many because anger is such a normal part of being human.
- Next, invite the children to position the words on the thermometer at the point they think represents how angry a person would be if this word was being used to describe them.
- As children place the words in different positions, ask them to think of something that might trigger a person to be that angry.
- Make a collection of triggers and decide as a group where each trigger would go. This will probably highlight that certain things make some people angrier than others.

 ## Extension ideas

- Draw angry words using bubble writing, including angry colours (eg, reds, oranges) and images (eg, volcanoes, grimaces, explosions, lightning).
- See whether the children can find more expressions or idioms for 'angry'.

 ## Note

With younger children, significantly reduce the number of words to add to the thermometer. More words can be added over time.

# A gold star for managing anger

 ## Objective

To consolidate how to manage anger well.

 ## Instructions

- Ask the children what a person who was not very good at managing emotions would do when they got angry.
- Ask the children to consider how a person who was extremely emotionally intelligent would manage anger.
- Ask the children to think of a potential trigger for anger.

- Next, ask them to draw a timeline of what an emotionally intelligent person does from the point when the potential trigger happens to the point when the situation is sorted. You could help with the following prompts:
  - the potential trigger;
  - noticing the physical symptoms of anger;
  - seeing the anger rise as it arrives;
  - knowing what has triggered the anger;
  - taking a pause before reacting;
  - seeing how the anger has affected their thoughts;
  - choosing helpful thoughts and challenging unhelpful ones;
  - wondering what might be going on for anyone else involved;
  - working out what the problem is;
  - working out what needs to be done to solve the problem; and
  - using 'I' messages to assertively state what needs to happen.

 ## Extension ideas

- The children could write exam questions for a test about managing anger well.
- The children could create and illustrate *Top Ten Tips* for managing anger.

 ## Note

I have asked children to approach this as if there were a scout or guide badge that could be achieved once a person was really good at managing anger – including designing the badge they could be awarded.

# Athan and his aggression

 ## Objective

To consider why sometimes we show anger when we're really feeling something else.

 ## What's needed?

Access to the information on the sheet *Athan and his aggression* (page 160).

 ## Instructions

- Explain to the children that sometimes we are taught not to be comfortable saying how we feel. This can be especially true for boys when they receive messages such as the following:

- o Man up.
- o Boys don't cry.
- o Be strong.
- Read through the sheet *Athan and his aggression* and ask pairs of children to discuss the questions on the sheet and then open up the discussion to the whole group. Key points that can be raised include the following:
  - o Sometimes we show anger in the form of aggression because we see it as a 'strong' and powerful emotion that can make us feel like we have more control than when we show other emotions.
  - o If we struggle to share how we are truly feeling when we're vulnerable, hurt, worried or frustrated, we often end up getting defensive or trying to control the situation. Unfortunately, these responses can sometimes mean we end up being verbally or physically aggressive; others can get hurt as a result, and we don't solve any problems that might exist.
  - o When we share our more vulnerable emotions, it usually helps others to connect with us.
  - o Athan needs help to feel secure enough to be able to ask for help from others.

 ## Extension ideas

- You could pretend to be Athan and let the children ask you questions and try to teach you how to manage your aggression better.

 ## Note

I have used this kind of social story with children who struggle with aggression and they work out some great advice for Athan without realising that his behaviour is very like their own. This social story distances a child enough from their behaviour so they can consider it without experiencing shame.

# Supporting someone who is angry

 ## Objective

To consider how it is best to respond to a friend who is angry

 ## Instructions

- Ask the children to consider what they think, feel and want to do when they see a friend is angry and ask them to share their answers. For example:

- we are usually startled into noticing an angry person – as they might be a threat that we need to get away from quickly (if it feels unsafe, getting away from the situation is always the best thing to do);
  - it often triggers a fear response in us;
  - if their anger is aimed at us, we might also become angry if we feel a need to protect ourselves;
  - if we think our friend is angry for a good or justified reason, we tend to sympathise and be supportive; and
  - if we are confused about why they are angry or if we believe they should not be angry, we might think they have no right to be angry and not be supportive.
- Now ask the children to consider what an angry friend might need. Although anger is an emotion that seems to be about warning people off, as long as we feel safe, we can still try to understand what is bothering a friend who is angry, which means we are more likely to try to help. To do this, ask the children to think of a time when they were angry and what anyone else could have done to help them. For example, a person who is angry:
  - often needs to feel heard and like someone has really listened;
  - probably feels an urgency that something needs sorting and want people to pay attention;
  - might want to talk about what has triggered their anger after they have calmed down and work out a solution to the difficulties they are having; and
  - might want either reassurance that whatever triggered their anger won't happen again or help to understand why the trigger of their anger happened or needed to happen.

 ## Extension ideas

- The children could compose their top three tips for helping someone who is angry.
- Exploring this issue with the children could start with a consideration of how they respond to other people's emotional reactions. You could ask the children to think of how they could respond supportively to friends experiencing other emotions such as sadness, embarrassment, anxiety, impatience etc.

 ## Note

During this activity, it's crucial to stress that if ever the children feel at risk from harm in the presence of an angry person, they need to first get away from the situation and then find trusted adults to tell until one of them helps.

# Where in the body do I feel anger?

Label this person with the things you feel or do when you're angry.

| Grit teeth | Clench fists | Eyes narrow |
|---|---|---|
| Muscles become tense | Eyebrows move down | Forehead creases |
| Face feels hot | Get a burst of energy | Mouth scowls |
| Tummy churns | Breathe quicker | Heart beats faster |
| Fidgets | Palms get sweaty | Anything else? |

# What can anger make us feel like doing?

When we feel anger, unless we are clever at dealing with it, it can make us behave in ways that can cause more upset or problems.

If Kasper called Violet stupid, which of the following do you think are good ways for Violet to respond and which do you think would probably make things worse?

| | |
|---|---|
| Violet tells Kasper that she hates him. | Violet calls Kasper stupid back. |
| Violet shouts at Kasper that she is going to tell the teacher. | Violet takes some deep breaths and then says, 'I feel sad when people say nasty things about me.' |
| Violet turns away from Kasper and talks to her friend Ezra. | Violet refuses to talk to Kasper for the rest of the day. |
| Violet jokes, 'Yes, I am a bit daft.' | Violet hits Kasper. |

If someone does something that means you end up feeling angry, what do you think is the best thing to do?

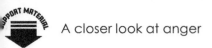

# Triggers of anger

Different things trigger different amounts of anger in different people. Two people can experience the same thing and one might end up furious but the other might not be bothered at all.

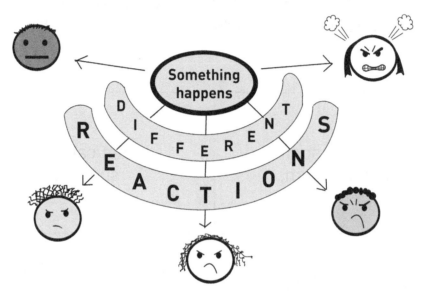

How angry do you think you would be if the following things happened to you?

| | |
|---|---|
| Someone ignoring you. | Someone talking all the way through your favourite TV programme. |
| Someone saying you can't play cricket with them because you're rubbish at it. | Someone grabbing your hat from your head and teasing you by not letting you have it back. |
| Someone laughing at your new coat and saying it looks awful. | Treading in dog poo. |
| A baby getting chocolate all over your clean clothes. | Being compared to a friend and being told you're not as good at drawing as they are. |
| Having a hole in your sock that your toe keeps poking through. | Someone barging in front of you in a queue at an ice cream van. |
| Getting a maths calculation wrong three times in a row. | Being told off by a teacher for something you didn't do. |
| Someone snatching your pencil off you and saying they need it more than you do. | Having a trip to the beach cancelled because it's raining. |
| Having a trip to the beach cancelled because the adult who was taking you forgot and had to do something else. | Completing a jigsaw puzzle to find there's one piece missing. |

# Cooling things down!

When we are angry, we don't usually make great choices. Because of this, when we're angry, it's a good idea to work out what would calm us and slow things down. Once we are calm again, we will be in a better place to work out what to do about what has happened.

Which of these do you think could work to calm you if you were angry?

| Take five really deep breaths. | Leave the situation if you can. | Rub the top of your head with your fingertips. |
|---|---|---|
| Think forward to a time when this won't bother you any more. | Use your finger to trace pictures of spirals. | Turn your head away from what has triggered your anger. |
| Imagine a red traffic light in your head and change it slowly to amber and then green, as you calm. | Close your eyes and count down from ten – or 100 if you need to. | Say clearly, 'I am struggling – can you help me?' |
| Distract yourself by squeezing your hand. | Think, 'I'm okay, I'm okay' over and over in your head. | If you can, do 20 star jumps. |
| Think of a happy memory. | Stretch and yawn. | Try smiling. |
| Hum a tune slowly and calmly. | Focus on what's happening inside your body. | Close your eyes and imagine a wonderful place. |
| Sing a silly tune in your head. | Blow several breaths out so that your cheeks puff out. | Think of something funny, like an ostrich with wellies on. |
| Go and find someone to talk to. | Think of someone you love. | Anything else? |

# Angry thoughts

When we're angry, we can have angry thoughts, which in turn can make us angrier. Angry thoughts tend to focus only on our side of the story. Alternatively, we can choose to think about any situation in a way that is more helpful.

| What happened | Angry thoughts | More helpful thoughts |
|---|---|---|
| Maya laughed at Finley's painting and said it looked like a two-year-old had painted it. | • 'Maya is really nasty.'<br><br>• 'I hate Maya.'<br><br>• 'I need to get Maya back for that.'<br><br>• 'I hate my painting now.' | • 'Maybe Maya is having a bad day.'<br><br>• 'Maybe Maya feels upset about something I did another time.'<br><br>• 'I guess this wasn't my best painting. I bet I could improve it.'<br><br>• 'I guess I have said mean things to people before too.' |
| Ayaan told Mabel she wasn't allowed to join in with their game of football. | | |
| Your mum told you to stop playing your computer game and still insisted, even when you told her you'd got to a really important bit in the game. | | |

# Anger - true or false?

Which of these statements about anger are true, which are false and which might you respond to with, 'Depends'?

1. Anger is an emotion that everyone feels now and then.

2. When we are angry, it's a good idea to react quickly

3. 'Exasperated' is one of many words that mean 'angry'.

4. When we are angry, it can affect how we think.

5. Anger makes some people aggressive.

6. When we are angry, we can struggle to make helpful choices.

7. Anger is wrong.

8. Some people get angrier than others – even if they have just gone through exactly the same thing.

9. We might not be able to stop ourselves from becoming angry, but we can choose what we do about it.

10. Anger tends to last for hours.

11. Anger has brought about some big changes in society.

12. Anger causes problems.

# Anger wisdom

| | |
|---|---|
| Anger is never without a reason but seldom a good one.<br>Benjamin Franklin | Speak when you are angry and you will make the best speech you will ever regret.<br>Ambrose Bierce |
| Being angry at someone is easier than telling them they hurt you.<br>Karen Salmansohn | Where there is anger, there is always pain underneath.<br>Eckhart Tolle |
| Anger is nothing more than an outward expression of hurt, fear and frustration.<br>Phillip C McGraw | Anger cannot be overcome by anger. If someone is angry with you, and you show anger in return, the result is a disaster. On the other hand, if you control your anger and show its opposite – love, compassion, tolerance and patience – not only will you remain peaceful, but the other person's anger will also diminish.<br>Dalai Lama |
| Holding on to anger is like drinking poison and expecting the other person to die.<br>Buddha | |
| Anger is an acid that can do more harm to the vessel in which it is stored than to anything on which it is poured.<br>Mark Twain | When angry, count to ten before you speak. When very angry, count to 100.<br>Thomas Jefferson |

# Words for 'anger'

There are lots of words that mean 'angry'. Some of them are angrier than others!

Place each word next to the anger thermometer at the position you think shows how angry it is.

| | | |
|---|---|---|
| **really, really angry** | Infuriated | Wound up |
| | Aggravated | Peeved |
| | Cross | Furious |
| **really angry** | Fractious | Maddened |
| | Agitated | Wrathful |
| **angry** | Relaxed | Serene |
| | Frustrated | Livid |
| | Seething | Raging |
| | Resentful | Exasperated |
| | Irritated | Incensed |
| **a bit angry** | Flew off the handle | Indignant |
| | Lose your cool | Vexed |
| | Riled | Hot under the collar |
| **a little bit angry** | Enraged | Blown a fuse |
| | Beside yourself | Irked |
| | Irate | Flipped your lid |
| | Boiling mad | Driven up the wall |
| **totally calm** | Peaceful | Fuming |
| | Annoyed | Up in arms |
| | Cheesed off | Pain in the neck |
| | Bothered | On my nerves |
| | Outraged | In a huff |
| | Grouchy | Sulky |

# Athan and his aggression

Athan is someone who only ever shows anger. He has not learned how to say what he is really feeling and is scared of looking weak or out of control. When Athan is feeling any of the emotions listed below, he always becomes aggressive – mostly insulting people, but sometimes kicking or punching them. Athan knows this always makes situations worse and he always feels bad after he has been aggressive.

| Shame (feeling worthless) | Really scared | Upset |
|---|---|---|
| Really guilty | Powerless | Really disappointed |
| Really embarrassed | Humiliated | Misunderstood |
| Jealous | Really worried | Being told what to do |

Discuss these questions:

1. Which of the following words do you think could be used to describe what it feels like to be angry?

   Powerful       Forceful       In control       In charge       Strong

2. Take each of the emotions in the table one at a time and decide whether you would prefer to feel that emotion or feel angry.

3. List some situations that could trigger Athan to feel some of the emotions above.

4. Why do you think Athan is scared to show how he really feels and why is this a problem?

5. What advice would you give Athan to help him be less aggressive?

# Chapter 5

# A FOCUS ON WORRY AND ANXIETY

## What's in this chapter?

This chapter explains what worry and anxiety are and explores tools to cope with them. It includes a number of tried-and-tested activities that can be used with children to help develop their understanding of anxiety – an emotion that many parents/carers and teachers often ask for support with.

I tend to use the terms 'anxiety' with older children and 'worry' with younger children – although, strictly speaking, anxiety is the emotion and worry is the thought process that can trigger it.

## *Activity notes*

- You will find a description of each of the activities in the first part of this chapter, followed by the relevant activity sheets.
- Activities are described with an objective, instructions, an indication of whether any further resources are needed (including printable resources from this book) and at least one suggested extension idea.
- The activities involve a variety of teaching and learning techniques, including discussion prompts, quizzes, agreement spectrums, sorting activities, drama activities, games and lessons that use printable worksheets.
- The age that each activity is suitable for has not been stipulated. Most activities could be simplified for younger children or adjusted to be more challenging for older children.

DOI: 10.4324/9781032690773-6

We are often presented with the notion of 'perfect lives'.

We rarely get time to sit quietly.

Our society generally pushes competition over compassion.

Our successes and failures are considered our responsibility in a way that creates pressure and little sympathy.

Many jobs have become more demanding.

We are 'sold' a perfect life.

Most of us carry trauma with us.

**No wonder we worry!**

We are bombarded with news - distilled down to the world's most shocking.

We can experience societal pressures heavily.

We are regularly painted a bleak view of the future.

It's a struggle to find time for both work and family life.

We often experience technology overload.

We often have to make frequent and/or difficult choices.

Relationships can easily become strained.

Life can be so busy!

We have learnt to torture ourselves with 'shoulds'.

We have a brain that evolved for a time when we lived quite differently.

We often have unrealistic expectations of ourselves.

***etc.***

# Key information about anxiety

| Topic | Further notes |
|---|---|
| Anxiety is in the fear family of emotions and it is an unenjoyable emotion | Fear evolved to help us deal attentively and immediately with danger. Anxiety evolved to keep us alert at times when danger might be a real possibility. Fear tends to last a short time and gives us an energy boost to get to safety quickly. Anxiety can last longer, as it is keeps us alert just in case a danger appears. |
| Fear and anxiety evolved at a time when we encountered danger far more often in our daily lives | We feel fear and anxiety even though today we rarely find ourselves in circumstances where we are at actual risk of being harmed, because our minds and bodies cannot tell the difference between real dangers that could injure us and things that we just find scary. (We can also find social situations frightening because we have developed a fear of rejection – for example, being ostracised or kicked out of the tribe – as this was once actually dangerous and reduced our chances of survival. However, again this is somewhat redundant today.) |
| We tend to react, think and behave in certain ways when we are anxious | Anxiety causes physical and mental reactions/symptoms, such as constant feeling of agitation, an upset stomach, broken sleep, an inability to focus on anything other than what is triggering anxiety, controlling behaviour etc. Anxiety can make us ruminate (ie, think unsettling thoughts over and over again) and catastrophise (ie, assume that everything that could go wrong will go wrong). |
| You need not feel anxious about feeling anxiety | Some people become anxious about feeling anxiety and its symptoms. Anxiety is a natural response, and although it can be really uncomfortable, it is not designed to harm us – it's designed to protect us. |

| Topic | Further notes |
|---|---|
| Is there more anxiety today? | Some people believe there is more anxiety today because:<br>• the internet gets us hooked on clickbait by continually triggering our dopamine/reward system. It also encourages us to compare ourselves with others. Both can be really agitating and unsettling;<br>• predictions for the future are presented as potentially catastrophic and young people are very aware of this;<br>• we are bombarded with extremely negative and disturbing news that is distilled from around the globe and delivered to us in a fast and furious way;<br>• some parents/carers may have overprotected their children in a way that has left them believing they cannot cope or be self-reliant, which makes them more anxious (Vigdal 2022); and<br>• individualism has encouraged us to be somewhat self-focused, which can lead to isolation and disconnection; whereas research tells us that connection with others can reduce anxiety (House 1988). |
| Anxiety is normal | Anxiety is a normal reaction to things that trigger worry. It gives us energy and helps us to focus on what is making us anxious. Anxiety becomes a problem only if it becomes extremely intense, lasts a very long time and gets in the way of us getting on with life. |
| What we worry about | Some worries are about concrete things we can actually do something about. Others are the result of our anxious mind getting carried away with searching for abstract possibilities to worry about. |
| Anxiety and change | When we face changes – especially those that may have a big impact on us – we often feel at least a little anxious. This is because change involves uncertainty, we can feel out of control and we may not trust ourselves to cope. |
| Comfort zones | Anxiety can prevent us from trying things that we anticipate will trigger worry or other unenjoyable emotions. If we always avoid the things that trigger anxiety, our brain will persist in believing that they are scary. |
| There are things we can do that will help us when we're anxious | Helping ourselves to manage anxiety often involves changing our thinking and behaviour, as well as finding ways to relax (or trigger our soothing, parasympathetic system). We can find things that soothe us to send our minds and bodies a clear message that there is no danger, which can help to reduce our anxiety. |

## Activities

# Relax!

 *Objective*

To consider how to relax (and trigger the parasympathetic system).

 *Instructions*

• Ask the children what it means to relax and tell them to collate their answers so that everyone can see them.

- Next, explain that relaxation helps the body to repair and rest, and that nature intended us to spend time relaxing because it is good for us.
- Ask the children what kinds of things they don't find relaxing. Sort their answers into things that can result in you feeling stressed and things that you can become quite excited about or have a real drive to want to do. Examples could include the following:
  - **Stressed:** Friendship troubles; worrying about how well you'll do in a test; finding a lesson difficult; having an argument with someone; going to the dentist; the night before school starts for the new year; performing on stage.
  - **Excited/driven:** Celebrating your birthday; opening a pile of presents; really hoping for a part in a performance that's not guaranteed; having a surprise visit from someone; deciding you're going to the beach; being told you're going to get a pet; really wanting to learn how to do something (eg, juggle); wanting to win a football match; really hoping someone wants to be your friend.
- Ask the children to consider what things they find relaxing and create a list of their answers. If the children have not mentioned the following things, discuss them and add them to your list:
  - Do a body scan to help you relax. Focus on each part of the body, starting with your feet, and tighten then relax the muscles as you scan up your body.
  - Focus on your breathing – especially if you take less time to breathe in than to breathe out. You could breathe in to a count of four and out to a count of five.
  - Find sensations that comfort you, such as massaging your feet, stroking a pet, playing soothing music or staring at the clouds.
  - Practise mindfulness by using all of your five senses to really notice something that you're doing (eg, eating an apple), to take you into this moment.
  - Try meditation, which reduces anxiety. Its effects build up over time the more you do it.
  - Do some exercise – this is great for regulating emotions as well as general health, and can leave you feeling relaxed afterwards.
  - Go outside – this is proven to have beneficial effects on your ability to relax, especially among the greenery of the countryside or parks.
- Ask groups of three children to create a TV ad for relaxation. Explain that the ad should persuade people to make time to relax and help them work out how to relax.
- When the ads have been created, invite groups to share them.

## Extension ideas

- The children could decide which ad was the most persuasive.
- The children could put the word 'relaxing' into a search engine and decide which pictures help them to relax the most.

- The children could devise a questionnaire and take it home to explore attitudes towards relaxation with the adult/s at home.

##  Note

We are not usually taught to relax unless we are suffering from anxiety. I think it is important to help children understand the value of relaxing and how it is recuperative for the body.

# What is anxiety?

##  Objective

To understand what anxiety is.

##  What's needed?

One copy of the sheet *What is anxiety?* (page 176) per pair.

## Instructions

- Ask the children what they think anxiety is and listen to their answers.
- Give pairs of children the sheet *What is anxiety?* and read through the definitions given at the top.
- Next, ask the children to complete the definitions scavenger hunt at the bottom of the sheet.
- Then ask the pairs to create their own definition of 'anxiety' without the help of the definitions sheet and share them with the whole group.

## Extension ideas

- The children could consider why anxiety evolved in humans – in other words, how it would have been useful to us in the ancient past (eg, when we're anxious we have more energy, which keeps us mentally alert, with a narrow focus on potential threats, and physically ready to react to danger).

##  Note

Although the terms 'worry'/ 'worried' and 'anxiety'/'anxious' are often used interchangeably, I find it useful to describe 'worry' as unhelpful thoughts that go round and round in your head, and 'anxiety' as what you end up feeling as a result of the worrying.

# What effect does anxiety have on us?

 ## Objective

To consider the physical and mental symptoms and impact of anxiety.

 ## What's needed?

Access to the information on the sheet *What effect does anxiety have on us?* (page 177).

 ## Instructions

- Ask the children to think of a time when someone might feel anxious (eg, before a test). State that it is perfectly normal to feel anxious in situations where we are not certain about how things will turn out. It is the body's reaction to worry.
- Next, give the children the information on the sheet *What effect does anxiety have on us?* and ask them to sort the effects into symptoms that are caused by anxiety and those that are not. The only one that is not is, 'It can make you fall asleep'. (Just to be clear, you can feel fatigued as a result of anxiety, but it's not known for actually triggering sleep.)
- Go through their answers.
- Explain to the children that anxiety and the symptoms themselves do not harm you – even though they are uncomfortable. They are a natural response to feeling threat or stress. Anxiety becomes a difficulty only if it lasts for a long period of time and stops people from getting on with the usual things they do in life.

 ## Extension ideas

- The children could label a blob person with all the symptoms of anxiety.

 ## Note

It's important to 'normalise' anxiety – especially for those who become anxious about feeling anxious!

# Could it trigger anxiety?

 ## Objective

To consider what can trigger anxiety.

# ✅ *What's needed?*

Access to the information on the sheet *Could it trigger anxiety?* (page 178).

# 🔍 *Instructions*

- Give the children access to the information on the sheet *Could it trigger anxiety?* This sheet helps them to reflect on the different things that can trigger anxiety – for example, perfectionism; worrying about what others think; believing that mistakes are terrible; thinking you will not cope; feeling that we haven't organised or planned enough for a certain situation, which therefore seems more chaotic than it needs to; facing uncertainty; feeling we have little control over things; facing things that bother us. (The only two statements that are unlikely to make situations trigger anxiety are: 'You've thought ahead, organised yourself and planned for something as much as you can', and 'You are confident that things will turn out okay').

- Next, ask pairs of children to consider what advice they could give to someone who is often anxious from what they have learned from the first part of this activity. Examples could include the following:
  - Everyone makes mistakes and we can learn from our mistakes, so they are generally a positive thing.
  - Uncertainty is part of life's adventure. Life would be dull and we would rarely be challenged and learn new things if we never experienced uncertainty.
  - Worrying about what others think is really unhelpful.
  - If you don't know much about a change coming up, see if you can find out more about it.
  - Rather than just worrying, check you have done everything you can to prepare yourself for something that is going to happen.

- Ask the children to share their advice with everyone. Pick out any themes that have been repeated.

# 🌀 *Extension ideas*

- The children could create a list of situations that can trigger anxiety (possibly relating to the criteria listed on the sheet) – for example, a test; moving house; starting a new school; changing class; bullying; parents splitting up; falling out with a friend; joining a club where you don't know anyone etc – and work out what it is about each trigger that bothers us (usually change, uncertainty, lack of control, fear of social rejection).

- Children could create anxiety advice posters.

**Note**

I tell children that it's totally normal to be anxious about anything we're not sure about, but that even if what we're dreading comes true, we will cope. Also, each time we cope should mean we feel less anxious the next time, as we prove to ourselves that we did cope!

# Challenging worries

 **Objective**

To learn to look for proof that your worry is unnecessary.

 **What's needed?**

Access to the information on the sheet *Challenging worries* (page 179).

 **Instructions**

- Talk through the idea that our brains can have a tendency to think the worst about any situation and that when we think negative things, they can really trouble us (our negativity bias). You could give the example of lots of people giving you praise but you only remembering the one comment that was slightly critical.

- Show the children the information on the sheet *Challenging worries* and discuss the different thoughts that each person has in response to what happened to them. Ask them to consider which thought in each pair seems more reasonable and realistic.

- Explain that we sometimes think in absolute terms of 'always,' 'never', 'every time', 'everyone' 'nobody' – generalisations and assumptions; but that we can nearly always find evidence that challenges such thoughts, as rarely are things 'always', 'never' etc.

- Ask the children to suggest helpful thoughts for the last three scenarios on the sheet. Obviously, there is no one right answer, but there are thoughts that could challenge the unhelpful ones that each child is having.

- Explain to the children that when we worry and feel anxious, we can convince ourselves that things will definitely go wrong, that we won't cope, that others will reject us, that the future will be unbearable. But these thoughts can always be challenged and we can often find evidence of times when, despite all our worries, everything turned out just fine.

*Extension ideas*

- The children could keep a worry diary for a week. They could note down each trigger and associated thoughts – helpful and unhelpful – and how the situation turned out, if relevant. This can often help children to realise consciously that their worries are often based on exaggerated negative expectations.

 *Note*

Some children really struggle to find thoughts that could challenge their own negative assumptions because they have a strong reluctance to believe that a positive outcome is likely. I spend time pointing out positive outcomes – 'See? It all turned out just fine!' – to help with this.

# Two types of worrying thoughts

 *Objective*

To consider worrying thoughts and how they can differ.

 *Instructions*

- Read the following worries to the children.
  - I am worried because I had an argument with my mum this morning.
  - I am worried that when I move house, I won't like my new bedroom. That makes me worry that I'll end up arguing with my sister because her bedroom will probably be better. I'm worried about my new route to school because it is along a busy road and it could be dangerous. I am worried that I won't make new friends at my new school, I won't like my teacher and the work will be too hard for me. I am worried that I'll be asked to do things that I get embarrassed about and that people will laugh at me. I'm scared of being asked to stand up in assembly or at the front of the class. I am worried that I won't know how to find my way around the new school and I might do something wrong because I don't know how the new school does things. I'm worried that the school won't be as fun as my school now and that the lessons won't be as interesting, so I will have problems concentrating and then I won't do well at school or get a good job, which could mean nobody likes me …

- Explain to the children that it's perfectly normal to worry about things, and there are two kinds of worry:
  - The first type (I am worried because I had an argument with my mum this morning) is based on something real. The worry is about what effect the argument might have had and how to make things better again.
  - With the second type (although it has been triggered by a big change coming up and the person doing the worrying is clearly anxious, as you would expect), the person gets carried away with worry, almost searching frantically for everything and anything to worry about. This kind of worrying 'makes up' things to worry about and is not really based on anything real. It is therefore hard to challenge, because one worry will simply be replaced by another.
- Explain that if you shared the thoughts you were having in the second example, people might think you were somewhat odd; whereas the first worry would seem totally valid. This is a good test for seeing whether a worry is based on something concrete.
- Also, explain to the children that being aware of the tendency to get carried away with worrying can help to calm it down.
- Finally, ask the children to write or act a creative and funny piece called 'Worrying about tomorrow' that includes runaway worrying. This brings humour and awareness to how bizarre worrying can become for some people.

 ## Extension ideas

- The children could reflect upon whether they are someone who gets caught up in runaway worrying or not.

 ## Note

I tend to use this activity with children who are 'worriers'.

# The emotions of change

 ## Objective

To reflect on the emotions of change and why they can be more unsettling than they need to be.

 ## What's needed?

Access to the information on the sheet *The emotions of change* (page 180).

# Instructions

- Ask the children to think of changes that they have experienced in their lives. There are some prompts on *The emotions of change* sheet if these are needed.
- Take a look at the sheet *The emotions of change* and check for understanding.
- Ask pairs or groups of children to discuss the questions on the sheet, making notes of any key points they discuss to share with the whole group. If groups do not mention any of the following, add them to the list:
  - Try to find and see the good things in each change.
  - Remember that change is good for learning new things – consider how dull life would be without it.
  - Find out as much information as you can – if we know very little this means more uncertainty, which can trigger anxiety.
  - It's good to get better at accepting that we can never be certain about how everything in the future will turn out.
  - How we feel before a change can depend on a variety of things, such as how much information we have; how confident we feel about how we will cope; whether we have experienced a similar change before; who else is involved in this change and how much we feel supported by them etc.
  - It's good to talk through any worries about change with someone you trust – this will help you to feel better.
  - Change might make you feel unsure for a short time, but you'll soon be back on track and everything will soon feel normal to you again.

# Extension ideas

- The children could discuss a life without change and the ways in which this could be problematic.
- The children could draw a timeline that contrasts a positive and a negative approach to change.
- The children could list and illustrate their top five tips for dealing with change.
- The children could draw a cartoon that illustrates that a change that we dread can be far worse in anticipation than in reality.

# Note

I often used this activity with children towards the end of Year 6 to prepare them for the transition to secondary school. However, it can be applied to any change.

# Anxiety and our comfort zone

 **Objective**

To consider how anxiety can reduce our comfort zone if we let it.

 **What's needed?**

Access to the information on the sheet *Anxiety and our comfort zone* (page 181).

 **Instructions**

- Ask the children what they think is meant by our 'comfort zone' (ie, all the places, activities and people that make us feel safe, comfortable and relaxed). Give an example of something that takes you out of your comfort zone and ask the children to volunteer some of theirs (eg, talking in front of lots of people; making mistakes in front of others; trying a new food; heights; holding a spider or snake; expressing that you need help; using a new gadget; filling in forms; accepting feedback; attempting to learn something you assume you'll be no good at; being given a new task to do and not being sure you'll be able to do it).

- Read through the information on the sheet *Anxiety and our comfort zone* and ask pairs of children to discuss whether they think anything on the sheet is outside their comfort zone and then work through the three tasks at the bottom.

- Discussion after the task can start with the following questions:
  - What part does anxiety play in preventing us from leaving our comfort zone?
  - What are the advantages of leaving our comfort zone (assuming it's safe)?
  - What encouragement could you give someone who is struggling to leave their comfort zone?

 **Extension ideas**

- The children could draw a circle labelled 'comfort zone' and place the things on the sheet – and anything else they can think of – inside or outside the circle to represent their level of comfort with each thing.

- The children could set themselves an 'out of my comfort zone' challenge.

 **Note**

Our comfort zone has a direct influence on how well we learn in school. With children, I use the term 'out of our comfort zone' to bring into awareness that we are likely to experience uncomfortable emotions when we learn and do things that we have never done before.

# What can we do about anxiety?

 **Objective**

To consider coping strategies for anxiety

 **What's needed?**

Access to the information on the sheet *What can we do about anxiety?* (page 182).

 **Instructions**

- Read through the information on the sheet *What can we do about anxiety?* and check for comprehension by asking some questions about the content.
- As an introductory activity, you could ask the children which of the strategies on the sheet involve changing the way you think about a situation. The reason for this is that many of the causes of worry relate to how and what we think about future situations.
- Ask the children to individually complete the activity outlined on the sheet.

 **Extension ideas**

- The children could give 'agony aunt'-style advice in response to a child saying how anxious they are feeling about moving to a new school.

 **Note**

I find that children usually have some strategies for dealing with feeling anxious even if they're not overly aware of them. As with adults, some of these will be healthy and others less so!

# What do we really fear?

 **Objective**

To consider the fear behind our worrying.

 **What's needed?**

Access to the information on the sheet *What do we really fear?* (page 183).

 **Instructions**

- Let the children see the information on the sheet and complete the activity in groups of four.
- Ask the children to share their thoughts as a whole group.
- Next, ask the children to work in the same groups of four to suggest some comforting advice for each of the worries at the top of the sheet and consider what thoughts or actions you could take that would really help in each of these situations.
- Ask each group to share their favourite piece of advice.

 **Extension ideas**

- Ask the children how they could persuade someone to be less worried about what other people think of them.

 **Note**

I would only do this activity with older children, but it can result in some very interesting discussions about social expectations, fear, needs, how the brain can get carried away with negative thinking, and how others generally forgive and actually feel more connected to people who mess up or show vulnerability.

# Threat, drive or soothe?

 **Objective**

To consider how we can soothe ourselves and what things can prevent us from relaxing.

 **What's needed?**

Access to the information on the sheet *Threat, drive or soothe?* (page 184).

 **Instructions**

- Emotions fall generally into those that are triggered because of threat, those that are responsible for driving and motivating us and the soothing or 'rest and digest' emotions (Gilbert, 2010).
- Using the information on the sheet *Threat, drive or soothe?*, tell the children about the three systems. Here is more detail about each system that you could share:

- The **threat system** (danger, anxiety, anger, fear, disgust) will override the other systems, as these emotions evolved first and foremost to ensure our survival and threats in hunter-gatherer times involved a greater risk of harm or death.
- The **drive system** (craving, happiness, love, excitement) evolved to motivate us to search for things that we also needed for survival – for example, food, a mate, social approval to avoid being kicked out of the tribe. This system can cause us to become addicted to things. Although it is a system that drives us to find 'rewards', our bodies can't always tell the difference between things that are genuinely good for us (eg, food, relationships) and things that are not so good for us (eg, too much screen time, too much food). Dopamine can keep driving us to find the wrong things, which can be unsettling and prevent our soothing system from kicking in.
- **The soothing system** (relaxed, caring, calm) evolved to allow our bodies to rest and repair, and avoid using up energy from being constantly in more energetic emotional states. Some people struggle to spend time 'resting and digesting' because they feel guilty; they spend too much time triggering dopamine with reward hits; they are anxious a lot of the time; they are wired to experience negative emotions more frequently and intensely than others; they don't understand how important it is to spend time relaxing etc.
- Work through the questions on the sheet and spend some time collecting ideas from the answers question 3. When we feel calm, we don't feel anxious!

## Extension ideas

- The children could debate whether playing on a games console or scrolling on a phone is actually relaxing or not.
- Quite often, anxiety prevents people from sleeping. Children could research what helps with good sleeping habits.

## Note

Some children are helped considerably by understanding the theory of these three systems, as they become more aware of what is stopping them from spending time feeling calm. I tend to use this with older children only.

# What is anxiety?

Here are answers that some people have given to the question, 'What is anxiety?'

| | |
|---|---|
| Anxiety is a normal response to many worrying situations. It's like a feeling of dread that's sometimes mild and sometimes a bit much. | Fear is what humans have to give them a burst of energy to get them away from danger. Anxiety evolved to keep us alert in case a danger came along. |
| Anxiety is triggered when you think, feel and assume that negative things are going to happen. It is what we feel when we think we won't cope with something or that something we have already done will cause something bad to happen. | Anxiety is in the fear family of emotions. Anxiety can cause problems if it lasts for a long time, triggers you to become fearful of many made-up worries in your head or stops you from doing many things because you're just too worried. |
| A little bit of anxiety can drive you to do something helpful, such as revise for a test, plan what you need to take with you the next day or avoid taking unnecessary risks. Your body is designed to use anxiety to keep you safe. Feeling anxious isn't unhealthy unless it becomes extreme. | When you're stressed, you feel anxious. Anxiety can make your tummy churn, make you restless, stop you from concentrating on anything other than what you're worried about, make you feel tense, make it hard to sleep, make you feel sick, give you headaches and make you have repeated unhelpful thoughts. |

## Definition scavenger hunt

From the definitions of 'anxiety' above, can you find ...:

- an effect that anxiety has on your body?
- a phrase that tells you what can trigger anxiety?
- a phrase that describes what anxiety is meant to do?
- an emotion that anxiety is linked to?
- a phrase that explains when or why anxiety is a positive thing?
- a phrase that tells you how anxiety can affect how you think?
- a phrase that tells you when anxiety becomes a problem?
- a phrase that tells you anxiety is usually linked to worrying about the future and what might happen?

# What effect does anxiety have on us?

Which of these do you think are true of anxiety?

| | |
|---|---|
| It can make you feel light-headed and dizzy. | It can make you restless and feel unable to sit still and relax. |
| It can make your palms sweaty and your hands shaky. | It can make you feel sick and sometimes give you a stomach ache. |
| It can make you feel agitated and give you a sense of dread – like something bad is going to happen. | It can lead some people to ruminate (have the same troubling thoughts going round and round in their head) and catastrophise (assume that anything that could go wrong will go wrong) |
| It can make you fall asleep. | It can make your heartbeat race and you breathe more quickly. |
| It can make your muscles tense, which can lead to pain – particularly in the neck and shoulders. | It can make it difficult to sleep. You can wake up with troubling thoughts going round and round in your head. |
| It can make you irritable and less tolerant of other people. | In small doses, it can drive you to get on and do something about whatever is worrying you. |

# Could it trigger anxiety?

**Decide which of the following describe a situation that could trigger anxiety.**

Could anxiety be triggered if...

- something bothers you so you think about it over and over?
- you feel a lot of pressure to do things perfectly?
- there a change you are going to go through that you know very little about?
- you are really worried about what others will think of what you're going to do?
- you know you might make a mistake but you understand that everyone makes mistakes?
- you've thought ahead, organised yourself and planned for something as much as you can?
- there's a story in the news that seems to cause a lot of upset?
- there's a change coming up that you think will make your life trickier than it is now?
- you're scared of something, even if isn't actually dangerous (eg, the dark)?
- you are confident that things will turn out okay?
- somebody is bullying you and you don't feel like you can stick up for yourself?

---

Can you think a piece of advice you could give someone to help them work towards becoming less anxious?

---

# Challenging worries

A lot of the worries that trigger anxiety are not based on facts.

| What happened | What they worried about | Proof this worry was unnecessary |
|---|---|---|
| Someone laughed at Sam because he fell over. | 'Nobody likes me.' | 'I have got lots of friends.' |
| Eliana let in a goal during her school football match. | 'I am a rubbish goalie. I'm always letting goals in.' | 'I have actually saved lots of goals.' |
| Luna is starting in a new class tomorrow as she moves into Year 6. | 'I don't think I will cope with moving to a new class.' | 'I coped last year when I moved up to Year 5 and it soon felt normal.' |
| Levi had a maths test yesterday. | 'I am worried everyone will laugh at me for getting a low mark.' | 'When I have done badly in tests before, nobody noticed and they didn't say anything nasty if they did.' |
| Maya is walking to the park. | 'I'm worried I might get lost like I did last time.' | |
| Simon has a speaking part in the school assembly tomorrow. | 'I'm worried I will mess my part up.' | |
| Luca's friend Matthew chose not to sit next to him yesterday. | 'I don't think Matthew likes me anymore.' | |

# The emotions of change

When we face changes in our lives, we can feel anxious because we cannot be sure about what will happen in the future and this uncertainty makes us worry that we might not cope.

This shows the emotions a person might experience after a change has happened in their life, such as moving classes or moving to a new town.

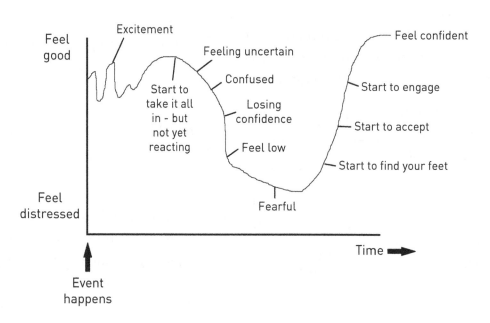

## Discuss these questions with someone:

- Think of some different changes you have been through – for example, changing classes, moving house, changing bedrooms, gaining new family members, making new friends, changing a routine etc. What kinds of things can make us look forward to a change and what can make us dread it?
- What is it about change that can make us worry or become anxious?
- What might this graph look like before the change happened and what might how we feel before a change depend upon?
- Do you think we feel most anxious about change before, during or after it has happened?
- Why do you think our anxiety usually decreases a while after a change?
- What advice would you give someone who was about to face a big change in their life to help them feel less anxious?

# Anxiety and our comfort zone

There are lots of situations where it's normal to feel anxious. Consider the following:

| | |
|---|---|
| Speaking with someone or several people you don't know. | Trying something new that you're not sure about (eg, a climbing wall). |
| Taking a bus for the first time on your own. | Standing up in front of a class or other group of people to say something. |
| Telling a friend that they need to stop helping themselves to your things. | Taking on a new responsibility (eg, walking a pet every day). |
| Staying away from home overnight on a school trip. | Starting a new topic in maths. |
| Joining a beginner's class in a martial art. | Asking for help from a trusted adult because you're being bullied. |

For each situation, answer the following questions:

- What specifically might a person in each situation worry and feel anxious about?
- If each situation triggered someone to become really anxious, what might they do?
- What advice would you give someone feeling anxious about each of these situations?

# What can we do about anxiety?

Here is a lot of different advice about what to do when you feel anxious. Choose the three pieces of advice you think would be most helpful to you.

| | | |
|---|---|---|
| Go for a walk. | Don't be a perfectionist – perfection does not exist and you'll be anxious trying to achieve it. | Trust yourself – remember all the times things have gone well for you. |
| Being anxious can make some people become very controlling – like being bossy or really, really tidy. You have to show yourself that if you stop doing these things, you'll still be fine. | You must be brave and face the things that make you anxious. Otherwise, your brain will hold on to the idea that they're scary forever, you'll keep avoiding them and the idea of them will keep making you anxious. | Be aware that anxiety can make you procrastinate, which means putting off things you need to do. Procrastination then makes you feel anxious about what you haven't done. You need to tell yourself: 'Just do it!' |
| Anxious people tend not to trust themselves to do a good job. You need to understand that you will almost definitely cope, whatever happens. | Don't look to others for reassurance. You might think this will help you be less anxious, but all the while you're looking for reassurance, you're still convinced it's not going to be okay. | Anxiety sometimes teaches us that we might need to change something. For example, we might need to change how we think about something, to learn something or to get on and sort something out. |
| You can never be certain about how things will turn out. Accept that uncertainty is part of life. | Picture what you're worrying about turning out just fine. That will soothe you. | Anxiety can be exhausting! You need to find ways to help relax yourself. |

# What do we really fear?

What do you think the following people are really scared of? Use the things written in boxes below to help you. It could be more than one of them:

- I have made a poster for the school fete but I am not sure it's good enough.
- I have fallen out with a friend. I can't stop thinking about it.
- I have planned my party in lots of detail but I still think it could be a disaster.
- I am in a school play tomorrow. I am so worried I will forget my lines.
- I am worried my dad won't like the present I have made for him.

| | |
|---|---|
| Making a fool of themselves in front of other people. | Messing up or making mistakes so others might think we're rubbish. |
| Disappointing someone we care about and/or want to impress. | Not being able to be certain about how something will turn out. |
| Thinking we won't be able to cope. | Many disasters actually happening and everything going wrong so that our life changes for the worse. |

# Threat, drive or soothe?

Dr Paul Gilbert is a psychologist who explains how three families of emotions evolved to help humans survive thousands of years ago:

- **Threat emotions:** The emotions that arise when we feel danger or a threat to our safety. These emotions override the others.
- **Drive emotions:** The emotions that motivate us to find things that reward us.
- **Soothing emotions:** The emotions we feel when we rest and recover from any stresses.

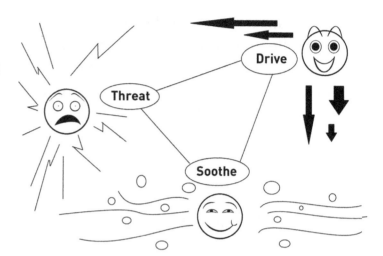

To which system do you think the following emotions belong?

Craving    Relaxation    Fear    Happiness    Anxiety    Love

Care    Disgust    Anger    Calmness    Excitement

For our bodies to rest and recover, we need to spend some time feeling emotions from the soothing system. What do you think can prevent people from feeling calm?

What things do you do to help you feel calm?

# Chapter 6
# RELATIONSHIPS AND EMOTIONS

## What's in this chapter?

This chapter explores the emotional aspect of friendships and other relationships. While it does not explore every aspect of relationships, it focuses in particular on emotions that are often triggered within friendships, developing empathy and raising awareness of how our behaviour can affect others.

## *Activity notes*

- You will find a description of each of the activities in the first part of this chapter, followed by the relevant activity sheets.
- Activities are described with an objective, instructions, an indication of whether any further resources are needed (including printable resources from this book) and at least one suggested extension idea.
- The activities involve a variety of teaching and learning techniques, including discussion prompts, quizzes, agreement spectrums, sorting activities, drama activities, games and lessons that use printable worksheets.
- The age that each activity is suitable for has not been stipulated. Most activities could be simplified for younger children or adjusted to be more challenging for older children.

## Notes about the topics covered in this section

Understanding our own emotions and the reactions of others, and being able to empathise are key to how well we manage our friendships and other relationships. Our ability to understand how we relate to others, both positively and negatively, can enhance our relationships and help us grow as individuals. This chapter explores many of the emotions that can be triggered within interactions that will further children's understanding of friendships and relationships.

DOI: 10.4324/9781032690773-7

Here are a few notes about the topics covered in this section.

| Topic | Notes relating to emotions and relationships |
|---|---|
| The value of friendships | Friendships bring a lot of benefits and it's valuable to reflect upon these. Aside from developing children's communication skills, increasing their sense of belonging, creating opportunities to practise social skills and contributing to self-worth, friendships also provide support and connection with others and have been shown to reduce anxiety and help us manage life's stresses better (Ozbay 2007). When we reflect upon the feelings triggered by friendships, it not only helps us to value them, but also sends us warning signs if something is going wrong in a relationship. |
| The ups and downs of friendship | It's beneficial when children understand that friendships have their ups and downs. Nearly all friends make mistakes and occasionally do things that trigger upset. This does not mean they are no longer a friend. It usually means that our upset needs to be communicated assertively to prevent situations or behaviour that can damage the friendship from happening again (as long as the friend is not engaging in persistently bullying or abusive behaviours). Sometimes an adult will be needed to help mediate this process. |
| Jealousy and envy | The word 'jealousy' is often used as a synonym for 'envy', but strictly speaking the two are different. Jealousy involves three people – where the jealous person feels more left out than they would like to be; whereas envy often involves just two people – where one person has something the other doesn't have, but which they desire. Both jealousy and envy can feature within friendships and can potentially be damaging. |
| Listening | Listening attentively is a powerful way to connect with others, make friends feel cared for and maintain friendships. There are tools that can be learned to enhance our listening skills (including the ability to empathise) and help another person to feel heard and understood. |
| Loneliness | It's good for children to reflect upon the idea of feeling lonely themselves as well as considering empathising with others who might feel lonely and considering what could help with this. |
| Asking for help | Some relationships can be unhealthy (including online relationships) and it's beneficial for children to know this. If a relationship with another involves considerable inequality in terms of 'give and take', if one person in the friendship is very controlling or manipulative or if there is bullying, a child's emotions are likely to alert them that something is wrong. If a relationship is causing a lot of anxiety or upset, they might need adult help to navigate the situation.<br>It's important to explain to children that if ever they find themselves in a situation they don't think they can manage themselves, they need to keep telling trusted adults until they get the help they need. |

# Activities

## When you think of friends ...

 *Objective*

To value friendships by considering the positive emotions they can trigger.

# ✅ *What's needed?*

Access to the information on the sheet *When you think of friends* (page 202).

# 🔍 *Instructions*

- Explain to the children that friends can be really good for us. Ask them to give reasons for why they think this is so (eg, they teach us about ourselves; they can be supportive; we feel we can be ourselves with true friends; we learn social skills though friendships; friends can help us when we're struggling; friends help us feel like we belong).
- Give the children access to the information on the sheet *When you think of friends ...* Explain that all of these words could be used to describe how someone feels when they think about friends, but that that we're unlikely to feel all of these emotions about just one friend, as we 'get' different things from different friends.
- Ask the children to identify any of the words they don't know the meaning of and spend some time defining these.
- Next, ask each child to choose one of the ways of feeling that they consider to be really important to feel in a friendship.
- Ask the children to find a partner and share their words, and then negotiate on which of the two words they can agree is more important (so that one word is 'ditched').
- Then ask the pairs of children to join into groups of fours and repeat the same process, negotiating on which feeling word is probably most important in a friendship. Have those groups join into groups of eight and repeat the process and so on, until the whole class has arrived at one word. The value in this activity is the discussion it triggers.
- Once the final word has been agreed, open up the discussion by asking, 'Why do you think it's important to feel this way in a friendship?' and listen to some of the answers.
- Next, ask each child to complete the sentence, 'In a friendship, it is important for me to feel ...' and see whether the children can explain their answers.

# 🌀 *Extension ideas*

- You could create a list of behaviours that would work against triggering positive emotions in friendships.
- A friendship display that is visible from the playground (if possible) could be created using the emotions considered in this activity (and possibly phrases created in other activities in this chapter).

# 📝 *Note*

It seems obvious that friends are a 'good thing', but I always find that activities such as this seem to instigate more kindness and connection within any group.

# The ups and downs of friendship

 **Objective**

To accept that friendships sometimes have difficulties and explore this by considering emotions.

 **What's needed?**

Access to the information on the sheet *The ups and downs of friendship* (page 203).

 **Instructions**

- Explain that it's totally normal for friends to sometimes do things that upset us. Nobody is perfect and we all make mistakes.
- Introduce the hypothetical friendship of Sophie and Noah. Explain that most of the time they get on really well, but that sometimes they upset one another. Ask the children to suggest the kinds of things they might do that could cause upset.
- Let the children see the information on the sheet *The ups and downs of friendship* and ask them to consider the question at the bottom of the sheet to explore the feelings further.
- Ask the children to consider the positive emotions on the sheet (love, compassion, grateful, forgiveness, admiration, pleasure, amused, accepting, excited, comfortable, supported) and consider what their friends do to trigger these emotions.

 **Extension ideas**

- The children could come up with other examples of times when each of the emotions on the sheet *The ups and downs of friendship* might be experienced in a friendship.
- You can explore the idea of hate with older children. It's something that many of us are taught is bad to feel, although most of us experience moments when we might feel contempt for someone – even those we love! We have more chance of moving on and forgiving if we accept that we sometimes feel contempt, rather than pretending that we never feel it.

 **Note**

In my experience, some children evaluate a friendship solely on the last thing that their friend did. This can mean they might write off a friendship because of a one-off negative action and forget the other positive aspects of the friendship as a protection mechanism. This is sometimes referred to as 'splitting' (Burgo 2012). It is beneficial to help children understand that we all make mistakes. We're all capable of doing 'good' and 'bad' things, and it's generally much better if we can learn to accept this and be more forgiving.

# Tricky behaviours

 ## Objective

To consider what makes a good friendship by considering the impact of behaviour.

 ## What's needed?

Access to the information on the sheet *Tricky behaviours* (page 204).

 ## Instructions

- Let the children see the information on the sheet *Tricky behaviours* and ask them to discuss in pairs how they would (or do) feel when someone engages in each of these behaviours. (You could also ask them why they think people sometimes engage in these behaviours.)

- Next, ask the children to create a list of the behaviours that are opposite to these (some behaviours don't have direct opposites, but this should generate discussion as they create the list) and consider what feelings these 'opposite' behaviours are likely to trigger in others.

- Pairs of children can then produce their top ten tips for a good friendship, considering all they have discussed.

 ## Extension ideas

- The children could privately reflect upon how 'good' a friend they think they are and consider which helpful and unhelpful behaviours they are personally aware of doing.

 ## Note

To keep shame to a minimum, I set a ground rule at the start of this lesson that we will never mention any names when talking about behaviour.

# Jealousy and envy

 ## Objective

To consider the emotions of jealousy and envy, understand how they are different and consider what helps us to manage these emotions.

## What's needed?

Access to the information on the sheet *Jealousy and envy* (page 205).

 ## Instructions

- Share the sheet *Jealousy and envy* and ask the children to complete the tasks outlined on it.
- Explain that both jealousy and envy are emotions that involve comparing ourselves with someone else and ending up feeling inadequate or rejected. To feel better, we often need to remember all the good things in our lives.
- Once the children have considered the strategies at the bottom of the sheet, ask them to share their ideas about what could help when you feel jealous and what could help when you feel envious.

 ## Extension ideas

- The children could put the words 'envious' and 'jealous' into an image search engine (or you could distribute a selection of pictures gained this way) and choose one image and attempt to explain what they think is happening in it – for example, who is jealous or envious? Why might they be jealous or envious? What else might they be feeling?
- Children could investigate what various expressions and metaphors relating to envy and jealousy mean – such as 'green-eyed monster', 'sour grapes', 'keeping up with the Joneses', 'a covetous eye', 'being the envy of ...', 'being green with envy' – and create pictures to illustrate them.

 ## Note

It's important to normalise jealousy and envy, as these are emotions that children are often told they should not feel. It's better to acknowledge that most of us feel these emotions now and then and discuss strategies that can help when we feel them.

# Feeling lonely

 ## Objective

To consider what triggers loneliness and what might help us manage it.

 ## What's needed?

Access to the information on the sheet *Feeling lonely* (page 206).

# 🔍 *Instructions*

- To encourage discussions, ask the children to complete the tasks on the sheet *Feeling lonely* in pairs or groups of three.

- Further points about loneliness you could explore together include the following:
  - As loneliness is about not feeling connected to others, you can feel lonely even when you're surrounded by others. Being lonely is not the same as being alone.
  - As our thinking is very linked to how we feel, we can sometimes get carried away with thoughts that enable us to feel disconnected from others – for example, 'Nobody likes me'; 'Everybody likes X more'; 'I have no friends.' It's usually easy to challenge these absolute statements and find evidence that contradicts them.
  - We can feel lonelier at different times in our lives – for example, when we go to a new place where we know nobody; when we're struggling to feel understood by others so that we feel like an outsider; when we lose a close friend because they have moved away.
  - Some of the best ways of tackling loneliness include making deliberate efforts to connect with others; doing something kind for someone else; reminding ourselves about all the positive things about the people we know.

- Next, take time to explore what the children could do if they realise that someone else is feeling lonely by asking, 'What could we all do to try very hard to prevent anyone in this school from feeling lonely?' Ideas might include the following:
  - Encourage everyone to look out for children with nobody to play with or talk to at break times.
  - Aim to make everyone feel included and not left out.
  - Reach out to children you might not often talk to and ask them questions that help you get to know them more.
  - Aim to be kind to everyone – including people you don't know.
  - Create a buddy system where older children check in on younger children.
  - Move children around in class so they don't always work with the same classmates.
  - Organise acts of kindness – for example, sending cards with compliments in them.
  - At breaktimes, deliberately play games that everyone can join in with.
  - Create a culture where people feel okay to say that they feel lonely or they would like someone to talk to.
  - Have a conversation bench in the playground for people to sit on when they feel like finding a new person to talk to.
  - Create a celebration of differences by asking pairs of children to list as many differences between them as they can find. They could also create a list of similarities.
  - Create conversation cards with entertaining questions children can ask each other, which can be accessed at breaktimes.

- Finally, finish by stressing that if anyone feels really lonely or excluded for a long time, they need to keep telling trusted adults until one of them helps.

 ## Extension ideas

- The children can consider the idea of making someone they don't know feel welcome and included. What makes another person feel welcome and included and what doesn't?
- The children can explore the difference between being alone and feeling lonely by discussing the question, 'What thoughts can contribute to making us feel lonely and which can help us stop us feeling so?'

 ## Note

Admitting to loneliness can make some older children feel quite vulnerable, so I tend to avoid asking anyone directly if they feel lonely and just explore the feeling in general terms.

# What does it feel like to be really listened to?

 ## Objective

To consider the emotions involved in being listened to.

 ## What's needed?

One copy of the sheet *Being listened to* (page 207) per child.

 ## Instructions

- Open up a discussion by asking the children to imagine telling two people the same thing, but one person really listens and the other doesn't. Which interactions would leave you feeling more positive? Which person would seem kinder?
- Next, ask pairs of children to take it in turns to share some information about themselves for a minute, with each pair alternating being the speaker and the listener. With the first conversation, ask the listener not to listen well. With the second, ask the listener to really listen carefully. This will mean four conversations in total, as each partner reciprocates. Ask the children to notice how being listened to and not being listened to feel. (Possible topics: what is your family is like? What do you think you'll be like as a grown-up? What would your perfect holiday look like? What is one of your happiest memories at school?)

- Share the table on the sheet *Being listened to* and ask the children to complete it using notes that reflect their experience of both being listened to and not being listened to. Ask those who are happy to if they can share some of their reflections.
- Discuss further how being listened to feels so much better than not being listened to.
- Also explore what can sometimes prevent us from listening well – for example, we are busy; we are struggling ourselves; we haven't learned to listen well; we're excited to say what we want to say; we haven't experienced being really listened to ourselves; we think that speaking is always better than listening etc.
- Finish the activity by asking the children to reflect privately upon how well they think they listen personally.

 ## Extension ideas

- The children could listen to conversations on the television and/or the internet at home and consider which involved good listening and which didn't, and feed back on anything they noticed. For example, who did the most talking? Did anyone become frustrated? Was there empathy? Did the people really pay attention to each other? If you had been the people in those conversations, how do you think you would have felt?

 ## Note

I often tell children that listening is a gift you give to others.

# Being a good listener

 ## Objective

To consider what makes a good listener.

 ## What's needed?

One copy of the sheet *Listening* (page 208) per pair; one plain sheet of paper per child; scissors.

 ## Instructions

- Give pairs of children a copy of the sheet *Listening* and ask them to cut out the cards and sort them as described on the sheet.
- Next, ask pairs of children to take it in turns to talk to each other, with one as the listener and the other as the speaker. In their first conversation, each should try to

include as many of the features of poor listening as possible; and in their second conversation, each should try to incorporate as many of the good listening skills as possible (making four conversations in total). The 'poor listening skills' part is quite hard to do but it can be entertaining and teaches the objective well. (Example conversation topics could include their favourite meal, the lessons they like most at school, the pet they would most like to own and what they love to do outside school.)

- Next, ask the children the following questions:
    - Which feels better – being listened to properly or not?
    - What irritated you most about not being listened to?
    - Did you find it easy to listen to your partner?
    - Did you find it hard not to listen to your partner?
    - What do you think makes you feel really listened to?
- Ask the children to fold a piece of paper and draw 'the world's worst listener' on the left and then 'the world's best listener' on the right and label what they both do.

 *Extension ideas*

- Older children could consider empathy (the ability to understand what another person's experience feels like) and consider which listening skills really help someone to feel understood with empathy.
- Children could set themselves a listening target. For example:

| Not so challenging > > > > | | More challenging |
|---|---|---|
| • Give others more time to speak than you in a conversation.<br>• Always ask a question when you first see someone and respond to their answer<br>• Don't let yourself be distracted from the conversation.<br>• Use 'Mmm', 'Go on' and other words of encouragement to show you're listening.<br>• Remember details about another person to ask them about.<br>• Pause more in conversations.<br>• Never interrupt. | • Aim to make the conversation more about the other person than you.<br>• Look for clues for how interested the person you're talking to is.<br>• Try not to bombard people with advice or tell them what to do.<br>• Notice when your thoughts wander away from a conversation and return to focus on what the other person is saying. | • Feed back on what you think the person is probably feeling, to show you have really tuned in to what they are saying.<br>• Try not to jump in on silence. Allow the other person to fill any gaps.<br>• Be more aware of any judgements you make about what someone is saying.<br>• Pay really close attention to what the other person is saying. |

**Note**

I find that children are usually very quick to sort the aspects that help and hinder listening in the above exercise. However, I find I have to encourage them to reflect upon whether they are truly a good listener. Adults can be poor listeners too and children can be told this!

# Empathy detectives

 **Objective**

To know what empathy is and how it can be helpful.

 **Instructions**

- Suggest a selection of emotions to the children (eg, happy, sad, angry, disappointed, irritated, worried, excited, hopeful, surprised, guilty, confused, lonely, misunderstood, nervous, jealous, regretful) – or let them choose their own – and ask them to think of a situation in which they felt a specific emotion that they would be happy to share.
- Ask pairs of children to take it in turns to tell each other about their situation without saying how they felt. Once the situation has been explained, ask the other child to guess what they think their partner was feeling during the situation. Encourage the children to guess more than one emotion word. Ask the speaker to feed back to the listener on how accurate their guesses were.
- Explain to the children that working out what another person is feeling is a skill called 'empathy'. Make it clear that it's helpful in relationships to think of empathy not as how you would feel in the same situation, but as how the other person is actually feeling (although how you would feel might sometimes give you clues as to how they are feeling).
- Ask the children where we can find clues as to how another person is feeling and listen to some of their suggestions (eg, the expression on their face, their tone of voice, what they are telling you, answers to questions you ask, how they hold their body).
- Ask the children, in groups of four, to discuss different ways in which empathy can be helpful and ask volunteers to share some of their answers (eg, helps you be kind to others; helps you work out what others might need; helps you connect with others; helps you communicate with others in a considerate way; helps you realise we all react to things differently; helps you be more forgiving; helps you solve emotional problems and conflicts with friends well; helps you understand different perspectives, which can make you wiser).

*Extension ideas*

- The children could draw an image that portrays empathy.
- The children could discuss the following idea: 'Empathy is not about thinking how you would feel in a situation; it's about understanding what another person is actually feeling.' What does this mean? Why might it be unhelpful if we assume that others feel the same as we do in the same situation?

 *Note*

I find using the idea of the empathy detective makes children want to try harder to work out what another might be feeling – like it's a puzzle to be solved!

# Being brave in friendships

 *Objective*

To consider how we might need to be brave sometimes within friendships, and that while this can be uncomfortable, it can ultimately make friendships stronger.

 *What's needed?*

Access to the information on the sheet *Being brave in friendships* (page 209).

 *Instructions*

- Tell the children that sometimes it can be a good thing to be brave in friendships and ask them what they think you might mean by this. Discuss some of their suggestions.
- Share the sheet *Being brave in friendships* and ask the children to consider which of the scenarios require no bravery (C and I) and which require bravery (all the others). Ask the children to discuss why some of these situations require bravery. Examples could include the following:
  - We can be scared of friends reacting aggressively or defensively if we challenge them in any way or are really honest with them.
  - We can worry that a person might reject, ignore, tease or stop liking us if we are really honest with them.
  - We can worry that we might get picked on if we stand up for a friend or don't join in with what most people are doing.
  - It can take bravery to admit we that have done something wrong or hurtful because it can make us feel uncomfortable, ashamed or that we are bad person.

- o We have to be brave to listen to criticism that a friend gives us and not just react negatively in a way that means we don't listen – or, worse still, say something nasty back. It takes bravery to consider criticism and whether you might need to do something about it.
  - o It can feel easier and more comfortable to just agree with others and not challenge them or their behaviour. 'Don't rock the boat' is an expression that describes this.
- Ask the children to imagine themselves in each of the situations on the sheet and consider how their emotions could influence what they would or wouldn't do, and then how being brave might change this.
- Ask pairs of children to complete the sentence: 'Being brave in friendships is a good thing because ...' and ask them to share their ideas with the whole group.

 ## Extension ideas

- The children can revisit 'I' messages (page 52) as a way of using your emotions to be assertive and express your needs.
- The children could roleplay one brave and one contrasting non-brave response to something that a friend did.

 ## Note

Being brave in friendships links very much to the idea of going outside your comfort zone – as explored in the activity *Anxiety and comfort zone* (page 172).

# Feeling hurt

 ## Objective

To consider what hurts us and what we can do when we feel hurt.

 ## What's needed?

Access to the table on the sheet *Feeling hurt* (page 210).

 ## Instructions

- Ask the children what we mean by 'being hurt'. Most children will describe being physically hurt, so you can move the discussion on to consider what being emotionally hurt means.

- Next, ask the children what can trigger hurt. Most children will give specific examples, but in general terms they will include things like:
  - being deliberately physically hurt by someone;
  - being criticised, especially when you think it's unfair;
  - being insulted;
  - hearing that a friend has been saying nasty things about you behind your back;
  - being deliberately excluded – like not being invited to a party;
  - being let down – expecting something from someone that doesn't happen;
  - someone not showing any appreciation for something you've put a lot of effort into;
  - someone falling out with you – especially if you don't really understand why;
  - someone you trust lying to you;
  - someone forgetting your birthday or something else that was important to you;
  - someone ignoring or dismissing your needs;
  - being bullied; and
  - anything else that we think is unfairly unkind that is done to us.
- Ask the children what being emotionally hurt feels like and discuss their ideas. For example, this could include feeling rejected, frustrated, misunderstood, sad, worried, ashamed, unlikeable or excluded, undervalued or underappreciated, wounded, disrespected and/or distressed; feeling that things are unfair or like you've not been not heard. What is hurting you can have a lot of impact and really bother you.
- Ask the children to complete the table on the sheet *Feeling hurt*.
- As a group, discuss ideas about how to deal with being hurt that would be better than those on the sheet – for example:
  - be more forgiving – we all do things that can hurt others, sometimes deliberately but sometimes not;
  - think past the hurt that is felt now and remember when the friendship was good;
  - tell the person how you feel using 'I' messages and give them an opportunity to apologise;
  - remember that even though you feel hurt now, you're unlikely to feel hurt (or as hurt) in the future, when what happened won't seem nearly as important;
  - try to see the funny side;
  - try hard not to ruminate on what happened and get carried away with further negative thinking;
  - try wondering about why your friend might have done what they did – they might just have been grumpy or have had a bad day; and
  - remember that unfair things happen all the time and we can decide to hold on to them or let them go – which will always help us to feel better.

*Extension ideas*

- The children could consider and investigate what forgiveness is, what it does and what helps you to forgive.
- The children could write guidelines for making up after a falling-out.

 *Note*

Although many situations that arise in friendships are best sorted out between the friends themselves, it's important to mention that bullying (deliberately and often repetitively physically or emotionally hurting someone so that they do not feel they can stick up for themselves) almost always needs an adult's help to sort out.

# Conflict

 *Objective*

To consider how to address conflict.

 *What's needed?*

One copy of the sheet *Conflict* (page 211) per pair.

 *Instructions*

- Ask the children what we mean by 'conflict' and discuss their answers (eg, conflict is when people can't agree about something and this creates a problem. People in conflict usually think, feel and/or want different things).
- Give pairs of children a copy of the sheet *Conflict*. Read the paragraph at the top and ask children what their first response to this situation is. (They usually say something like, 'It's silly because they wasted time arguing and didn't get to play.')
- Ask pairs of children to complete the table on the sheet to explore what might be going on for both children and how this conflict could be sorted. There is no one correct answer, but points that often come up include the following:
    - On the surface, they both just want to play the version of marbles they know.
    - Both Sally and Sakshi might be a bit scared they won't understand the new rules or not want to take time to learn them.
    - Sally might be thinking that they should play her version of marbles because the marbles belong to her. Sakshi might believe her uncle's version will be better.

- The conflict is likely to be triggering anger, irritation, frustration, indignance and lots of other feelings that conflict can trigger. These can get in the way of focusing on solutions and tend to make people just focus on 'winning' and getting their way.
  - If a conflict triggers anger, this emotion tends to make people consider their own needs over those of others. The problem solving needed to find suitable ways forward in a conflict is best sorted when everyone is calm.
  - The 'need' of both children was to be entertained by a game of marbles – although they might also have had other needs, such as not wanting to learn something new, wanting control, etc.
  - They could both 'win' this conflict if they listened to each other's thoughts and feelings, made an effort to understand them and focused on how to solve any problems and find a way forward that would help everyone feel comfortable and content.
  - Often remaining in conflict can prevent solutions being found because people are more determined to be right than to be creative in their problem solving.
- Ask the children what helps and what doesn't help in conflicts and anything they think they have learned about them.

 ## *Extension ideas*

- Two children (or one or two adults) could play Sally and Sakshi and 'hot seat' (sit in a chair and answer questions in role) just after they had come in from break. The rest of the children can ask them questions with the aim of solving the conflict.
- The children could consider other conflicts in the same way (eg, two children arguing over the same piece of equipment; a conflict over whose artwork is best; a conflict about the fairness of being given different jobs, such as washing up and drying).
- The children could read Aesop's fable 'The North Wind and the Sun' and consider what message it gives us about conflict.

 ## *Note*

Quite often, children assume that conflict is something negative to be avoided. I always talk about the positive aspects of conflict as a potential opportunity for learning and making beneficial changes.

# Feelings as warnings

 ## *Objective*

To consider when relationships are unhealthy and what to do about them.

# 🔍 *Instructions*

- Explain to the children that not all relationships and friendships are healthy. This can be because within a friendship, there is manipulation, control, bullying, disrespect of boundaries, lack of trust, lack of respect and/or anything else that means the friendship is really unfair or unequal, or causes physical or emotional harm. Explain that this is different from two friends occasionally falling out or having conflict. If a relationship is harmful, it tends to often be harmful. Also make it clear that online relationships can be unhealthy too, not just those where you interact in person.

- Explain to the children that when we feel strong uncomfortable emotions consistently towards someone we know, the chances are that there is something wrong with the friendship or relationship. Ask the children what feelings these might be – for example, dread, anger, powerlessness, confusion, humiliation, anxiety, feeling drained, feeling judged, always feeling like you're the one putting the effort in, being ignored or dismissed, not having any of your needs met, feeling exploited or taken advantage of.

- Add that when relationships make you feel like this – especially if you're being bullied – you will almost always need a trusted adult's help to you work out what to do about this relationship.

- Ask the children to identify at least five adults each that they would turn to if they needed this kind of help. They could draw a picture of them and label them 'my support network'.

- Next, emphasise that if ever they find themselves in a situation they don't feel they can sort themselves, they need to keep telling a trusted adult until someone helps. The best place to start would be with the five adults they have just identified.

# 🌀 *Extension ideas*

- The children could find ways to advertise the Childline number in school to ensure that every child in the school knows about it.

- The children could create a list of questions that could be used to check whether a relationship is unhealthy.

# ✍️ *Note*

I regularly repeat the message that if a child finds themselves in a situation they don't feel they can sort themselves, they need to keep telling adults they trust until one of them helps. The exercise in which the children identify these adults will hopefully keep these people readily available in the child's mind should their help be needed.

# When you think of friends

Friendships are valuable things. Close your eyes and think of some good friends. How do you feel? Here are some words that could help you:

Warm   Enthusiastic   Affectionate   Supported

Joyful   Valued   Liked   Grateful   Pleased   Happy

Proud   Connected   Content   Amused   Inspired

Safe   Relaxed   **Friends** Caring   Admiring

Accepted   Trusting   Encouraged   Appreciated   Calm

Respected   Honoured   Cherished   Understood

Reassured   Rewarded   Playful   Comfortable   Excited

Comforted   Empathetic   Optimistic   Inspired

Loyal   Nurtured   Heartened   Engaged

Affirmed   Fulfilled   Uplifted   Stimulated

Cheerful   Committed   Reassured   Entertained

# The ups and downs of friendship

In a friendship, you could feel ...

| | | |
|---|---|---|
| **Jealous**<br>when a friend spends more time with someone else than you. | **Rejected**<br>when a friend doesn't want to spend time with you. | **Loved**<br>when a friend greets you with a big smile and looks pleased to see you. |
| **Misunderstood**<br>when a friend didn't get what you meant and decided you meant something nasty. | **Compassion**<br>when a friend has hurt themselves falling over and you want to help them feel better again. | **Confused**<br>when a friend does something that you didn't like and you can't understand why. |
| **Grateful**<br>when you appreciate everything you like about a friend and the fact they are your friend and there for you. | **Envious**<br>when a friend gets something for their birthday that you have always wanted. | **Hate**<br>when a friend has done something nasty and it's all you can think about and you've forgotten what you like about them. |
| **Forgiveness**<br>when a friend says sorry for upsetting you and that they didn't mean to. | **Admiration**<br>when your friend achieves something amazing – like painting an incredible picture or scoring a fantastic goal. | **Irritated**<br>when a friend keeps interrupting you so you don't feel like you've been able to say what you needed to say. |
| **Pleasure**<br>when you enjoy playing a fun game together. | **Amused**<br>when a friend tells you something really funny. | **Accepting**<br>when your friend is clearly different from you but you still enjoy each other. |
| **Betrayed**<br>when you hear a friend moaning about you behind your back. | **Hurt**<br>when a friend says something unkind about you. | **Disappointed**<br>when a friend said they would do something and then they don't. |
| **Excited**<br>when you know you're going to spend the day with a friend doing something really fun. | **Comfortable**<br>when you feel so relaxed with your friend, you can completely be yourself. | **Supported**<br>when a friend stands up for you when someone says something nasty about you. |

Which of these feelings help you to feel connected to your friends and which feelings can cause difficulties?

# Tricky behaviours

We all behave in different ways at different times for different reasons. Sometimes our behaviour is kind or helpful to others, and sometimes it's unkind or unhelpful. Consider how you feel when people behave in the following ways.

| | | |
|---|---|---|
| Laughing at you | Telling you lies | Boasting |
| Being unreliable: not doing what they said they would | Turning everything into a competition | Telling someone something you didn't want shared |
| Criticising you | Not helping you when you're upset | Ignoring you |
| Insulting you | Cheating in a game | Being bossy |
| Not listening to you | Often comparing you to someone else | Teasing you |

## Some feelings to choose from:

Disappointed   Upset   Sad   Annoyed   Irritated   Hurt   Rejected   Confused   Indignant

Deflated   Abandoned   Deceived   Insecure   Betrayed   Angry   Furious   Frustrated

Helpless   Mistrustful   Curious   Unconfident   Doubting   Nervous   Wary   Withdrawn

# Jealousy and envy

People often confuse 'jealousy' and 'envy', but the two emotions are slightly different:

- **Envy** is the unenjoyable emotion you can feel when you really want something that someone else has.
- **Jealousy** is the unenjoyable emotion you can feel when you think you are going to lose someone or something to someone else.

Which of these are examples of envy and which are examples of jealousy?

| | |
|---|---|
| I am worried my friend Briony doesn't like me as much as she likes Jodie. I don't think she wants to spend as much time with me as she used to. | Logan always scores goals in our school football match. I have only ever scored one. It upsets me that I am not as good at football as Logan. |
| Zoe got an electric scooter for her birthday. I have always wanted one of those. Every time I see her with it, I wish it was mine. | I used to go to the park with Mason all the time. Now he wants to play computer games with his cousin. I feel really left out and rejected. |

Which of these pieces of advice would be better for when you feel envious and which would be better for when you feel jealous – and which might help with both?

- Accept what you're feeling and know it's a normal part of being human.
- Remember all the good things in your life that you feel grateful for.
- Try really hard not to compare yourself with other people. Only ever compare yourself with how you used to be.
- Remember that friendships change over time and it's normal to move on and make different friends as time goes on.
- Work out what you need and problem solve to work out whether and how you can get it.
- Distract yourself by finding something fun to do.
- Talk to someone you trust about how you're feeling.
- Remember that friends can be shared – it doesn't mean they like you less.
- Anything else?

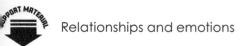

# Feeling lonely

- If you were writing a recipe for feeling lonely, which of these ingredients would you include?

  Left out   Alone   On your own   Misunderstood   Disconnected   Overlooked

  Feeling unliked   Separate   Excluded   Outsider   Withdrawn   Ignored

  Rejected   Lack of support   Not being noticed   Jealous   Sorry for yourself

- Describe loneliness in your own words.

- At which times in a person's life might they be more likely to feel lonely?

- Mark the following out of ten for how well they might work to help someone cope better when they were feeling lonely.

| | | |
|---|---|---|
| ☐ Talk to someone about how they are feeling. | ☐ Remember that everyone feels lonely now and then. | ☐ Plan to do a secret act of kindness for someone. |
| ☐ Think about what they could do to make themselves an even better friend. | ☐ Make a plan of something they could do with a friend tomorrow. | ☐ Decide to join a new club or group that will mean they meet new people. |
| ☐ Remember all the nice things people have said about them in the past. | ☐ Remember that feelings come and then go and they won't feel like this for ever. | ☐ Have a look at some old photos of themselves with friends and family having fun. |
| ☐ Decide to start a conversation with someone as soon as the opportunity arises. | ☐ Make some cards for some friends telling them what they like about them. | ☐ Draw a picture of their favourite people. |
| ☐ Find something relaxing to do. | ☐ Make the effort to be kind to a new person. | ☐ Write down how they feel. |

# What does it feel like to be really listened to?

| | Being really listened to | Not being listened to |
|---|---|---|
| What does a person do to make you feel like you're being really listened to/not being listened to? | | |
| How does this make you feel? | | |
| Why is listening a kind thing to do? | | |

# Being a good listener

Some of us have learned to listen better than others but nearly all of us could be better at it. Which of the following things do you think would help a person feel like they are being really listened to and which do you think would make them feel like they were not being listened to?

| | |
|---|---|
| Looking at the person's face. | Making encouraging noises, such as 'Mmm' and 'Uh huh.' |
| Looking at the clock while they are speaking. | Looking interested. |
| Telling the person that they must be exaggerating. | Asking the person questions about what they are saying. |
| Interrupting the person speaking. | Feeding back what you think the speaker might be feeling. |
| Changing the conversation so that it becomes more about you. | Allowing some silent moments for the person speaking to think. |
| Really paying attention. | Looking like what they are telling you is irritating you. |

Do you think you're a good listener?

# Being brave in friendships

Sometimes we need to be brave in our friendships. Which of these do you think are brave and which are not? Complete the table below to show what you think.

| A Telling a friend that something they said triggered you to feel a bit angry. | B Disagreeing with a friend over different opinions. |
|---|---|
| C Telling a friend that you like their painting just as it is when you actually have an idea about how they could make it even better. | D Telling a friend about something that is really upsetting you that you would not want everyone to know. |
| E Standing up for a friend who a few people are picking on. | F Saying sorry for something you did that caused your friend to become upset. |
| G Explaining to a friend that you find it difficult when they sometimes ignore you. | H Listening to a friend tell you they need you to ask before you borrow their things, and choosing to respect this and do what they said. |
| I Teasing someone you like, just because everyone else was. | J Being the first to reach out to a friend after you have fallen out. |

| Brave | Not brave |
|---|---|
|  |  |

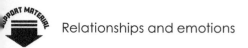

# Feeling hurt

- Rudra and Henry had been friends since the start of infant school. When Henry laughed at Rudra because he had started bird-spotting with his dad, Rudra never spoke to Henry again.
- Mila could not forgive Grace for deciding to go ice skating with her cousin rather than coming to her birthday party. Mila told everyone how horrible Grace was.
- Jacob laughed at the present Tom gave him and said it was babyish. Tom told Jacob that he hated him and that he'd get him back some time.

|   | What triggered the hurt? | What did the hurt person do? | What could the hurt person do instead that would have been better? |
|---|---|---|---|
| A |   |   |   |
| B |   |   |   |
| C |   |   |   |

# Conflict

Sally brought some marbles to school and asked Sakshi if she'd like to play marbles with her at breaktime. They were both excited about this idea. When breaktime arrived, Sally got the marbles ready and told Sakshi how to play. Sakshi had played marbles with her uncle and insisted that Sally had got the rules wrong. Sakshi wanted to play the way her uncle had shown her, but Sally didn't like Sakshi's version and wanted to follow her own rules. They argued all breaktime and went back to lessons without playing a single game of marbles.

| | Sally | Sakshi |
|---|---|---|
| What does she want? | | |
| What do you think she is thinking? | | |
| What do you think she is feeling? | | |
| What do you think she needs? | | |
| How could they sort this conflict? | | |

# Chapter 7

# EMOTIONS AND LEARNING

## What's in this chapter?

This chapter includes activities that explore the emotions associated with learning, challenge and extending beyond our comfort zones. It acknowledges that the process of learning – and many things worth achieving – often need us to take the risk of feeling some uncomfortable emotions.

## *Activity notes*

- You will find a description of each of the activities in the first part of this chapter, followed by the relevant activity sheets.
- Activities are described with an objective, instructions, an indication of whether any further resources are needed (including printable resources from this book) and at least one suggested extension idea.
- The activities involve a variety of teaching and learning techniques, including discussion prompts, quizzes, agreement spectrums, sorting activities, drama activities, games and lessons that use printable worksheets.
- The age that each activity is suitable for has not been stipulated. Most activities could be simplified for younger children or adjusted to be more challenging for older children.

## Emotions and learning: an overview
### *Schools are full of emotions!*

As learning in schools seems to be about thinking and using our brains, it might be easy to think that making links between emotions and learning is not particularly useful. However, lessons – and school generally – usually involve a lot of emotion. A busy classroom will be full of emotions. For example, a child could be:

DOI: 10.4324/9781032690773-8

- excited about breaktime or an activity coming up;
- angry about being told off;
- irritated because their pencil keeps snapping;
- envious because someone else has been praised a lot by the teacher for what they have achieved;
- feeling hatred towards someone calling them nasty names;
- worried about having forgotten their homework or not understanding the work properly;
- feeling empathy with someone who is struggling;
- feeling rejected because a friend has just ignored them;
- full of admiration for someone else who has done something really well;
- grumpy because they're too hot, hungry or tired; or
- feeling apathetic and not wanting to do anything.

It's no surprise that many emotions are experienced in schools, as they are busy places where children and adults spend a lot of their time, with many different things happening each day and numerous social interactions.

## *The emotions of learning*

Emotions are not just triggered by the hustle and bustle of school life; there are also emotions associated more specifically with learning. This is because learning requires us to take risks, maintain motivation and concentration, enjoy success and cope with failures – all within the busy, noisy setting of a classroom. Some emotions hinder learning and others help. For example, in any lesson, a child might feel:

- hopeful that they will produce a really good piece of work;
- anxious about failure;
- confused about not understanding something;
- satisfied and proud of doing something well;
- shame if they get something wrong or make a mistake;
- embarrassed if they answer a question incorrectly;
- joyful and surprised if they succeed in something they initially really struggled to do;
- curious about something interesting;
- nervous about answering a question in front of the class;
- bored if the lesson is too hard or too easy;
- frustrated when they keep trying but just can't achieve success; or
- irritated if a friend stops them from being able to concentrate.

These examples illustrate that there is rarely any learning experience that does not trigger emotion.

## *Being aware of the emotions around learning*

It can be helpful to explore the emotions that are triggered in lessons so that the children further understand what they might struggle with. Raising awareness of the emotions of learning can help children embrace beneficial risk, help them cope when they find something difficult, ensure that they welcome mistakes as the learning opportunities they are and help them develop healthier learning habits

# Emotions that help us learn

It's also important to remember that some emotions enhance learning – those that help us to stay focused, make us pay attention and assist us in remembering things. As a teacher, I know that triggering surprise, enjoyment, curiosity, hope, anticipation, intrigue, determination, joy, enthusiasm and pride helps my pupils learn more effectively. Research (Fredrickson 2001) also tells us there is more creativity and willingness to learn when we're happy!

## Activities

## At the start of a lesson ...

 *Objective*

To reflect on feelings about learning.

🔍 *Instructions*

- Explain to the children that you're going to read out some sentences. If they agree with the sentence, they should give a 'thumbs up' sign; if they disagree, they should give a 'thumbs down' sign. If they are unsure, they can indicate this by positioning their thumb horizontally.
- Do a test run with statements such as: 'The sky is blue today'; 'I think kittens are cute'; 'I love tomatoes' etc.
- Explain to the children that you will use the thumb gauge to see how they feel about lessons and learning.
- Choose one or two statements from the below to begin this exploration of lessons and learning. Each statement can prompt further questions – some examples of extra questions are given below. 'At the start of lessons ...':
  ○ I am always interested to see what we are going to do. (Do you feel excitement at the start of a lesson or something else?)

- I am sometimes a bit worried I won't understand what we are going to do. (What can we do when we don't understand?)
- I always feel ready to learn. (What can happen sometimes that might mean we don't feel ready to learn?)
- I always want to do things as well as I can. (Do we always do things really well? Why might we not do as well as usual some days?)
- I always want to try hard. (What helps us try hard? Do you think a teacher cares more about children getting everything correct or trying as hard as they can?)
- I get a bit worried that I will make a mistake. (Why might we worry about making mistakes? Are mistakes 'bad' things?)
- I like that we are going to learn something new. (What does it feel like when we learn how to do something for the first time?)

 ## *Extension ideas*

- You could create a checklist for a positive mindset at the start of lessons – for example: At the start of lessons ...:
  - I will accept I might make mistakes.
  - I will ask for help if I don't understand.
  - I will try hard to listen and work out what I need to do.
  - I will try hard even if it looks difficult.'

 ## *Note*

This activity has a very similar learning objectives to some of the activities below but is more suited to younger children. This activity can be used repeatedly at the start of different lessons if you change the statements so they are not about lessons in general, but instead specifically about the lesson that is about to happen.

# Learning something new

 ## *Objective*

To consider the emotional journey of learning something new.

 ## *What's needed?*

Access to the information on the sheet *Learning something new* (page 223).

## Instructions

- Let the children see the information on the sheet *Learning something new* and discuss what the timeline is showing.
- Ask pairs of children to discuss the questions on the sheet.
- Ask the children what it feels like when you're not very good at something; then ask them what being successful and achieving something feels like and contrast the two.
- Extend the discussion by asking the following questions:
  - Does being good at something feel better than not being good at something? Ask them to explain their answers.
  - To get good at something, do you nearly always have to put up with uncomfortable emotions?
  - If you could not put up with uncomfortable emotions, what do you think would happen?
  - Do we feel more enjoyment when we succeed at something easy or something difficult?
  - Why is it sometimes hard to stay determined to get good at something?
  - What are we feeling when we give up?

## Extension ideas

- The children could label some emotions that Ben might have felt at different parts on his timeline.
- The children could think about the 'ingredients' of success and possibly write a recipe for success.
- The children could draw their own timeline for something new that they learned this week – or better still, give them a difficult task that requires learning (eg, juggling, knitting, a dance routine, playing a tune, remembering a poem off by heart, tying a specific knot) and ask them to record how they feel at different moments as they try to learn it.

## Note

I have found this activity very effective for raising children's awareness of the emotions linked with learning. After completing this activity, we ended up using the shorthand question, 'Have you dipped below the line?' when children were struggling with the emotions affiliated with learning.

# What might you feel?

 **Objective**

To consider why learning can trigger uncomfortable emotions.

 **What's needed?**

One copy of the sheet *What might you feel?* (page 224) per child.

 **Instructions**

- Tell the children that whenever any of us are asked to learn something new, we can feel a mixture of emotions depending on the task.

- Ask the children to think of a lesson they don't always look forward to and ask them how they might feel when this lesson starts. Also ask them what thoughts they might have and how these influence what they end up feeling.

- Explain that – particularly with lessons we find difficult – we can end up thinking unhelpful thoughts and feel uncomfortable emotions that can put us off trying before we have begun. These thoughts and emotions certainly don't encourage us.

- Give each child a copy of the sheet *What might you feel?* and read through the occurrences in the left-hand column. Explain that each of these can mean we have to put up with unenjoyable emotions.

- Ask the children to complete the right-hand column of the table.

- Once all children have completed this, ask them to consider what the best response would be to each of the things happening (and why what you feel might prevent someone from responding in this way).

- Ask the group to discuss how feelings can affect how enthusiastic we feel about learning.

 **Extension ideas**

- Ask the children to complete the following sentences:
    - If you feel X about making a mistake, remember...
    - Learning can sometimes feel difficult, but ...
    - Things that help us to get better at learning include ...
    - The good thing about being challenged is ...
    - If someone gives us a suggestion about how to improve our work, we could ...

 **Note**

Helping children tune into their emotional awareness and attitudes to learning can in itself create more determination to engage, accept mistakes and be motivated.

# Getting ready to learn

 ## Objective

To consider what helps us develop a healthy attitude to learning.

 ## What's needed?

Access to the information on the sheet *Getting ready to learn* (page 225).

 ## Instructions

- Explain to the children that when we are asked to learn something in school, sometimes we are in a better place to engage with learning than others. Ask the children what can affect how keen we are to learn and create a list from their suggestions.

- Give the children access to the information on the sheet *Getting ready to learn* and ask how many of these things are on their list. Are there any missing? Are there any additions?

- Acknowledge that quite a lot of things can affect our attitude to learning – some that we can do something about and some that we can't change (other than how we think about them).

- Ask pairs of children to complete the task at the bottom of the sheet and feedback on their thoughts. If you're happy to, explain that if they can make some suggestions that are easy to implement, you will aim to act on these as far as possible.

 ## Extension ideas

- The children could create, 'Are you ready to learn?' leaflets with advice on approaching learning with a resourceful attitude.

 ## Note

Sometimes in this activity, children make some unachievable suggestions, such as 'Make all lessons like a computer game.' At other times, however, they will make suggestions that are quite achievable, such as including some relaxation breathing at the start of lessons; acknowledging feelings or readiness to 'have a go' once a task has been introduced; promoting mutual encouragement in lessons that children acknowledge they find more challenging; introducing fewer difficult tasks just before lunch etc.

# Attitudes to mistakes

 *Objective*

To consider and possibly reframe how we think about making mistakes.

 *What's needed?*

'Agree' and 'Disagree' signs, and the means to stick them in two places some distance apart, so that everyone can see them.

## Instructions

- Create a space to use as an agreement spectrum by sticking one sign that says 'Agree' on one side of a room and 'Disagree' on the other, so there is space for the children to stand at any point along the imaginary spectrum. Explain that you are going to read out statements and that the children are to stand in a position that represents how they feel about each statement. Add that it is okay for them to stand in the middle if they are undecided or unsure of what they think.

- Read out the following statements one at a time and invite children to find the position that represents how they feel about the statement. After people have found their position invite discussion by asking, 'Would anyone like to say something about where they're stood?'

  - Everyone makes mistakes.
  - I can remember the last mistake I made.
  - I remember how I felt when I last made a mistake.
  - I experience strong uncomfortable emotions when I make a mistake.
  - I can be really hard on myself when I make a mistake.
  - The 'voice' in my head (my thoughts) are really mean to me when I make a mistake.
  - Making mistakes sometimes puts me off continuing what I was doing.
  - I would rather avoid doing something than risk making a mistake.
  - I see mistakes as failures.
  - I think making mistakes can make a task more interesting.
  - When I correct a mistake, I usually feel an enjoyable emotion.
  - I always put more effort in after I have made a mistake.
  - I think I learn more in tasks where I make a mistake at first than tasks where I make no mistakes.
  - Mistakes can be an opportunity.

- Continue the discussion by asking pairs of children to write a list of reasons:

  - why mistakes can be a problem; and
  - why they can be an opportunity.

Discuss the lists the children create as a whole group. Finish the discussion by asking pairs of children to think of the most persuasive argument they can for mistakes being a beneficial thing and ask volunteers to share these.

 ## Extension ideas

- The children could look for sayings about mistakes on the internet and reflect on their messages.
- The children could consider the 'voice in their head' and what positive things it could say immediately after they have made a mistake.
- The children could consider what the risks are when learning something new (eg, getting frustrated; making mistakes; making a fool of yourself; feeling shame, which makes you tell yourself you're useless; comparing yourself with others; feeling the discomfort of not being in control; others laughing at you or mocking your efforts) and what emotions they trigger.
- The children could create ads selling the benefits of making mistakes.

 ## Note

I nearly always find that children do not like making mistakes and that you have to work hard to create a culture that truly celebrates mistakes as opportunities.

# Feeling positive about learning

 ## Objective

To consider healthy attitudes towards learning.

 ## Instructions

- Ask groups of three children to create a set of guidelines for learning, using the prompts: 'mistakes', 'effort', 'comparisons', 'encouragement', 'determination', 'understanding', 'concentration', 'uncomfortable emotions' and 'success'. Explain that these are just prompts and they don't necessarily need to use them all.
- Share each group's ideas and develop some guidelines for the whole class. Some ideas you might like to share to prompt further thinking include the following:
  - We should try really hard not to see mistakes as failures. The idea of failing can trigger feelings of inadequacy and shame, which can be very unenjoyable; but we need to see and feel the benefits of mistakes.

- Learning can mean that we have to endure some uncomfortable emotions, but this is true of many things worth doing.
- It's helpful to develop a 'give it a go' attitude, whatever the task and however difficult we think it might be. Try not to be scared of having a go at something you think you will find difficult.
- It's not always helpful to compare what we have done with what other people have done. It's better if we just focus on our own work and our own achievements.
- It's helpful to develop pride in the effort we put in and our willingness to have a go – even with things we know we are not naturally talented at. In fact, putting effort into tasks we know that we usually find difficult is more praiseworthy than putting effort into activities we find really easy.
- It can be great to encourage other people to learn to create a supportive classroom.

 ## Extension ideas

- The children could create motivational posters based on the guidelines they produce.
- The children could list aspects of learning that they struggle with and work in pairs to consider how to overcome these.

 ## Note

I ask children to create catchphrases to continuously motivate learning positively – for example, 'Mistakes are great!'

# Anxiety and learning questionnaire

 ## Objective

To consider which aspects of learning cause most worry and what could be done about them.

 ## What's needed?

Access to the questions on the sheet *Anxiety and learning questionnaire* (page 226); scrap paper as graffiti sheets for feedback.

 ## Instructions

- Explain to the children that they are going to interview each other about worries they might have in lessons and ask them to find a partner they would be comfortable sharing this information with.

- Give access to the questions on the sheet *Anxiety and learning questionnaire* and ask the children to interview their partners while noting down anything that triggers worry.
- Write the following titles on different sheets of scrap paper and spread them out across tables in the room.
  - Different subjects
  - Who you sit next to
  - Being uncomfortable
  - Being put on the spot
  - Group work
  - Seeking help
  - Completing work
  - Quality of work
  - Concentration
  - Making mistakes
  - Others criticising what you do
  - Being bored
  - Finding work too easy or too hard
  - Reading aloud
  - Anything else?
- Ask the children to feed back on the sheet any issues they discovered from interviewing their partners, without using names.
- Look at the sheets one at a time as a whole class with the aim of identifying the things people struggle with and any problems, and create a list of these.
- Allocate different problems and issues to smaller groups to discuss what could be done to help.

 ## *Extension ideas*

- The children could consider what makes classmates helpful and unhelpful when it comes to learning.

## *Note*

Because this activity gives feedback (nearly) anonymously, it can give any teacher food for thought!

# Learning something new

This timeline shows the emotions that Ben felt when he learned how to do long division.

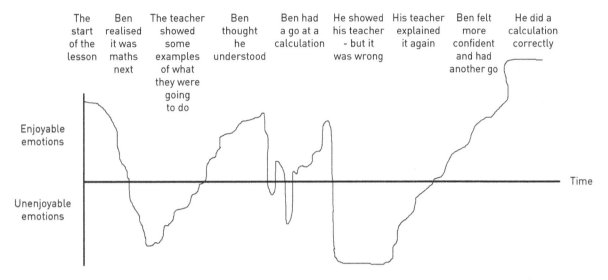

See if you can work out the answers to these questions:

- It was breaktime just before the maths lesson. Do you think Ben enjoyed his breaktime?

- Do you think Ben likes maths?

- Do you think Ben's confidence grew as his teacher explained what he needed to do?

- When Ben had a go himself at doing a calculation, do you think he was certain he had got it right?

- How do you think Ben felt when he realised he had made a mistake?

- When did Ben feel the most enjoyable emotion?

Emotions and learning

# What might you feel?

Your teacher explained what you're doing in this lesson and you are getting on with it. How would you feel if ...

| | |
|---|---|
| You didn't really understand what you are meant to do | |
| You're taking longer than everyone else to complete the task | |
| You make a mistake | |
| Someone criticises what you've done so far | |
| You don't feel that you're doing a very good job | |
| Your teacher just asked you to make improvements | |
| You realise you've done it all incorrectly so far | |
| You think it's boring | |
| You're finding it really difficult | |
| You keep making mistakes and don't seem to be able to get it right | |

**Feelings you could choose from:**

Shocked  Overwhelmed  Unsettled  Intimidated  Annoyed  Silly  Excited  Dread

Frustrated  Ashamed  Enthusiastic  Disappointed  Embarrassed  Dismissive  Uninterested

Bothered  Nervous  Interested  Bored  Foolish  Angry  Surprised  Irritated  Scared  Anxious

Daunted  Upset  Determined  Undeserved  Disengaged  Accepting  Happy  Pleased

# Getting ready to learn

When we are about to start a lesson and learn something new, our attitude can be affected by a lot of different things, such as:

- our mood;
- how much we like the subject;
- how easy or difficult we think we will find the task;
- how interesting the lesson is;
- the way the lesson is being taught (eg, reading, writing, drama, drawing, discussing, working on your own);
- how much success or failure we've had in the past;
- whether we enjoy the opportunity of being challenged or we see it as a big problem to overcome;
- whether we think of learning as enjoyable or it makes us anxious;
- how much we compare ourselves with others;
- how much we want to improve;
- how important we think learning is;
- how we think what we do will be judged by others;
- how comfortable we feel physically (eg, not too hot, tired or hungry); and
- what else is going on in our life or school day.

Can you think of anything else that could affect our attitudes to learning?

> If you were giving a teacher some advice on how to help their class be ready to learn, what would that advice be?

# Anxiety and learning questionnaire

Let's think specifically about feeling anxious or worried about things in lessons. While a little worry can drive you to do better, too much can occupy your thoughts and distract you from learning. Answer the following questions to see if any of the following things about lessons cause you to worry at all:

- Do you dread some subjects? Explain your answer.
- Do you dread some lessons – perhaps because you might not like who you sit next to or where you sit in the classroom?
- How do you feel when you are put on the spot by teacher asking you a question or asking to do something without warning?
- Does working in groups sometimes cause you difficulties?
- Do you sometimes feel too worried to ask for help?
- Do you worry that the teacher might not help you even if you ask for it?
- Does the idea of not finishing your work in time bother you?
- Do you sometimes worry that you might not understand the lesson?
- Do you sometimes worry that your work won't be good enough?
- Do you sometimes worry that you'll get distracted – by other classmates, for example – so you can't focus or concentrate?
- Are you scared someone might tease you about the quality of your work?
- If you make a mistake, how do you feel?
- Do you sometimes worry that your work is not neat enough?
- If nobody notices when you do really well in a lesson, does this annoy you?
- Do you compare what you have done with others and give yourself a hard time if your work is not as good – or if you think it's not as good?
- What happens if you find a lesson boring?
- How do you react if the work is too easy?
- How do you react if the work is too hard?
- Do you mind being asked to read aloud?
- Is there anything else that causes you to worry about lessons?

## Final question:

- If any of these things causes you to worry or become anxious, does the worrying drive you to try harder or does it get in the way of you learning?

# Chapter 8

# EMOTIONAL INTELLIGENCE AND SUPPORTING BEHAVIOUR

## What's in this chapter?

This chapter explores how children's behaviour can be supported using emotional intelligence. It explains how behind most challenging behaviour there is strong emotion (eg, overwhelm or anxiety). It suggests some proactive and reactive tools for supporting children's behaviour and addressing their underlying needs, with the aim of preventing behaviours getting stuck 'on repeat'. It also invites any adult who works with children to look at their own thinking and emotional reactions when facing behaviour that challenges, in order to become more conscious of those responses and gain even greater control (and therefore flexibility) over how they approach challenging behaviour.

## Supporting behaviour that challenges
### Reasons for children's unhelpful and challenging behaviours

There are several reasons why some children engage in unhelpful behaviours, but it is always helpful to see behaviour first and foremost as communicating a need. Even the most low-level behaviours are probably communicating something such as boredom, tiredness, a bad mood, over-challenge, insecurity a need for connection or discomfort. Children also engage in some behaviours simply because they have not yet been taught, learned or accepted that a particular behaviour is unhelpful.

DOI: 10.4324/9781032690773-9

When children engage more frequently in more extreme behaviours, however, these can be driven by far deeper issues relating to self-worth and/or a perceived need to protect themselves. Such children, in my experience, show many of the following:

- They tend not to trust easily.
- They are very easily triggered to engage in extremely unhelpful or damaging behaviours.
- They are often hypervigilant.
- They 'test' adults and try hard to push them away.
- They can become extremely controlling.
- They experience negative emotions more extremely and/or frequently than most.
- They can 'zone out'.
- They can be extremely competitive and can interpret others' success as their own failure.
- They may demand constant attention.
- They may have an extremely small comfort zone and easily feel over-challenged.
- They may have very low expectations of themselves and others.
- They can become overwhelmed and anxious extremely easily.
- They may resist showing vulnerability and/or asking for help.
- They can be very self-absorbed and unable to empathise.
- They have a very poor understanding of themselves – their emotions, needs and how their behaviour can affect others.
- They exhibit self-loathing in a variety of ways – some directly, others indirectly.

## Attachment theory

When I first learned about Bowlby's (1958) attachment theory, it made absolutely sense to me in evolutionary terms: that the environment into which a child is born influences the wiring of their brain for optimum survival. If a child is born into a reasonably stable, nurturing, attentive and secure environment, they can metaphorically relax and trust others to steadfastly meet their needs. They therefore have no need to engage in self-protective behaviours as they feel safe and fully trust that the adults in their lives have their best interests at heart, and will therefore be generally compliant.

The reasons why a child might end up with tendencies such as those outlined above are many and varied, but often relate to trauma they have already experienced in their lives. They might have had fearful experiences of chaos, extreme unpredictability and/or violence; their physical needs might not have been met; they might have been shamed, rejected and/or ignored, and/or made to feel that their existence was not overly welcomed. Some of these behaviours can also be the result of excessively anxious and over-protective adults in their lives, which can also leave children with exaggerated feelings of threat and poor self-reliance.

Such trauma understandably results in powerful emotions that can often lead a child to engage in controlling and defensive behaviours. The child makes ineffective attempts, through this behaviour, to make themselves feel safe and secure using strategies that might have had some kind of protective impact in the past, but are generally unhelpful and damaging now. To help children learn new ways of managing their emotions and behaviour requires patience and genuine care. The most effective help involves viewing a child's emotions and behaviour as a mystery to be solved, not something to be oppressed.

## Helping children with trauma

When working with children with trauma, there are no magic wands or quick wins. 'Progress' – in the form of beneficial changes in behaviour – is nearly always slow, often involves tiny steps at a time and can take months.

I nearly always find that I need to convince a child that I am consistent, reliable, available, present and completely accepting of them – 'warts and all' – if I am to have any chance of securing their engagement. Eventually, this means the child relaxes enough with me so they can let me help them.

## *Explore your reactions*

The behaviours that can potentially trigger strong reactions in adults tend to include defiance, emotional escalation and dysregulation, insults and rejection, and sometimes low-level but persistent unhelpful behaviours. How we react to these behaviours varies from person to person and from day to day, but reflecting on them can highlight how unsettled certain behaviours can sometimes leave us. We might sometimes find ourselves caught emotionally off-guard, which is likely render us less able to respond in the best possible way.

Although no response towards children's behaviour that challenges is guaranteed to help, it is important that adults remain as calm and predictable as possible. If children – especially those prone to dysregulation – are eventually going to learn more helpful behaviours, they need to feel safe and secure with the adults who work with them. This requires a calm and accepting approach towards all aspects of a child's emotions and behaviour. Children need to feel that all of them (including all emotions and behaviour) can be tolerated, managed and accepted as communicating something.

# Our reactions towards behaviour

When I help teachers to consider their emotional (and intellectual) reactions to dealing with behaviour that potentially challenges, it often becomes clear that most people who work with children do not generally do this. When you make your reactions more conscious, you not only have more control over them, but also become calmer and more consistent in how you respond.

It is quite common for teachers to admit to an adrenaline rush, feelings of inadequacy, concern over how colleagues might judge how they deal with the situation and a strong feeling of rejection in the face of some children's behaviour. Acknowledging these feelings and realising that they are quite typical can help; as can having concrete tools to use that enable you to respond calmly.

## Different approaches to behaviour

Historically, children's behaviour tended to be suppressed using authoritarian approaches that made them scared of the adults in their lives. This approach involved punishment, blame and shame. It also dictated what children had to do and meant they had no voice or impact in what happened. This might have worked to control behaviour, but it did not help children learn how to self-regulate.

More recently, there has been a tendency for some parents and carers to be more passive or 'hands-off' in their approach to behaviour. This approach is also unhelpful, as it allows children to do whatever they wish and ignores the fact that they don't always behave in ways that are helpful. It means children are left without guidance. Another observation I have made about adults who are passive with respect to children's behaviour is that when rattled by their child's extreme behaviour, they can revert suddenly to authoritarian measures.

In the main, I find that parents/carers and others who are responsible for children rarely reflect upon which approach they adopt and there can be confusion about what the best approach should be. As with most things, a healthy ground can be found in a middle way: the authoritative approach.

# Authoritarian approaches

I often use the analogy of the speed camera to explain why authoritarian approaches are not in a child's best interests and an authoritative approach is better. Take the example of the person in a rush, driving from A to B. They are driving fast, over the speed limit, until they see a speed camera. For the duration of the time it takes to drive past the camera, the driver reduces their speed. But as soon as they are past the camera, they begin speeding again. The camera acts to suppress the speeding temporarily but does not address the attitude that allows it to happen.

A more authoritative approach would help the driver to understand why speeding is dangerous. It would explain how driving above the speed limit increases the risk of fatalities should an accident happen. Speeding also makes accidents more likely. Securing full 'buy-in' to the reasons for the more beneficial behaviour means the driver is more likely to learn and be motivated to self-regulate.

## *The authoritative approach*

The aim of the authoritative approach is to teach children positive and beneficial ways of behaving so they eventually learn to self-regulate. It recognises that children sometimes do things that are unhelpful and aims to teach them better ways of behaving when this happens. It does not use blame, shame or punishment, but works with children to understand what might be going on for them to trigger their unhelpful behaviours and points out better ways of behaving in a non-judgemental way, as if you're problem-solving together. It assumes that the adult has greater responsibility (and wisdom) in addressing the behaviour, but it does not use the power imbalance between adult and child to dominate and control. The authoritative approach makes it clear that it is down to the adults in a child's life to help them disengage in unhelpful behaviours through guidance that develops the child's understanding of their behaviour.

The authoritative approach uses emotions to be curious, kind and empathetic when a child engages in unhelpful behaviour. It helps the child not only become more self-aware, but also understand the effect of their behaviour on others. The tools in the next section can be used to adopt the authoritative, emotionally intelligent approach towards behaviour that challenges.

## Tools for supporting children's behaviour using emotional intelligence
### *Being the soothing, steady 'rock' that children need when dysregulated*

When a child has escalated emotionally, I find they need more than ever for their responsible adults to remain a calm and soothing presence. This is most obviously true of young children who have become overwhelmed with emotion, as they have not yet learned how to regulate themselves and need an adult to help soothe them. This is also true, however, of older children who have not been given the opportunity to develop the tools of self-soothing so that uncomfortable emotions always seem insurmountable and tend to trigger strong reactions.

The consistently steady and comforting presence of an adult eventually helps a child understand that their 'enormous' emotions can be managed, as you effectively help them see that these can be endured. Staying calm communicates, 'I am clearly okay, so it is obvious we will cope with this situation.'

Once children start to endure their uncomfortable emotions with less panic, they can become comfortable enough to let you help them make sense of them: to understand what their need is and to work out better ways of dealing with them.

## When children escalate

I find that little guidance is given to adults about what to do when older children have a tantrum. We tend to assume that older children who behave in a way that's more typical of younger children are doing so wilfully and 'should know better'. Children do not enjoy emotional outbursts or tantrums. It's better to understand that dysregulated older children have missed out on the tools they need to regulate themselves and are in a state of genuine distress. Once I fully acknowledged their distress, I knew they really needed my help and understood more than ever that I cared.

To soothe a distressed child, aside from remaining calm and accepting, you could:

- remind the child that you care about them;
- gently remind them that you're there to help when they're ready. You can occasionally ask, 'Are you ready for my help yet?' so they know you're still holding them in your awareness;
- give them the time and space they need to calm themselves if they won't yet accept help;
- acknowledge and show acceptance of their distress – for example, say, 'I can see how upset you are';
- maintain boundaries as these also help a child feel safe. Don't back down from a request – even if it is what triggered the child's upset – and don't allow dangerous behaviours;
- rub the top of their back gently in a circular motion if they are comfortable with touch;
- hug them sideways with a hand on each of their upper arms; and
- use a calm soothing voice that implies sympathy and care.

## *Linking emotions to behaviour*

When a child is struggling with behaviour, it is useful to speculate about what they might be feeling, as this will often be driving how they are behaving. This can make a child feel extremely 'seen', connected to and cared about. It also increases their awareness of the impact of their emotions; helps them link their emotions to their triggers and behaviour; helps them focus inwardly on what is going on for them; and can help slow things down so that impulsive reactions become less likely.

As well as speculating about what a child might be feeling, you can also acknowledge and validate it. There are a few tools you can use to do this, such as:

- using the term, 'I wonder if ...' (eg, 'I wonder if you're feeling a bit upset/rejected/frustrated etc because Harry didn't play with you?') Don't worry if you 'wonder' incorrectly – the child will soon correct you;
- speculating with, 'I think you're feeling a strong emotion. Am I right?';
- empathising out loud (eg, 'I would be feeling really sad if I had just lost my toy');
- asking the child to reflect upon where in their body they are feeling the emotion that's visiting them;
- verbalising any observations you have when a child struggles (eg, 'I notice you always start to look uncomfortable when it's time to go out to play');
- acknowledging and validating emotions (eg, 'I can see you're angry,' or, 'I understand why you're upset. I would be too'); and
- using affective statements relating to how the child feels (eg, 'I feel sad that you feel sad. I hope you will let me help you soon').

Something else to note is that some children are extremely reluctant to speculate about their emotions in front of their peers – especially older children. I therefore tended to help children connect with their emotions individually and quietly with others out of earshot.

## There are always opportunities to learn

I remember a child once asking me, 'Why are you always banging on about my emotions, Miss? It's really annoying!' In my early years of teaching, I might have reacted in a defeated way. Instead, I saw this as an opportunity to open up a discussion about how emotions link to what we think and how we behave, and to explain that when we can notice and understand them better, it helps make everything easier. The child did seem to accept this as solid reasoning for me 'banging on about emotions'! I think many things children do, including anything dismissive or rejecting, is potentially an opportunity to learn.

## *Managing children's shame well*

Shame (an emotion that can leave you feeling worthless) is a powerful and difficult emotion for most people to endure. Some children experience it more frequently and strongly than others, and children with trauma can experience it so it becomes all-consuming and will easily trigger extreme reactions and unhelpful behaviours.

Although some shame is unavoidable, there are things adults can do to reduce its impact when it comes to supporting children who are struggling with their emotions and the resulting behaviour. These include:

- not challenging a child so much beyond their capabilities as to cause overwhelm and too much anxiety;
- quickly observing when a child's shame starts to be triggered because they are finding something too challenging and stepping in to help break down a task into smaller, more manageable steps;
- never lingering on any kind of negative feedback (eg, having to tell a child not to do something, explaining that a child has made a mistake and swiftly moving on to make it clear you still value them – for example, by commenting on something they must be proud of or stating you enjoyed something they did); and
- using social stories to explain why some behaviours are difficult and make situations worse. This helps a child consider their behaviour, but the social story distances it enough not to trigger shame.

## Social stories

I frequently use simple social stories to describe a child's behaviour to them. I might tell them about a child who used to throw his maths book across the room every time he found something a bit difficult. Invariably, the child does not realise I am describing them and often offers some well-considered advice about what that child should do instead!

## *Avoiding defiance*

When a child refuses to do what has been requested of them, it's usually because they have a hidden need. It could be that they are actually nervous, insecure, overwhelmed and out of their depth, and thus feel the need to take aggressive, defensive or controlling measures. You can explore this using the tools described in *Linking emotions to behaviour* (page 233).

If a child is defiant and speculating that what is going on for them does not work, there are other tools you can use to reduce the likelihood of emotional escalation. These tools help you avoid locking horns with the defiance and give the child time and space to feel more secure to find a better way forward.

Here are some tools you can use:

- Be very clear about the request/next step you need the child to take. Keep this as simple as possible – for example, 'Go and sit in the reading area', 'You need to pick those up' or 'I need to talk with you.'
- Deliver your request and then if a child refuses to carry it out, say brightly and breezily, 'When you're ready.' I have used this many times. It's easy to keep things calm when using this tool, as it is so simple. It also helps you keep any other children in the room 'on board', as you can calmly state, 'X knows what she needs to do. She's struggling at the moment but she'll do it when she's ready.'
- Hide your request within a false choice. If you wish the child to start writing, for example, you can ask, 'Would you like to write with your pencil or my special pencil?'
- Another way of using language to avoid defiance is to use the negotiation of 'when … then …' – for example, 'When you have put the paints away, then we can go out to play.'
- Keep the energy you direct towards the child being defiant minimal. Let them know you're still there for them and acknowledge you know they are struggling, but focus most of your attention on other children and leave the struggling child with time and space to reconsider.
- Linked to the idea of minimal energy is to deliver requests quickly and turn away, giving the (almost arrogant) air that you have no doubt they will do what's been requested of them. This kind of delivery leaves little opportunity for the child to challenge.
- State that you are happy to help the child carry out what has been requested of them, if appropriate. For example, if you have asked a child to pick up some books they have knocked on the floor, once they start picking them up, offer to help them. This offer can help instigate a change of heart from the child, makes the child feel supported and can help demonstrate there are no residual 'hard feelings'.
- Another tool I have used to remove a child who is being defiant from a situation (and have repeatedly been surprised by its effectiveness) is to say, 'I'd like a word with you over there/in the classroom/in the reading corner,' and then take myself over to where I stated I wanted a word. Resist the urge to look back at them or check in on them. It sometimes takes a (very long) two minutes, but it has never failed to eventually trigger the child to come and find me. Their curiosity always kicks in. Of course, you have to think of something to say to them once they come to you. I found humour was often enough.
- If you have another adult in the room and a child has dug their heels in with you, a change of staff can often 'break their stubborn trance' enough to enable the child to reconsider what they're going to do next.

- Another tool that always worked for me is to give a request and instead of saying 'please', say 'thank you'. 'Please' is very like a request. 'Thank you' conveys a sense of *fait accompli* and seems more assertive.

## *Rejection and insults*

It is imperative that adults working with children do not appear to take their insults or acts of rejection personally. I would almost say it's part of a teacher's job description! It's good to remember that invariably, the adults that children insult are those they feel closest to and trust enough to be able to cope with any challenge they dish out. Here are two tools for dealing with insults and rejection:

- Agree with the insult humorously – for example, if a child calls you stupid, you could reply, 'Yes, I know – it's amazing I put my shoes on the right feet!' This takes the sting out of the child's insult and reduces the hidden shame they would likely feel if they did genuinely upset you.
- State how much you still care – for example, 'You might be struggling with me at the moment but I still care about you.'

## *Using emotion to 'praise'*

There has been much consideration of the potentially damaging effects of praise in the classroom in recent years, as it can leave children feeling only as worthy as their last good deed. This is especially true of children with trauma, who are often uncomfortable receiving praise, resist it, challenge it and/or don't believe it.

Being valued for who you are, and not what you do or don't do, can help build trust, confidence and willingness to take learning risks and tackle difficult tasks. Although it can be hard to stop using praise altogether in the classroom (one swift round of praise for those paying attention soon gets everyone on board!), an adult can move towards using more detailed observations linked to emotions and the effect behaviours have on other people. Examples include the following:

- You must be very proud of that picture you painted. You did it so carefully. You've included loads of detail.
- You must be feeling very pleased with yourself because you helped Davy so kindly. I can see it meant a lot to him.
- I feel pleased when I see you really getting stuck into your maths and not being put off, even when you don't find it really easy. You must feel pleased with yourself too!

## *Using emotions to problem solve and develop self-reliance*

When children bring a problem to us, we tend to bombard them with advice, be dismissive in an attempt to make them feel better ('It's no big deal') or try to sort everything out for them – even if their problem isn't really anything to do with us. This is because as adults, we tend to feel this is our responsibility. A far better approach is to give children as many opportunities as possible to sort out their own problems. This not only increases their self-reliance, but also can reduce their anxiety in the long run as they grow to trust themselves to sort out their own situations more.

The best way to do this is simply to reflect the likely emotions behind a child's problem to them. By doing this, the child feels really listened to, which will usually help them feel comfortable enough to open up a dialogue. This dialogue will not only help them feel better, but also could help them work out a solution to their problem. Here are some examples of fishing out the emotion behind what a child is saying.

| Child | Adult |
|---|---|
| 'I don't want story time.' | 'I can see you don't want to stop doing what you're doing because you're enjoying it so much.' |
| 'I hate you.' | 'I know you're annoyed because I am asking you to do something you don't want to do.' |
| 'I don't want to let him have a go.' | 'I can see you don't want to stop playing with it but he will feel sad if you don't let him have a go.' |
| 'Nobody plays with me at break time.' | 'I can hear you're feeling left out at break.' |

## *Using scripts*

As a teacher, I became a fan of scripts – especially when they became so embedded that everyone in the school was using the same ones. 'Scripts' are short phrases that are easy to repeat and that can be used to address behaviour and promote values and learning. They are best developed as a whole staff group, but here are some examples of scripts that I have used in the past:

- 'Kind hands, thank you' – if a child hits.
- 'What's the plan?' – if you want a child to stop and think about what they are doing.
- 'Good ignoring!' – when children are not joining in with another child engaging in challenging behaviour.
- 'Check and change' – to put a positive spin on making a mistake.
- 'Use your words' – when a child is using their physicality to express their distress.
- 'We need to keep you safe' – a way of showing concern for dangerous behaviours and to state our intention.

- 'Where inside are you feeling it?' – to take a child's focus inwards to consider the emotions they are experiencing and make outward impulsive reactions less likely.

## Low-level behaviours

Children often engage in low-level behaviours that seem to be designed to irritate adults. When this happens, unless the behaviour is preventing learning or causing damage or harm, it is usually best managed through tactical ignoring. However, if it persists, you could:

- swiftly remove any offending item (eg, a tapping pen), say nothing and smile kindly at the child; and/or
- speak to the child at another time and be honest about your irritation. If the child subsequently uses this knowledge against you to irritate you, it creates further opportunity to talk about why they deliberately want to irritate you and what their need is.

## Using emotions to help resolve conflict

When conflict arises, many of us quite often remain determined to be affronted. We can become consumed with how we have been misunderstood or our needs not considered; we often wish to prove another person wrong and ourselves right; and we struggle to see the other side of the issue. If we approach conflict with the idea that we need to 'win' and the other person needs to 'lose', things will often remain stuck.

Using emotion to address conflict can be a useful way to break any stalemate and help start to consider others' needs. With children, a mediator is often needed to enable a conversation that goes beyond the affront to look at the feelings and needs. Some children learn to manage conflict themselves without adult intervention.

Using emotion to address conflict can involve a variety of tools, such as:

- allowing equal time for each person in the conflict to state their version of the issues;
- fishing out the emotions behind what each child states (eg, 'It sounds to me like that upset you');
- using what triggered any emotion as a clue to finding out the child's underlying needs (eg, 'It sounds to me like you need X to understand that what they did triggered you to become upset and that they should do it differently next time'); and
- once needs have been identified, working out what could be done to address those needs by problem solving together.

# Conflict resolution

Sometimes children's conflict is extremely heated. Any chance of cooling it down usually needs a calm, assertive adult who is prepared to take the conflict seriously and help the children negotiate a resolution. I often find that children need to offload their version of what happened quite urgently; I listen attentively and clarify my understanding, but do not allow too long for this as it can retrigger strong emotions in both parties. I tend to assert that each child has a set amount of time – for example, two minutes maximum – to explain their side of the story.

Once the conflict resolution moves on to how the situation made everyone feel, things tend to cool down and the mood of the conflict can be coaxed towards solutions rather than perpetuating the conflict. When a child starts to consider the emotions of the person they are in conflict with, it helps to move their focus more compassionately away from their affront and beyond their own needs. This then leads on helpfully to what needs to happen for everyone to feel better and how everyone can engage in problem solving.

## *Being proactive as well as reactive*

We deal with behaviour reactively in the moment it occurs, but it can also be helpful to take time to address behaviour proactively. While not possible or practical with every incident of unhelpful behaviour, there is always a benefit to some kind of follow-up once a situation has cooled down – especially for children who regularly struggle with behaviour. In this follow-up, it can be really useful to discuss how the situation could have been managed in a better way.

If a child's aggression and resulting defiance often cause difficulties, any aggression needs to be dealt with in the moment; but it can also help to discuss what happened once the child has cooled down. Examples include the following.

| Reactive responses | Proactive actions |
|---|---|
| • Stay calm.<br>• Ensure the child, you and others are safe.<br>• Validate emotions: 'I can see you're angry.'<br>• Link reaction to trigger: 'I wonder if ...'<br>• Soothe – be a calm, accepting presence and suggest cooling-down activities.<br>• Make a clear suggestion about what needs to happen next that the child can follow 'when they're ready' – for example, go and sit in the reading area.<br>• Use scripts – for example, 'Use your words'; 'I want to understand.' | • A follow-up chat or check-in once the child is calm again.<br>• Teach that anger is normal (we all feel it) and consider the physical symptoms.<br>• Consider how aggressive responses are nearly always unhelpful and make situations worse.<br>• Talk about strategies for putting a gap between the trigger and the response.<br>• Use a social story to describe what happened and discuss how the child could have managed the situation in a better way.<br>• Work towards helping the child eventually express their needs in a healthy way – using 'I' messages.<br>• Teach children to look for the problem that needs solving when we become angry and attempt to work out how to solve it. |

## Presence

Quite often in the busy school environment, adults rarely get much one-to-one time to spend with a child. However, with children who need a high level of support, even a couple of times of week proactively dedicated to checking in with them can work wonders! In that time, you can just make yourself available for the child, aiming to allow them to:

- have your full attention;
- be attentively listened to with interest;
- feel fully accepted by you; and
- talk about anything that might be bothering them.

It's also worth bearing in mind that all children benefit from being sought out by adults to constructively spend time together. It helps them feel valued. Imagine if you were the one who always initiated connection with a friend – you'd soon feel your friendship was very one-sided. It is often the case with children – especially in school – that to get attention from an adult, they have to initiate it.

## Unconditional positive regard

Receiving unconditional positive regard (Rogers 1959) can be incredibly nurturing – for adults as well as children. Many of us were praised or told off for things we did or didn't do as children. This led us to believe that our worthiness was based not on who we are, but on what we did. (Praise can feel positive but it can leave us believing that we are loveable only when we do something praiseworthy.) Unconditional positive regard is about making someone feel accepted just as they are. When we are consistently on the receiving end of it, we can eventually relax our self-protective and controlling behaviours enough to allow others to connect with, guide and support us.

Children who most often receive disapproval or feel rejected usually develop poor self-worth. For children with poor self-worth, unconditional positive regard is crucial if they are to start accepting support from the adults who work with them.

To help a child feel unconditional positive regard, remember to:

- always be pleased to see them;
- regularly initiate positive interactions with them;
- use affective statements eg, ('I feel really pleased that you helped me pick those up', or 'You must be really proud that you've learned to do that'), rather than going overboard with praise;
- listen attentively and make it clear their opinions and thoughts count; and
- acknowledge their emotions and show concern for what they are feeling.

## The need for compassion

After years of working with children with trauma, it's clear that what they need most is compassion. As an adult who works with them, my compassion means I want to alleviate their suffering. I find it is easy to be compassionate when I remember that no child would choose to behave 'badly' and they feel distress when they do so – even if it's hidden.

# Chapter 9

# A WHOLE-SCHOOL APPROACH TO EMOTIONAL INTELLIGENCE

## What's in this chapter?

This chapter provides several ideas that schools can use to put emotions well and truly on their agendas. It explores how to use a whole-school approach to implement policy, practice and programme; and offers further ideas for increasing awareness of emotions and emotional intelligence within the school community.

## A whole-school approach

As with any initiative, the impact on a school is far more effective if the whole school community is involved in its implementation. If a school is to value and promote emotional intelligence, it will do so most effectively if all school staff are involved (teaching assistants, school cleaners, teachers, midday supervisors, leadership etc), together with the children, the school council, parents/carers, governors and possibly some people from the closest community beyond school.

## Action plan for becoming an emotionally intelligent school

In broad terms, becoming an emotionally intelligent school involves securing 'buy-in', first and foremost; followed by implementation of policy, practice and programme. The following outlines a possible step-by-step action plan for developing an emotionally intelligent school:

- **Appoint a 'champion':** Initiatives are most successfully implemented when one person (or sometimes a group of people) is assigned to champion the initiative. This will mostly

DOI: 10.4324/9781032690773-10

likely be the school's personal, social, health and economic education (PSHE) lead; but it could also be an interested governor or teaching assistant, for example.

- **Carry out an audit:** An audit is a good place to start in terms of finding out what is already happening within the school with emotional intelligence. The audit could be used to investigate:
  - what already exists within the PSHE curriculum relating to emotional intelligence;
  - everyone's understanding of emotional intelligence and its benefits;
  - how assemblies are contributing the development of emotional intelligence;
  - how confident staff feel to develop children's emotional intelligence, both proactively through the curriculum and reactively (eg, through modelling);
  - other places where the 'soft curriculum' is delivered and anything else that might put emotions on the agenda;
  - whether and how teaching staff acknowledge the impact of emotions on learning;
  - how children who struggle with self-regulation are currently supported;
  - whether the school's behaviour policy acknowledges the part emotions play in unhelpful behaviours; and
  - attitudes towards emotional intelligence and how important different members within the school community consider it to be.

- **Consult with children:** A consultation involving all of the school's children, a selection of children from each year group or the school council could be carried out to investigate the perceived strengths and weaknesses in terms of emotional intelligence within the school and/or an informal assessment of the children's understanding of aspects relating to emotional intelligence. Consultation could be undertaken though questionnaires, interviews, graffiti walls (adding comments to a large displayed sheet of paper) etc and could explore, for example:
  - What children feel they struggle with most when it comes to emotions;
  - what tools they have learned to help them manage uncomfortable emotions such as anger, worry or sadness;
  - what they know about being assertive;
  - how they think emotions impact on learning;
  - how well they think they manage when they fall out with a friend;
  - what support there is when they are struggling emotionally;
  - how much they feel listened to and supported by school staff; and
  - an emotional exploration of the school day (using a timeline) and/or the school building (using a map), labelling the emotions children associate with different times of the day or places within the school grounds.

- **Consult with parent/carers:** Informing parents/carers that your school is moving towards developing children's emotional intelligence further and inviting views from them helps to put emotional intelligence on the agenda, secure 'buy-in' and increase interest in the topic. Parents and carers can be involved in a consultation in a variety of ways. Here are some examples:

- Invite parents/carers to share resources, books and ideas they have used to help their children with different aspects of emotional intelligence (eg, communication, managing anger, dealing with worry, making mistakes, challenging behaviour, conflict, motivation).
- Use a questionnaire to investigate parents' and carers' understanding of emotional intelligence, the impact it has and what they currently do to help their children manage their emotions.
- Use an anonymous questionnaire to investigate which aspects of their children's emotions and behaviour they struggle with most.
- Ask older children to create an emotion poster that can be sent home to younger children's parents/carers near the beginning of term. Deliver the instruction, along with the poster, that it can be used at the end of the day to reflect on the emotions of the day. Ask parents/carers if they noticed any beneficial impact of this daily check-in at the end of the term.
- Set PSHE homework based on exploring different emotions and how to manage them using questions that will prompt discussion between children and their adults, and ask parents/carers to feed back on their experience of the homework.
- Invite parents/carers to read any policies you develop relating to emotional intelligence and ask for feedback.

- **School staff training:** Dedicate professional staff development to enhancing awareness of emotional intelligence. You could include topics such as:
  - what emotional intelligence is;
  - how it benefits children;
  - what can be taught – the key principles;
  - emotionally intelligent interactions;
  - how emotions impact on learning; and
  - how to use emotions to support children's challenging behaviour and conflicts.

- **Consider modification of relevant policies:** It is helpful to identify which school policies might need modification as a result of an increased focus on emotional intelligence next time they are reviewed. Common policies that might be affected include:
  - the behaviour policy;
  - the anti-bullying policy;
  - the safeguarding policy;
  - the PSHE policy;
  - the mental health and wellbeing policy;

- the inclusion and equal opportunities policy; and
- any statements of values.

- **Devise a programme:** Create a curriculum for all of the year groups in your school to ensure progression. This can be allocated to year groups as a series of learning objectives or delivered in greater detail as activity ideas or lesson plans to support teachers who are less confident with this area of the curriculum. This is usually embedded within the PSHE curriculum.

- **Review progress:** The impact of the policy and programme to increase emotional intelligence and any strengths or weaknesses could be reviewed a couple of years after initial implementation. This would ideally involve children, parents/carers, governors and school staff. The methods used in the original audit and/or consultations could be repeated to facilitate a direct comparison of results. Information gained from the review could then be used to make useful modifications.

## Further ideas for a whole-school approach to the development of an emotionally intelligent school

This section is a miscellaneous ideas bank for further opportunities to promote emotional intelligence in a school community.

### Check-ins

One of the simplest ways to increase awareness of emotions and their impact is to do regular check-ins with children and staff about how they are feeling. This can be done in a number of ways, such as the following:

- Conduct an emotion check-in (see page 32).
- Stick a laminated poster of emotions near to the classroom door and write the children's names on pieces of card. The children can be invited to place their name on the emotion that best describes how they feel each day as they arrive.
- Conduct a quick check-in (thumbs up, thumbs down or horizontal thumbs) to ask children to reflect on how they feel and share in an assembly.
- Invite the children to draw a smiley, neutral or sad face at the end of a piece of written work to indicate how they felt about it at the point of completion.
- Issue the children with emotion diaries and invite them to collect their personal triggers for different emotions.
- Use emotion trackers (see below) over a period of time (eg, within a lesson) to invite the children to share how they feel and explore what possible triggers contributed to them feeling that way.

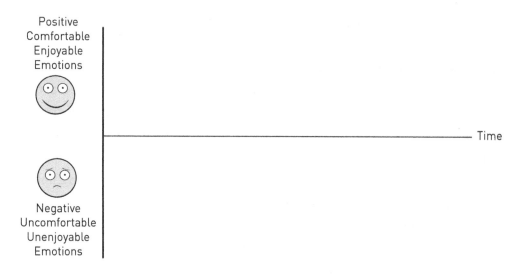

## The value of emotion check-ins

With emotion check-ins, it's important to remember that their value lies in getting the children to reflect on how they feel. In a full class, you are unlikely to be able to follow up on what might be concerning every child who indicates they are experiencing an unenjoyable emotion. The proactive work you do in helping children to expect and endure unenjoyable emotions, as well as any coping strategies you have explored, can be regularly referred to.

## *Assemblies*

Assemblies are brilliant opportunities to deliver messages about emotions. In addition to those led by an adult – who could explore different emotions, their triggers, coping strategies or stories illustrating different aspects of emotional intelligence – you could, for example, invite the children to:

- find or write stories that present helpful messages about emotions that an adult could read and explore in assembly;
- create a 'magazine'-style assembly based on one emotion – for example, an assembly based on anger could involve:
  - a short play about anger;
  - some advice for managing anger;
  - wise sayings about anger;
  - poems inspired by anger;

- a trigger spectrum – from reasons why someone might only feel slightly angry to really angry;
    - a tour of the physical features of anger;
    - cooling-down strategies; and
    - the use of assertiveness as a resourceful response to anger;
- create an assembly that shows a learning situation in a classroom and provides a running commentary of all the emotions the different children are experiencing as they try to master something new;
- create an assembly where different emotions are personified. Each child playing a different emotion could illustrate the kinds of thoughts, words, physical sensations and actions they would have and how they would interact with others in the playground;
- create an assembly that gives top ten tips for managing emotions well; or
- create an assembly about conflict management – starting with how conflict can sometimes make us forget that other people have feelings too.

## *Emotional intelligence displays*

Displays about emotional intelligence can be posted in school communal areas. Ideas for displays include:

- an emotion vocabulary wall, illustrated by a possible trigger;
- a display of different children's faces labelled with the emotion their face is expressing;
- a display of emotions that need us to take a pause and slow down, and ideas that can help us pause;
- a display of choices about what can we do when somebody upsets us;
- a display of the messages that different emotions might be sending us;
- illustrated inspirational quotes about different emotions;
- a display of ways to feel better when we feel sad, angry or worried;
- an empathy display, on which children write examples of where they showed kindness and empathy towards others;
- a display focused on one particular emotion (eg, anger, excitement, boredom, fear, sadness, worry, embarrassment, happiness), featuring:
    - stories by the children of times when they felt that emotion;
    - pictures or poems inspired by the emotion; and
    - quotations about the emotion;
    - a display of advice of what to do to help when you feel it or examples of other people feeling it in a song, a film etc;
- a display of suggestions for what to do when we fall out with a friend; and/or
- an illustrated cartoon on how to manage conflict.

## Whole-school compositions

In the school office or outside the headteacher's office, you could invite children to add to an emotion compilation of some kind. For example:

- create a trigger collection scrapbook, in which children stick representations of emotions they felt recently and what triggered it;
- a box of cards of strategies for dealing with uncomfortable emotions that children can add to; and/or
- a book of emotions, where the children complete emotions profiles (page 91), which are then clipped into a folder.
- a displayed list of pieces of music and the emotions they trigger in the child who listed each piece.

## An emotional intelligence charter

Creating, displaying and sharing a charter for emotional intelligence can enhance awareness and help everyone understand why your school has decided to value and promote it. A charter could include:

- a definition of 'emotional intelligence' as something you are all aiming for;
- the reason why emotional intelligence is valued (ie, its benefits);
- they way emotional intelligence is valued (eg, the acknowledgement of emotions and their impact);
- how emotional intelligence will be applied within the school (eg, validating emotions, supporting behaviour, supporting learning, successful conflict resolution, improving interactions, supporting and valuing friendships);
- how people will aim to express their emotions (eg, resourcefully; not hurtfully; through 'I' messages; knowing when and how to seek help; using effective coping strategies); and
- the outcomes expected as a result of increased emotional intelligence (eg, improved listening skills, better self-regulation, increased self-reliance, stronger friendships, increased empathy).

## Assessment

Assessment of PSHE and emotional intelligence enhance their status within a school. An informal assessment could be carried out at the beginning and end of a period in which emotional intelligence topics have been taught, in order to chart progress. There are a number of ways this assessment can be done – for example, the children could:

- list three things they have learned;
- draw spider diagrams with different emotions in the middle and add what they know and think about those emotions;
- create a presentation of the most important things about emotions that they have learned;
- create a portfolio of their main learnings in each lesson and add to it over time;
- complete a question sheet on how they manage anger (eg, what does it feel like? What does it make you feel like doing? Where in the body do you feel it? What triggers your anger? How many different words can you think of for anger? Do you have any methods for cooling yourself down when you're angry before responding? Do you know how to create an 'I' message?);
- list advice for someone who is struggling with anxiety;
- self-reflect by considering and reporting back on what they think is the most difficult aspect about emotions;
- create a list of top ten tips for managing emotions well; and/or
- write and post in an anonymous post box, 'What I find helps me most with emotions.'

## Information-sharing sessions with parents and carers

In my experience, the most useful information-sharing sessions with parents and carers are those which focus on the following topics:

- an introduction to emotional intelligence, what it is, how it benefits people and how to get more of it;
- how to help children become more emotionally intelligent;
- supporting behaviour using emotional intelligence;
- how to help children manage anxiety; and
- helping children manage their anger more resourcefully.

## Emotion ambassadors

Emotion ambassadors are children who are prepared to listen attentively to other children when they feel sad or worried. The process of becoming an emotion ambassador requires some training, support and supervision delivered by an adult and the job description needs careful consideration. This could include, for example:

- 'I will be on duty ...' (describe duty times).
- 'Children will know how to find me because...' (eg, 'I have a badge').
- 'I will listen to someone attentively when they are worried or sad.'

- 'I will notice and accept how they feel.'
- 'I will listen until they feel better.'
- 'If I suspect they or anyone else is at risk of harm, or if the problem seems like something children won't manage to sort out themselves, I will tell an adult.'

## *Staff modelling*

School staff are highly influential when it comes to increasing emotional intelligence. Most modelling will involve staff expressing how they feel and what triggered their emotion, using 'I' messages (page 52).

# APPENDICES

## A possible programme

| Year group | Possible learning | Possible activities |
|---|---|---|
| R | **Emotions**<br><br>• Understand that we all feel emotions (and it's a normal part of being a human).<br>• Increase emotion vocabulary.<br>• Identify whether you are experiencing an enjoyable or unenjoyable emotion.<br>• Start to identify where inside the body you feel the sensations of different emotions so that you can point to the sensations.<br>• Identify the facial expressions triggered by happiness, sadness, anger and fear.<br>• Identify something that triggers happiness and something that triggers sadness. | • Teddy's day<br>• Emotion hunt<br>• Emotion whispers<br>• Emotion check-in: smiley face or frowning face?<br>• Happy or sad? |
| 1 | **Emotions**<br><br>• Understand that it's normal to feel enjoyable and unenjoyable emotions, and start to notice which you're feeling.<br>• Increase emotion vocabulary.<br>• Know the physical symptoms of anger, sadness and excitement.<br>• Consider what triggers happiness, sadness and anger (and a few other emotions).<br><br>**Specific emotions**<br><br>• Understand that anger can make us react in ways that can make situations worse, so we need to try to pause before we react. | • I'm a potato<br>• Emotion check-in<br>• Enjoyable and unenjoyable emotions (with a few words)<br>• Is this a yes or no moment?<br>• Where in the body do we feel it (excitement, sadness and anger)<br>• Trigger runaround<br><br><br>• Angry Anira |
| 2 | **Emotions**<br><br>• Increase emotion vocabulary.<br>• Be able to reflect upon the emotions experienced in a day.<br>• Identify the physical symptoms of a greater number of emotions.<br>• Start to realise that the same situation can trigger different emotions in different people.<br>• Start to be able to 'read' the possible emotions of others.<br><br>**Specific emotions**<br><br>• Increase understanding of fear.<br>• Increase understanding of boredom. | • Emotion check-in<br>• I'm a potato<br>• Emotion diary<br>• What might she be feeling?<br>• Where in the body do we feel it?<br>• Max's day<br><br><br><br>• Fear<br>• Boredom |

DOI: 10.4324/9781032690773-11

| Year group | Possible learning | Possible activities |
|---|---|---|
| 3 | **Emotions**<br><br>• Increase emotion vocabulary.<br>• Start to consider in more detail what different emotions feel like, to encourage introspection.<br>• To learn how to focus inwardly when we experience an emotion, so that we can eventually work out the best way of responding.<br>• To understand that emotions can affect our behaviour and our behaviour can affect other people's emotions.<br>• To start to read what others might be feeling.<br>• To know that we can experience emotions with different strength.<br><br>**Specific emotion**<br><br>• Understand what makes us happy. | • I'm a potato<br>• Describing feelings<br>• A simple question<br>• Happy and sad<br>• Symptom checker<br>• What faces can tell us<br><br><br><br><br><br><br><br><br>• Feeling happy |
| 4 | **Emotions**<br><br>• Increase emotion vocabulary.<br>• Link more emotions to their likely triggers.<br>• Become increasingly aware of emotions at the moment they arrive.<br>• Understand that emotions come and go.<br>• Develop our understanding of how emotions affect us when they visit.<br>• Link emotions to what they might makes us feel like doing.<br>• Learn about empathy.<br>• Learn 'I' messages.<br><br>**Specific emotions**<br><br>• Understand excitement.<br>• Understand disappointment.<br><br>**A focus on anger**<br><br>• Know the physical symptoms of anger.<br>• Understand that anger can trigger us to behave in ways that can make situations worse and that we need to find ways to cool down to prevent this.<br><br>**A focus on learning and emotions**<br><br>• Acknowledge the emotions involved in learning and especially learning something new.<br>• Considering what helps us develop a positive attitude towards learning. | • Emotion check-in<br>• Happy, angry, sad or scared?<br>• Emotions as visitors<br>• How would you feel?<br>• Name that feeling<br>• Can we find emotions to name?<br>• A park full of feelings<br>• Which emotions might make you want to ...?<br>• Can we work out what they might be feeling?<br>• 'I' messages<br>• Excitement<br>• Disappointment<br><br><br><br>• Where in the body do I feel anger?<br>• What can anger make us feel like doing?<br>• The triggers of anger<br>• Cooling things down<br><br>• At the start of a lesson ...<br>• Learning something new<br>• What might you feel?<br>• Getting ready to learn |

| Year group | Possible learning | Possible activities |
|---|---|---|
| 5 | **Emotions**<br><br>• Increase emotion vocabulary.<br>• Understand that emotions send us messages – some that are useful and others that are not.<br>• Learn some strategies that can help us deal with unenjoyable emotions.<br>• Learn to use 'I' messages to express how you feel.<br><br>**Specific emotions**<br><br>• Understand embarrassment.<br>• Understand sadness and the strategies that can help with it.<br>• Consider the benefits of feeling grateful.<br><br>**A further focus on anger**<br><br>• Revise the need to find cool-down strategies when our anger is triggered so that our reactions are less likely to make situations worse.<br>• Increase our vocabulary for describing different levels of anger.<br>• Understand how anger can affect our thinking.<br>• Make responses when angry more conscious.<br>• Understand that aggression is sometimes expressed when we are actually feeling vulnerable.<br>• Understand how to respond to someone who is angry.<br><br>**A focus on friendships**<br><br>• Acknowledge the emotions that can be triggered within friendships.<br>• Understand the difference between jealousy and envy and know what can help when you feel them.<br>• Know what helps when you feel lonely or someone else does.<br><br>**A focus on learning and emotions**<br><br>• Learn to reframe mistakes by considering what emotions they trigger in you.<br>• Develop greater resilience and a positive attitude towards learning. | • Enjoyable and unenjoyable – with many emotion words<br>• Lots of words for emotions!<br>• 'I' messages revision<br>• An emotion profile<br>• What messages can emotions send us?<br>• Feeling better<br><br>• Feeling sad<br>• Embarrassment<br>• Gratitude<br><br>• Angry thoughts<br>• Words for anger<br>• How do you respond when you're angry?<br>• Anger – true or false?<br>• Anger freeze-frames<br>• Anger wisdom<br>• A gold star for managing anger<br>• Athan and his aggression<br>• Supporting someone who is angry<br><br>• When you think of friends …<br>• The ups and downs of friendship<br>• Tricky behaviours<br>• Jealousy and envy<br>• Feeling lonely<br><br>• Attitudes towards mistakes<br>• Feeling positive about learning |

| Year group | Possible learning | Possible activities |
|---|---|---|
| 6 | **Emotions**<br><br>• Increase emotion vocabulary.<br>• Understand the effect of different emotions on our thinking.<br>• Understand that what we think about whatever happens has an impact on what we end up feeling.<br>• Understand that being good at enduring uncomfortable emotions means we can sort things out better and achieve more.<br>• Learn strategies that can help us feel better.<br>• Understand that it's beneficial to be curious about what an emotion might be telling us and take time to work out what's best to do each time a strong emotion is triggered.<br>• Revise 'I' messages as a means of being assertive.<br><br>**Specific emotions**<br><br>• Understand the emotion of guilt.<br>• Know what shame is and how to deal with it.<br><br>**A focus on worry and anxiety**<br><br>• Understand the importance of relaxation and how to relax.<br>• Understand what anxiety is and the impact it can have.<br>• Understand the kinds of situations that can trigger anxiety and worry, including change.<br>• Understand how to challenge worrying thoughts.<br>• Understand how anxiety can impact on our confidence and reduce the likelihood of us trying some things.<br>• Learn strategies that can help with anxiety<br><br>**A focus on friendships and other relationships**<br><br>• Understand how to listen well and the impact this can have.<br>• Understand how you might be able to work out what another person is feeling.<br>• Acknowledge that emotions can be clues as to how healthy a friendship or relationship is.<br>• Know what to do when friendships go wrong.<br>• Know when to seek help from a trusted adult.<br><br>**A focus on learning and emotions**<br><br>• Investigate and attempt to problem solve aspects of learning that trigger anxiety. | • 'I' messages revision<br>• Emotions affect how we think<br>• We sometimes jump to conclusions<br>• Accepting uncomfortable emotions<br>• What could they do?<br>• If emotions could talk<br>• Low-mood menu<br><br><br><br><br>• Guilty!<br>• Shame<br><br><br><br>• Relax!<br>• What is anxiety?<br>• What effect does anxiety have on us?<br>• Could it trigger anxiety?<br>• The emotions of change<br>• Challenging worries<br>• Two types of worrying thoughts<br>• Anxiety and our comfort zone<br>• What can we do about anxiety?<br>• What do we really fear?<br>• Threat, drive or soothe?<br><br>• What does it feel like to be really listened to?<br>• Listening<br>• Empathy detectives<br>• Being brave in friendships<br>• Feeling hurt<br>• Conflict<br>• Feelings as warnings<br><br><br><br>• Anxiety and learning questionnaire |

# Suggested emotion vocabulary progression

| Year Group | Added vocabulary/emotions to explore for each year group | | |
|---|---|---|---|
| R | Happy<br>Sad<br>Scared<br>Angry | Surprised<br>Bored<br>Calm<br>Worried | Excited<br>Grumpy<br>Tired<br>Annoyed |
| 1 | Confused<br>Disgusted<br>Relaxed<br>Upset<br>Tired<br>Shocked | Cheerful<br>Irritated<br>Hopeful<br>Furious<br>Lonely<br>Loving | Miserable<br>Disappointed<br>Pleased<br>Trusting<br>Joy<br>Playful |
| 2 | Panicked<br>Hurt<br>Guilty<br>Embarrassed<br>Infuriated<br>Delighted | Grateful<br>Thrilled<br>Terrified<br>Determined<br>Carefree<br>Terrified | Amazed<br>Enthusiastic<br>Satisfied<br>Impatient<br>Energetic<br>Amused |
| 3 | Jealous<br>Envious<br>Exhausted<br>Suspicious<br>Interested<br>Nervous | Confident<br>Brave<br>Shy<br>Appreciative<br>Admiring<br>Proud | Content<br>Peaceful<br>Affectionate<br>Misunderstood<br>Pitying<br>Selfish |
| 4 | Curious<br>Petrified<br>Astonished<br>Hesitant<br>Flabbergasted<br>Distressed | Ashamed<br>Cautious<br>Mischievous<br>Relieved<br>Impressed<br>Empathy | Alert<br>Thoughtful<br>Full of dread<br>Motivated<br>Offended<br>Inspired |
| 5 | Rejected<br>Inspired<br>Flustered<br>Awkward<br>Doubtful<br>Regretful<br>Accepted<br>Enchanted<br>Self-conscious<br>Yearning<br>Appalled<br>Repulsed | Overwhelmed<br>Insecure<br>Agitated<br>Optimistic<br>Tense<br>Foolish<br>Exasperated<br>Forlorn<br>Compassionate<br>Disapproving<br>Awed<br>Serene | Baffled<br>Concerned<br>Contempt<br>Unsettled<br>Timid<br>Uncertain<br>Tempted<br>Vigilant<br>Anxious<br>Withdrawn<br>Euphoric<br>Alarmed |
| 6 | Stressed<br>Adored<br>Blissful<br>Ashamed<br>Intimidated<br>Fulfilled<br>Melancholic<br>Remorseful<br>Sentimental<br>Craving<br>Nostalgic | Ecstatic<br>Distractible<br>Passionate<br>Perplexed<br>Tentative<br>Resigned<br>Apprehensive<br>Discouraged<br>Self-pitying<br>Indignant<br>Vengeful | Humiliated<br>Anticipatory<br>Vulnerable<br>Preoccupied<br>Triumphant<br>Pensive<br>Expectant<br>Humble<br>Paranoid<br>Obsessed<br>Devoted |

# PSHE Association: PSHE Programme of Study – learning opportunities relating to emotional intelligence

## *Key Stage 1*
### *Wholly covered by the contents of this book*

H11. About different feelings that humans can experience

H12. How to recognise and name different feelings

H13. How feelings can affect people's bodies and how they behave

H14. How to recognise what others might be feeling

H15. How to recognise that not everyone feels the same at the same time, or feels the same about the same things

H16. About ways of sharing feelings; a range of words to describe feelings

H17. About things that help people feel good (eg, playing outside, doing things they enjoy, spending time with family, getting enough sleep)

H18. Different things they can do to manage big feelings, to help calm themselves down and/or to change their mood when they don't feel good

H19. To recognise when they need help with feelings; that it is important to ask for help with feelings; and how to ask for it

R7. How to recognise when they or someone else feels lonely and what to do

R8. Simple strategies to resolve arguments between friends positively

R9. How to ask for help if a friendship is making them feel unhappy

R20. What to do if they feel unsafe or worried for themselves or others; who to ask for help and vocabulary to use when asking for help; the importance of keeping trying until they are heard

R21. About what is kind and unkind behaviour, and how this can affect others

### *Partly covered by the contents of this book*

H1. About what keeping healthy means; different ways to keep healthy

H4. About why sleep is important and different ways to rest and relax

H9. About different ways to learn and play; recognising the importance of knowing when to take a break from time online or TV

H20. About change and loss (including death); identifying feelings associated with this; recognising what helps people to feel better

H24. How to manage when finding things difficult.

H27. About preparing to move to a new class/year group

H29. Recognising risk in simple everyday situations and what action to take to minimise harm

R1. About the roles different people (eg, acquaintances, friends and relatives) play in our lives

R2. Identifying the people who love and care for us and what we can do to help them feel cared for

R5. The importance of telling someone (such as their teacher) if something about their family makes them unhappy or worried

R6. About how people make friends and what makes a good friendship

R7. About how to recognise when they or someone else feels lonely and what to do

R10. That bodies and feelings can be hurt by words and actions; that people can say hurtful things online

R11. About how people may feel if they experience hurtful behaviour or bullying

R12. That hurtful behaviour (offline and online) – including teasing, name-calling, bullying and deliberately excluding others – is not acceptable; how to report bullying; the importance of telling a trusted adult

R16. About how to respond if physical contact makes them feel uncomfortable or unsafe

R19. Basic techniques for resisting pressure to do something they don't want to do and which may make them unsafe

R24. How to listen to other people and play and work cooperatively

## *Key Stage 2*
### *Wholly covered by the contents of this book*

H17. To recognise that feelings can change over time and range in intensity

H18. About everyday things that affect feelings and the importance of expressing feelings

H19. A varied vocabulary to use when talking about feelings; about how to express feelings in different ways;

H20. Strategies to respond to feelings, including intense or conflicting feelings; how to manage and respond to feelings appropriately and proportionately in different situations

H29. About how to manage setbacks/perceived failures, including how to reframe unhelpful thinking

R10. About the importance of friendships; strategies for building positive friendships; how positive friendships support wellbeing

R13. The importance of seeking support if feeling lonely or excluded

R14. That healthy friendships make people feel included; recognise when others may feel lonely or excluded; strategies for how to include them

R17. That friendships have ups and downs; strategies to resolve disputes and reconcile differences positively and safely

R18. To recognise if a friendship (online or offline) is making them feel unsafe or uncomfortable; how to manage this and ask for support if necessary

R19. About the impact of bullying, including offline and online, and the consequences of hurtful behaviour

### *Partly covered by the contents of this book*

H3. About choices that support a healthy lifestyle, and how to recognise what might influence these

H8. About how sleep contributes to a healthy lifestyle; routines that support good quality sleep; the effects of lack of sleep on the body, feelings, behaviour and ability to learn

H15. That mental health, just like physical health, is part of daily life; the importance of taking care of mental health

H21. How to recognise warning signs about mental health and wellbeing and how to seek support for themselves and others

H22. That anyone can experience mental ill health; that most difficulties can be resolved with help and support; and that it is important to discuss feelings with a trusted adult

H23. About change and loss, including death, and how these can affect feelings; ways of expressing and managing grief and bereavement

H24. Problem-solving strategies for dealing with emotions, challenges and change, including the transition to new schools

H36. Strategies to manage transitions between classes and key stages

R9. How to recognise if family relationships are making them feel unhappy or unsafe, and how to seek help or advice

R11. What constitutes a positive healthy friendship (eg, mutual respect, trust, truthfulness, loyalty, kindness, generosity, sharing interests and experiences, support with problems and difficulties); that the same principles apply to online friendships as to face-to-face relationships

R16. How friendships can change over time; about making new friends and the benefits of having different types of friends

R16. How friendships can change over time, about making new friends and the benefits of having different types of friends

R20. Strategies to respond to hurtful behaviour experienced or witnessed, offline and online (including teasing, name-calling, bullying, trolling, harassment or the deliberate excluding of others); how to report concerns and get support

R28. How to recognise pressure from others to do something unsafe or that makes them feel uncomfortable and strategies for managing this

R29. Where to get advice and report concerns if worried about their own or someone else's personal safety (including online)

R30. That personal behaviour can affect other people; to recognise and model respectful behaviour online

# References

Bowlby J (1958) 'The Nature of the Child's Tie to His Mother', *International Journal of Psychoanalysis*, Vol 39 Issue 5 pp 350-373.

Burgo J (2012) *Why Do I Do That? Psychological Defense Mechanisms and the Hidden Way They Shape Our Lives.* New Rise Press.

Busch FN (2009) 'Anger and Depression', *Advances in Psychiatric Treatment*, Vol 15, 271-278.

Feldman BL, Lindquist KA and Gendron M (2007) 'Language as Context for the Perception of Emotion', *Trends in Cognitive Sciences*, Vol 11 Issue 8 pp 327-332.

Fredrickson, BL (2001). 'The Role of Positive Emotions in Positive Psychology: The Broaden-and-Build Theory of Positive Emotions', *American Psychologist*, Vol 56 Issue 3 pp 218–226.

Gilbert P (2010) *The Compassionate Mind: A New Approach to Life's Challenges.* New Harbinger Publications.

Goldberg LR (1990) 'An Alternative "Description of Personality": The Big-Five Factor Structure', *Journal of Personality and Social Psychology*, Vol 59 Issue 6 pp 1216-1229.

Hoffman S (2016) *Emotion in Therapy: From Science to Practice.* Guildford Press.

House JS, Landis KR and Umbertson D (1988) 'Social Relationships and Health', *Science*, Vol; 241; Issue; 4865 pp; 540-545.

Ozbay F, Johnson C J, Dimoulas E, Morgan CA, Carney D and Southwick S (2007) 'Social Support and Resilience to Stress', *Psychiatry MMC*, Volume 4 Issue 5 pp 35-40.

Rogers CR (1959): 'A Theory of Therapy, Personality and Interpersonal Relationships as Developed in the Client Centred Framework', *Psychology: A Study of Science*, Vol 3 pp 184-256.

Sutherland R (2018) *Tackling the Root Causes of Suicide.* NHS Blog post.

Vigdal JS and Brønnick KK (2022) 'A Systematic Review of "Helicopter Parenting" and Its Relationship with Anxiety and Depression', *Frontiers in Psychology.* 25 May.

For Product Safety Concerns and Information please contact our EU
representative GPSR@taylorandfrancis.com Taylor & Francis Verlag GmbH,
Kaufingerstraße 24, 80331 München, Germany

Printed and bound by CPI Group (UK) Ltd, Croydon, CR0 4YY
08/06/2025
01896981-0011